CLUBLAND UK

Steven McLaughlin is a former member of the elite Royal Green Jackets. He has served on operational tours in Iraq and Northern Ireland and in his critically acclaimed memoir *Squaddie* wrote movingly of his experiences as an infantry soldier in one of Britain's toughest regiments. As a prominent 'voice from the ranks', he has featured as a military commentator on numerous international news channels, including Sky News and the BBC World Service.

He has served as a volunteer for the Prince's Trust charity, helping to lead and mentor young adults through its challenging 12-week Team programme. He has also undergone conflict resolution leadership training and has participated in peace talks with individuals who have been involved in violent armed struggles, either as victims of terrorist attacks or as enemy combatants, belonging to organisations such as the IRA, the UVF and the PLO.

An accomplished sportsman, he is a qualified Master Scuba Diver and experienced martial artist. He has been awarded an associate diploma in acting from the London Academy of Music and Dramatic Art (LAMDA), is a member of Equity and the Society of Authors, and has passed the Cambridge University CELTA course. He has backpacked across the United States and Poland.

A former doorman on some of Blackpool's busiest clubs, he holds a black belt in shotokan karate. *Clubland UK* is his second book.

CLUBLAND UK

On the Door in the Rave Era

STEVEN McLAUGHLIN

MAINSTREAM
PUBLISHING

EDINBURGH AND LONDON

First published in Great Britain in 2013 by

MAINSTREAM PUBLISHING COMPANY

(EDINBURGH) LTD

7 Albany Street

Edinburgh EH1 3UG

ISBN 9781780575988

A catalogue record for this book is available
from the British Library

Printed in Great Britain by
CPI Group (UK) Ltd, Croydon, CR0 4YY

1 3 5 7 9 10 8 6 4 2

For John Rad and Zenon Malkuch
We met for a reason
What men you are

and

Rifleman Damian McLaughlin 1975–2001
You are somebody
You always were

If you always put limits on yourself and what you can do, physical or anything, you might as well be dead. It will spread into your work, your morality, your entire being. There are no limits, only plateaux. But you must not stay there, you must go beyond them. If it kills you, it kills you.

– Bruce Lee, martial artist (1940–73)

CONTENTS

AUTHOR'S NOTE

PARTS OF THIS BOOK HAVE BEEN WRITTEN IN ANGER. THIS IS A book about the person that I used to be and not the man I am today – I wish to emphasise that. I worked in the nightclubs of Blackpool for approximately three years in the early 1990s at the height of the so-called rave era. The events that I write of here took place over 20 years ago. Much has changed since then – especially in me. Some of the things I did I am proud of; some of them not so. I suspect most of us could say the same, so I will only ask that you don't judge me too harshly – for what is the journey of life supposed to mean if we don't learn anything along the way?

When I was working on the doors, I never imagined that one day I'd be writing about it. The idea came about almost by accident, in fact. I had just left the army and was immersed in writing my military memoir, *Squaddie: A Soldier's Story*. Never having written a book before, I decided to simply start from the very beginning of my life, from childhood onwards. When I got to my nightclub years, the memories flooded back and I wrote a couple of meaty chapters that jolted me with nostalgic adrenaline, of the sort that I used to feel nightly. It utterly pained me to cut them from *Squaddie*, but, as my publisher pointed out, I was writing a military book, not a clubland one and the 'bouncer stuff' belonged in a different book.

I was dismayed but also secretly glad, as I realised I had been so focused on writing my army story I had almost overlooked an equally significant chapter in my life: my time as a doorman in Blackpool. This period was every bit as life-changing for me as my military service and taught me just as much. And that is how *Clubland UK* was born – the results of which are now in your hands.

This has been a difficult and emotional book for me to write, but a necessary one; when you're forced to confront and analyse life-changing decisions that you've made – in a bold black-and-white print that streams from your consciousness – well, it gives a whole new meaning to the word 'clarity'.

I have written this book in a harsh language because that is how we communicated back then. It is not how I speak, think or act today, but out of respect for the young hothead that I was, and his story, I have reverted back to that rawness and coarseness. I have become reacquainted with my old self. And yes, it does embarrass me – but hey, that was me.

For reasons of privacy, I have chosen to change the names and personal details of certain individuals and places. In some cases, I have also subtly altered the details of certain events, for the same reason.

1

BEDSIT LAND

THE BARMAID BEGAN SCREAMING HYSTERICALLY, HER CRIES SO pain-ridden and anguished that I can still hear them to this day. The dance floor emptied like someone had lobbed a grenade into it. The DJ's decks ground to a halt. A herd of burly bouncers charged towards me, roughly elbowing drinkers aside.

At the sight of all the chaos and drama I had wrought, I rapidly began to sober up. I felt a sudden sickening realisation of the enormity of what I had done. As a friend's shirt was being tightly wound around my arm, I mumbled a faint apology to the barmaid, who was sitting on a stool, knees tucked into her chin, with her thin arms tightly wound round herself, curled into a foetal ball, rocking backwards and forwards in a state of comatose shock. Her gasping pale cheeks shone with tears and her crisp white blouse was spattered with blood. Her eyes blinked pitifully, like those of a trapped and frightened animal. At the sight of the crumpled girl, I felt a sharp stab of guilt and self-hatred. I realised that my actions had damaged not only myself but others too: innocents who didn't deserve to be dragged into my intensely private – but now all too public – drama.

Thanks to the efforts of a now bloodstained bouncer, the torrent of red pouring from my arm had slowed itself to a grossly pulsing trickle and a modicum of calm returned to the atmosphere. As soon as the ambulance arrived, I shuffled into it – my eyes firmly glued to the floor, unwilling and unable to meet the concerned gazes of my friends.

Once inside I began to weep silently.

Not from pain – but shame . . .

* * *

When a young man seeks out violence, he suffers from unresolved issues. And I sought it in bruising clumps. To trace the roots of my self-destructive behaviour and the source of bubbling anger that fuelled much of my youth, I merely have to cast my mind back to the fragmented wreck of my childhood.

As a child, I was unfortunate enough to enjoy the attentions of a stepmother who at times seemed colder than the Arctic itself. Her conflict with my brother and me wasn't of a sexual or overtly physical nature; instead it was a decade-long campaign of military-style discipline, icy rejection and spirit-sapping emotional abuse.

To the outside world, we were compelled to present a false smile and cheery resilience. For us, it felt like nothing mattered more to my stepmother than 'what the neighbours might think'. Our silence and submission were misread by others as quiet obedience; unfortunately, it was a damaging and toxic anxiety nestled within the family itself.

To her, the troublesome flesh and blood that I wore was an ever-present reminder of my father's first love, the woman who had given birth to me – now expelled from our lives, driven away by cruel circumstance, and agonisingly beyond my stepmother's reach. I, however, remained conveniently within range. I eventually came to understand that she wasn't really scorning me: her scolds were meant for my mother.

My mother had courageously stood up for us, fighting with all of her strength for access to my little brother and me – a bitter struggle she won in the courts. But in the end she realised that, despite her victory, the campaign against her and use of us as emotional pawns would never cease and ultimately we children would suffer. So, for our sakes, she graciously sacrificed her own happiness and stepped away from our lives. She left the door open to us and told us that when we were old enough to understand she would be there and waiting for us – and she was, as the fullness of time proved.

My stepmother seemed an expert manipulator. During my childhood, she was a near unbeatable figure, running rings around my mother and anybody else who dared to confront or challenge her.

One of her pastimes was to sit us on the back doorstep and casually tell us, as she dragged on a cigarette, that she wanted us 'gone' by the time we were 16 because we 'weren't hers'. What never failed to chill me was the calm and conversational tone she used, as if it was perfectly reasonable; in fact, it was as if we ought to have been ashamed of ourselves for not seeing it and for getting in the way. When you're a small child and every day of your life you are drip-fed that kind of cold propaganda from a powerful adult, it can make you or break you. In contrast, my father was as kind and gentle a guardian as a son could ever wish to have.

When they had first met, my stepmother had won my hard-working father's affections by conveying warmth and innocence, projecting a persona of loving contentment. However, once firmly established within the family home and with a wedding ring safely on her finger, the atmosphere changed: my father's loving and non-confrontational nature was soon dominated by a seeming hardness in my stepmother.

He desperately wanted his second marriage to work and for our new family unit to bond together tightly and, sensing this, my stepmother took full advantage, comfortable in the knowledge that my father would try to keep the family together at all costs. The divisive force of what followed was like a tidal wave that engulfed the entire household: my father found himself swiftly overwhelmed and he became a victim of the surge, too. At the end of it all, my stepmother reigned gloriously supreme.

My childhood yielded many important lessons, but it was an education no child should ever receive. Now that I am an adult and have forged an identity of my own, I can see how plainly wrong those lessons were and I have cast them aside. But there is one special gift that I remain grateful for and I cling to it to this day: it taught me how to endure.

I left school at the age of 15 with barely a qualification to my name. At the time I was greatly ashamed by this fact and felt like an abject failure because I had become exactly what my stepmother had predicted: a schoolboy dropout. She gleefully reminded me that this would undoubtedly be the first of a great many failures in my destined-to-be-crap life. I resolved to prove her wrong, but the cold reality was that I was a teenage boy: I was hard on the outside but as weak and vulnerable as a cracked bird's egg on the inside. It wouldn't have taken much to crush me, no matter how grandiose my dreams.

By the age of 16, I had realised that my employment prospects were practically zero. So, in a desperate attempt to prove myself and find a sense of purpose, I pledged to join the army. Bursting with youthful energy, I naively assumed my entrance was a forgone conclusion; I foolishly allowed a sense of destiny and pride to build within myself. I was intensely angry at my lost childhood and vowed to use my rage as fuel to aid my escape through my undoubted acceptance to the army. I couldn't wait for the adventure to begin so I could start proving her wrong. This flimsy bubble of expectation and confidence that I had cocooned myself in was soon ripped away and I was once again naked and cruelly exposed. She was proven right.

I was summarily rejected for military service because I was severely short-sighted – so much so that I couldn't even enlist as a cook. The military rejection was a hammer blow to my morale and a crushing disappointment. (Back then I had no way of knowing that in the distant future, after successful surgery on my eyes, I would achieve my goal of becoming a professional soldier and serve in the famed Royal Green Jackets on operations in both Iraq and Northern Ireland.)

My failure to become a soldier was the last straw, in my stepmother's eyes. It confirmed my utter uselessness. After an intensified round of emotional blackmail I left the family home.

Throughout my early 20s, the contamination of my childhood was a raw and open wound: I made the mistake of honouring this period with too much power and allowing the memories to make me angry. Eventually, I learnt to live with and accept what my brother and I had been through, with as much grace and equanimity as I could muster. But writing about it has brought it all back. My eyes moisten and my hands tremble. It has reminded me that no matter how hard I work to put my childhood troubles behind me and make something of myself, a residue of loss will always remain in my heart.

The inescapable fact is that she made good on her promise, just as I knew she would, and by age 16 we were both gone.

Many years later Damian and I would return home to build bridges, make peace and restore the family ties that had so ruinously fallen away – but not until long after our stepmother was gone. We got there in the end but the scars took a long time to heal and it was an incredibly difficult journey. Damian went on to become a respected soldier, serving six years in the Royal Green Jackets, and was loved by his comrades, proving wrong the woman who had gleefully proclaimed that he'd amount to nothing. He died aged 25, the victim of a tragic car smash, but not before making his mark on this world.

I have never hit a woman in my life and I regard men who do so as nothing more than inadequate bullies – sniffling, insecure cowards who offer feeble and pathetic excuses that say more about their own weaknesses than those of their unfortunate victims. To me, such gross bullying represents humiliation of the worst sort: every time such men strike out in anger, they lose whatever remaining vestiges of self-respect they have, so they're not only wounding their victim but also destroying themselves. But I do confess that back in my younger days, when I was still foolish and immature enough to let my childhood spectres haunt me, whenever I was involved in a particularly bloody brawl, be it in a back alley street fight or a rumble on the door of a nightclub, it was often the grinning ghosts of years past that I saw crumpling beneath my fists.

And it wounded me with shameful joy.

Within a matter of months, I found myself inhabiting a seedy bedsit in the twilight world of Blackpool's backstreets. I got there via an enjoyable stint at my grandparents' house, which came to an abrupt end, thanks to the machinations of my stepmother. Oddly enough, once I got over the shock of my sparse and shabby surroundings, for the first time in my life I began to feel like I had found a place called home.

For decades, the seaside resort of Blackpool has drawn youngsters to it like moths to a flame. Taken at face value, its bright lights, glittering tinsel and bawdy colours invoke warm stirrings of sunshine and laughter, mirth and merriment, and present a seductive palette. However, scratch a little below the surface, visit the town when the riotous summer season comes to an end or take a detour off the tourist trail and the town takes on an altogether darker and colder hue.

For the princely sum of £30 a week, I shared a decrepit,

filthy and needle-strewn house with a motley crew of benefit cheats, drug addicts and petty thieves. We each lived in separate bedsits but had to share a damp and decaying bathroom, riddled with mould and a vile green slime that clambered up the tiles like an alien spawn. The bedsit I occupied was on the ground floor and, to this day, I have yet to see a more squalid abode.

Despite my many faults, I have always prided myself on being a clean and hygienic person: back then I always believed that no matter how poor you were, you could always spare fifty pence for a bar of soap and a scrubbing brush. I fully believed in that wholesome philosophy until I attempted to clean – or, more accurately, sterilise – my new 'home'.

The room had an unmistakable odour of stale urine, dried sweat and rotting wood. In the twenty-first century, I don't think a landlord could get away with charging rent on such a shitheap; in fact, he'd probably be arrested. But back in the late 1980s, apparently nobody cared.

For two whole days, I scrubbed and disinfected the place, but no matter how hard I toiled I couldn't get rid of the rancid smell. I swiftly identified the mattress as the main culprit and furiously set about soaping it clean, in my naivety thinking that a vigorous rub would wash away pools of dried piss, flaky cum stains and sheens of matted sweat. Next I attacked the curtains, which were cloaked in a dense, choking dust, and then the windows, which were covered in a layer of Vaseline-like grease that stank of chip fat.

I had difficulty sleeping, almost gagging at the noxious whiff of the bed sheets, which came with a built-in body odour that never went away, no matter how many times I washed them. I came to grimly appreciate that years-old human sweat truly is a remarkably persistent essence.

I eventually realised I was wasting my time and resolved to live in shit, if only on a temporary basis. In truth, the bedsit didn't really need cleaning – it needed to be fucking demolished.

In a twisted kind of way I held a curious admiration for the landlord's ruthless application of Darwinian economics – he genuinely didn't give a toss just so long as he got his money. Every square inch of his property had been converted into rental living space; some of the bedsits were so tiny I'd have sworn they were originally broom cupboards.

Crap accommodation and slum landlord aside, I thoroughly enjoyed living in my shitty bedsit. Amongst fellow misfits and oddball tenants, I made some good, albeit fleeting friends. I came from a background that was solidly working class and although we had never been poor or hungry, not a single member of my family had ever earned any real wealth. Throughout my childhood I had always been proud of my working-class roots, but the abject poverty I witnessed and endured in that bedsit made a profound and lasting impression on my adolescent mind.

There is working class and then there is poor, and there is but a tenuous and flimsy tightrope between the two. With a helpful shove, I had taken a big tumble backwards and was now, briefly, one of the poor. If I was to get out, I would have to fight like a wounded tiger. Thanks to the combined influences of my stepmother, the stingy landlord and his chaotic tenants, my survival instincts were beginning to stir.

I struggled by on scraps of money from short-term, menial jobs, interspersed with spells on the dole. I'd done an unfulfilling stint as a window cleaner, and become a failed YTS apprentice, an office temp, a supermarket shelf-stacker and a temporary shift worker in a factory. When I wasn't working, I got to know some of my flatmates. They were a motley bunch of rascals and misfits, most of whom had never done a decent day's work in their lives – that is if you discount 'thieving and dealing' as work. I generally steered clear of them and tried to avoid hearing too much about the scams they were involved in, but when you're an impressionable soul living in the same house as a bunch of scallys, even the best of intentions can go awry.

I became particularly close to my Irish next-door neighbour Seamus, a small-time drug dealer who'd frequently knock on my door in the middle of the night and offer me free cannabis. After a token display of feeble refusal, which he always waved away, I'd invite him in and sample his free hashish. Seamus had a heartbreaking tale of his own to tell and if I thought my childhood had been harsh, well, it was like a fairy tale compared to his. He'd lost family members to IRA punishment beatings and knee-cappings, to drug overdoses, suicides and lengthy repeat prison sentences.

In his mid-20s, Seamus had fled to Blackpool intending to make a clean break from his criminal past and wasted youth. By his own admission he was like a misguided pinball, having no ideas, ambitions, role models or skills that might enable him to turn his life around. Within one year of his arrival he was a full-on pothead and borderline heroin addict. The trouble with Seamus was that his head was still in the same place – drug-running for the IRA – only the geography had changed.

Seamus and I had a nice little routine going: he'd talk and I'd listen, smoking his free pot. I learnt many things during our conversations; he introduced me to a darker side of life that I hoped never to visit again. Seamus was a drug addict and a thief, but he was also a human being who had lived and experienced life at its rawest and most agonising. I never allowed myself to grow too close to him and I restricted our friendship to our occasional nightly joints, but I am certainly glad I met him.

Our association came to an abrupt end when the landlord found him collapsed in the toilets with a needle poking out of his thigh. In his typical 'couldn't give a shit' style, Seamus had chosen the worst possible day of the week to get high.

Friday was rent day and with pin-sharp punctuality the landlord turned up at 6 p.m. to collect his money.

I was bursting for the loo and wearily trudged upstairs to use our grotty shared toilet. The door was slightly ajar, so I gave it a cautionary tap and gently pushed it open. Seamus was sprawled on the toilet seat in a state of total collapse. I knew he was a druggie and suspected that he injected, but I had never seen him in such a state before. His skinny, hairless white legs poked out before him, his filthy soiled jeans tangled carelessly round his ankles. A needle stuck out of his bare thigh, half-covered by his pale, green-veined hand and a crisp white towel. A thin stream of bright red blood was running down his leg, glistening in pock-like tracklines and congealing round half-healed scabs and open sores from previous injections, spotting the towel with crimson and dripping noiselessly onto the piss-stained carpet. His eyes registered no shock at my presence or any hint of embarrassment or shame.

I quietly shut the bathroom door and sat on the stairs, numbed at what I had seen. For an hour I waited for the door to swing open and the toilet to flush, but the sound never came. With my bladder about to burst, I returned to my bedsit, stood on my tiptoes and flopped my cock against the cold metal sink. As I watched the straw-yellow fluid bubble against the rusted grey bowl, the relief I felt was tempered with worry about what fate awaited Seamus. The answer came with the dreaded landlord's arrival. Once he'd pocketed his precious rent money, he forcibly and noisily evicted my pothead friend.

I never saw him again.

Sometimes in life you need to witness a shocking scene, or even participate in that sudden and frightening event, in order to wake up and see things clearly. I had just experienced such an episode with Seamus. Sitting on my torn and tattered couch, with its cigarette burns, burgundy wine stains and decayed digestive crumbs, looking at the crumbling hovel I inhabited, having just given my landlord a slice of rent money that I could ill afford, I vowed to make a change.

My thoughts were disturbed by the drip, drip, drip from the corner of the room, where two large buckets were gradually filling with water, thanks to a gaping hole in the ceiling just beneath some leaking pipes. The hole had exploded with a bang in the middle of the night several weeks earlier, when I'd awoken with a start, thinking it was a brick being thrown through my window. From then on, it had been like Chinese water torture, the drip keeping me awake at nights.

I had warned the landlord about the growing bulge in the ceiling, which, as it swelled with water, began to resemble a pregnant ewe's tits, but each week, as he solemnly stepped into my room, a bit like an ashen-faced Boris Karloff, with his back ramrod straight, staring down at me imperiously from his great height and silently stretching out his long arm to collect the rent (he'd quite deliberately stand as far away as he could while maintaining an efficient money-grabbing distance) he'd stare at the ceiling with his best poker face, scratch his chin and mumble under his breath . . . then he'd walk out and do sod-all about it. The cold reality of my situation and surroundings, as well as the potential threats and future hazards it represented, hit me in the face with a hard slap and I knew instantly that it was time to leave. I had enough common sense in me to know that if I hung around much longer it might be me being flung onto a concrete pavement and angrily kicked out into the streets. I didn't want to end up like Seamus. It was time for me to find a new home.

With the remnants of my meagre savings, I scraped together enough for a deposit on a new bedsit. My new dwelling was still decidedly poky (I was becoming used to such places), but it represented a significant step up in class from my old one: the landlord was a warmer sort and it was closer to the town centre. I felt pretty positive about it – apart from the small but significant problem of being barely able to afford the rent.

My financial woes were further compounded by the discovery that the electric meter, which I would rely on heavily for warmth during Blackpool's infamous windswept winter, devoured fifty-pence coins like a rabid Pac-Man. With a weary and reluctant sigh, I acknowledged that my new home meant I would also have to find a decent, permanent job – and fast.

I began sniffing round for opportunities wherever I could and found myself becoming increasingly inventive and creative as I adapted to my new situation. I would cheerfully wander the streets, knocking on the doors of various shops and businesses, peering at adverts in windows and constantly looking for a break. Whenever a series of knockbacks threatened to get me down, I'd retreat to the sanctuary of the library and lose myself in the oasis of books and the fantastic possibilities that they represented.

The library became a second home to me and a place of safety from the outside world. Whilst there I'd scour the job ads and constantly pester the librarians for any tips and leads. Sure enough, I soon spotted an advert in the paper for trainee clerks in a huge office complex that seemed to employ half of Blackpool. To my restless teenage spirit, it sounded soul-sapping – but the pay wasn't bad and it seemed secure, which was what I needed more than anything else.

The only problem was my complete lack of qualifications. Supposedly, the job required a grand total of five GCSE passes, which I just didn't have at that time; for all I cared, they may as well have been asking for an Oxford University PhD. After giving it about five minutes' thought, I cheerfully decided to lie through my teeth – I was going to get this job no matter what because I needed it to survive and to put food in my belly.

Growing up under my stepmother's glacial gaze forced me to become resourceful and adaptable, so I'd developed a vivid imagination and a sharp emotional intelligence. At school I had been a complete failure – disruptive, aggressive, sullen and withdrawn – but at home, where I was forced to spend hours banished to my bedroom, I discovered that I had a natural talent for writing and escaped to far-off worlds through the pages of books. Circumstances had forced me to develop my voracious reading habit and by the age of 13 I was racing through several books a week, learning at an exponential rate and becoming a knowledge-hungry autodidact. I couldn't have told you anything about science or maths, and I could barely add up, but when it came to the written and spoken word I was already way ahead of my contemporaries. My technical grammar skills weren't that great and I didn't yet have the well-rounded writing ability that I have now, but when it came to stringing sentences together that 'felt good' and expressing myself on paper, very few people could compete with me. I had a strong and constantly improving 'writer's voice' which I had enhanced with all of the reading that I'd been doing for years on end. It was this that enabled me to embellish my non-existent qualifications to such an extent that I would pass the job interview. It came down to survival skills.

Two weeks later the soggy, longed-for brown envelope telling me I'd got the job landed on my grime-stained porch. But what I couldn't have known then, in the midst of my joyous celebrations, was that within a matter of months I'd be plunged into a grave personal crisis that would have profound, life-changing consequences and leave me fighting for my sanity; in fact, for life itself. All that I had worked for would come crashing around my feet and conspire to plunge me into an abyss.

And, worst of all, the blood that would be spilt would all come about from my own angry hand . . .

2

SUICIDE SOLUTION

THERE ARE CERTAIN POINTS IN AN AVERAGE MAN'S LIFE WHEN HE cannot help but compare himself with his peers and agonisingly analyse how little he's achieved. If he is anything like I used to be, then he will dwell on how generally crap he is doing and how impotent he is to make his few dreams come true. I think it is primarily a disease of the young: the younger we are, the more competitive and insecure we tend to be. Wiser heads tell us that the only race we should be concerned with is the private one with ourselves to achieve our own potential and I've found that the older I get the more I realise the timeless truth of this advice: no matter how successful you think you are, sooner or later you come across somebody younger, better-looking, richer, with a hotter girlfriend and a bigger dick. And that's just the way life works.

On the flip side, there'll always be somebody with a damn sight less than you, too.

At some point in our lives we'll all probably experience a bit of both and we'll either be on the up or on the down. So I guess none of it really matters; it's foolish to make comparisons and you just do your best to be happy and fulfilled in your own skin. But how the hell are you supposed to know all that when you're barely 18?

As soon as this so-called milestone age loomed before me, I felt a cloud of depression easing itself onto my sagging shoulders, its black weight crushing me into the floor. And the more I fought against the burden, the heavier and stronger it became. When I looked around at my contemporaries, they were carefree, their casual talk about college parties and girlfriends; I felt a great deal older, more rushed, pressured and tightly wound, like a coiled-up spring. Despite settling into my new home and job with a minimum of fuss, I had a nagging feeling that life was somehow passing me by; my precious youth was draining away like a drunkard's piss down a grimy Friday night drain. A sense of powerlessness and loss gripped my every waking moment. I was adrift. Depression beckoned with its warm and welcoming hand.

I yearned for Seamus, with his spidery spliff-rolling fingers, his tobacco-stained teeth and mischievous grin, and the green Irish eyes that twinkled like emeralds. I wondered what had become of him. I sorely missed the kind of non-judgemental conversations we had shared.

I missed his free pot, too.

I found myself getting extremely angry that I had been forced to leave behind my beloved younger brother Damian. I had barely seen him since I had left home, where I remained a *persona non grata*, and I missed him a great deal. He was practically forbidden to come near me and it only deepened my pain.

I simply couldn't shake off my feelings of despair and an impending sense of doom. I was sliding ever deeper into a dangerous depression and I just didn't know how to break out of it. As a last resort, I called Damian. Fuck it, I decided. I needed cheering up and to hell with any objections. I couldn't be hurt any more than I already had been, for the scars ground deep and the damage was wrought.

I arranged to meet my brother outside his school gates to

catch up on old times. It was an awkward meeting, as so much time had passed and so many things had changed, and we were both reluctant and embarrassed to acknowledge it. Whereas before we had enjoyed an easy-going banter and deep rapport, now there was a stilted nervousness and uncertainty to our chatter. I noticed Damian looked at the floor a lot, avoided eye contact, and fidgeted and glanced around, as if fearful that our stepmother would burst from a hedge and surprise us – catching him red-handed, breaking her most sacred iron rule. He was clearly desperately unhappy and it pained me to see him in such a perilous state. His whole being seemed cowed and subdued. I managed to coax out of him what his plans were and how tough a time he was having at home. He confided that now he was a teenager vice-like pressure was being applied to force him into an early exit. Our stepmother wanted him out of the house.

On the upside, he had joined the Marine Cadets and was doing surprisingly well, winning the 1989 Cadet of the Year award and the coveted 'best shot' trophy for marksmanship. He said that, like me, he was thinking about a military career, as he reckoned it was the quickest and best way to get away from 'her'.

I tried to gee him up, congratulating him on his success and telling him what a massive achievement winning those two awards was, and how profoundly pleased and proud he'd made me. I wished him well and told him that I hoped he'd have better luck with it than I did. We shook hands and parted.

As I watched Damian trudge off, with his hands in his pockets and gaze glued firmly to the floor, his mind swirling with God only knows what fears and anxieties, I felt several conflicting emotions. The first was an intense wave of love and concern for him. Love because this beautiful blond kid with such a warm heart and pure soul was my brother; concern because, like me, he faced an uncertain future and bore the

27

same scars as me like an invisible but gruesome tattoo.

The second emotion was a hot stab of hatred that he should have to suffer under such a stultifying weight and crushing oppression. He was being suffocated, with his hopes and dreams smothered and his doubts and fears stoked.

Far from cheering me up, this meeting made me feel a hundred times worse. I returned to my grubby bedsit with a heavy heart. There was a dark storm gathering within me.

It is only now, years later, when I look back on those bleak and lonely times, that I realise how incredibly deeply my childhood had wounded me. The complete and utter rejection of my entire being had left me feeling like a worthless wretch. Outwardly I tried to put a brave face on things, but inwardly I nurtured a gnawing sense of isolation.

In retrospect I can see that it was an error to move so close to the thumping heart of Blackpool. I foolishly believed its gaudy temptations would bring me happiness. But it's hard to sit alone in a cold, dingy bedsit when you can hear the constant sound of revelry on your doorstep. When the famous tower was lit up, the illuminations were bouncing off my walls like some green-tinged ghost train!

Despite living in the epicentre of Britain's undisputed wildest party town, I became consumed with an aching loneliness. Shortly after meeting Damian, I began on a downward spiral from which I would not emerge until the following year. As I found myself getting involved in more and more scrapes, my personality began to darken and fracture. I embraced the seedy twilight world of Blackpool at its worst and deliberately entered into conflicts and situations that could have had tragic and permanent consequences. I eagerly took on the stereotypical role of the 'angry young man' and could only see the world through the bleakest of eyes, choosing always to view myself as a wronged victim and cynically using this as an excuse to generally wreak havoc. For a long time, I'd summarise myself as someone not easy to get along with or like – probably because I didn't like myself.

In fact, I fucking hated myself.

My newly adopted face was an ugly one.

At night-time, I'd wander the streets and find myself staring up at multistorey car parks, debating whether or not to jump off them and wondering what I'd look like splattered on the floor. On one occasion that still causes me to shudder I'd drunk a bottle of Bacardi and cheap cola on my sofa before stumbling out well past midnight. The streets were almost deserted, as it was out of season and midweek. I came to a car park that had caught my eye earlier, but I couldn't get into the damn thing; its rust-ridden steel shutters closed off the entrance/exit completely. I tried to climb onto the first floor by jumping up and getting a handhold on the chipped concrete ledge, with the intention of hauling myself into it with brute strength and quiet determination. But luckily for me it was harder than it looked and it defeated my furious scrabbles with ego-bruising ease. After several failed attempts, I collapsed against the wall and knelt down against it to regain my strength and soothe my scraped knees. My hands were grazed and bleeding, thanks to the harsh stone, and my fingernails split and cracked, but I'd resolved to ignore the pain as it felt strangely cathartic. It only added to the occasion – to the struggle. Death, like life, was not supposed to be easy.

Somehow the blood, the phlegm in my throat, the grit in my fingers, my aching knees and throbbing tiredness, the silence of the night and empty streets – it all felt right. I didn't have to pluck up any courage because the certainty that it was my time enveloped me like a warm blanket and comforted me as a dear and trusted friend.

As I was readying for a fresh leap, a police car slowly cruised up to me, its blue lights eerily and silently flashing as its lone driver pulled to an ominous stop. He waved me over and I stood before him with my chest heaving, blowing cold hoops of air into the moonlit night, wiping my dusty hands down on my ripped jeans. He wound his window down, all the time silently and warily staring at me, then tilted his head out and peered up into the darkness, scanning the car park's shadowy nooks and crannies, before slowly swivelling his gaze back to me and eyeing me calmly. My heart began thundering as I readied myself for a bollocking and desperately fumbled for an explanation that might somehow save me from arrest.

'Go home, son,' was all he said. He didn't even ask what I was doing, although I'm sure he must have guessed.

The sight of the solemn-faced policeman, with his strangely calming stare, brought me round and I nodded wordlessly in reply before reluctantly taking his advice and trudging back to my darkened bedsit, hands in pockets and grief-deadened eyes glued to the grey pavement cracks, a haze of numbed confusion under his watchful lawman's eye. There was something compelling in the blank way he looked right through me that seemed to trigger a hypnotic obeisance. If he hadn't turned up at that exact moment, then God only knows what I would have done, either at that car park or somewhere else, because in my heart of hearts I felt calm and ready that night. And that's what scared me: I knew that the policeman's divine-like intervention was only a temporary stay of execution. I felt so low I was almost willing something to happen and I wouldn't rest or recover until it did.

I had another near miss when, on an impulsive whim, I decided I was going to take a pill overdose. I trawled round the chemists of Blackpool town centre buying up packets of paracetamol to down with my usual tipple. The chemists will only sell you one packet at a time and even then they'll question you if you look suspicious. I managed to get about five packs before I was refused outright and couldn't buy any more. It made me wonder if they had some kind of 'round-robin' telephone warning system for unstable-looking individuals . . . but no matter, I reasoned, I had more than enough to get the job done.

As soon as I got back to my bedsit, I placed the pills on the mantelpiece and plonked myself down on my stale settee, feeling oddly elated and resolute as I began necking the Bacardi, with one eye on the pills.

I was going through a phase of being slightly obsessed with Simple Minds and I had fallen in love with their 1989 album *Street Fighting Years*. (I still adore the band and in 1991 saw them perform live on their Real Life tour at the Birmingham NEC.) I decided to listen to it on my Walkman and ended up drifting off to sleep, enjoying the music, half-drunk, forgetting about the pills. I awoke with a jump when I heard loud banging on my window that just wouldn't stop. In retrospect, like the policeman's timely warning, this was another divine intervention.

I groggily opened the door to let in a drinking buddy, who was actually a very decent guy and had grown concerned about me. I sparked up in that weird kind of manic way that is often a signal of somebody fighting depression. And for some reason – I don't know why – I told him that I was going to take a load of pills once he'd gone. It was no idle threat: I fully intended to do it – so much so that I was soon ushering him out of the door in a drunken haze.

I decided to listen to *Street Fighting Years* one last time, though – and yet again I drifted off to sleep, guzzling from my precious Bacardi bottle. This time when I awoke it was with a startling clarity that I must take the pills. But when I went to the mantelpiece they had gone. My friend had taken them while my back was turned.

So there were no pills left for me to swallow.

I paced about the room, cursing and chuckling, feeling intensely confused, slightly offended and strangely euphoric all at the same time. Eventually, I drifted off again and the temporary crisis passed. When I awoke next day, it was with the sensation that I had avoided something terrible – but deep down I knew it was only a temporary reprieve.

I didn't have to wait long for another opportunity.

On the occasion of my 18th birthday my despair erupted in a predictably violent and bloody episode – the physical scars of which I still carry to this day. To celebrate my coming of age, I agreed to go on an all-day drinking binge with a group of booze buddies. It wasn't the sort of thing I was normally into, but as it was supposed to be such a special and happy occasion I found myself feeling obliged to go along with it. In truth, I didn't need much persuading, even if I feigned protest.

We must have visited damn near every pub in Blackpool and by the end of the night I was so drunk I had vomited several times. Our final destination was a tacky seafront nightclub that had seen better days. Up until that point it had been a great night, without a hint of trouble – but like the selfish idiot I was, I couldn't bear to see others happy when I wasn't, so I had to go and spoil it. In the past, I had always been a happy drunk – I found that the more I drank, the better I felt – but not that night. I began to experience a powerful sense of melancholy, and I became weepy and giddy, fighting a constant urge to reach out and touch my companions. As the ale flowed and the night wearily wore on, the music and fog of white noise grew louder in my head till I sought solitary refuge on a step by the bar.

I sat by myself watching my little gang of pals dancing and enjoying themselves, revelling in the drink-fuelled madness of youth. I felt humbled that I had such friends and deeply moved that they had chosen to honour me with a party, which in a spirit of self-loathing I began to feel I didn't deserve. Sitting on the step, as easily as a drunk falls from a stool, I slipped from melancholy to ruminations to recriminations to violence – and all of it aimed at myself.

That fleeting thought was all it took. In a blinding flash, I awoke from my trance and sat bolt upright. The answer had come. The moment had arrived. Or so my warped mind told me.

I marched to the bar and asked the barmaid if I could have an empty glass. She hesitated for a second, perhaps sensing my intentions, before dismissing her ridiculous fears, flashing me an uncertain smile and helpfully giving me what I had asked for. For the briefest of moments, I examined the shining glass before smashing it on the gleaming bar rail. I buried the jagged edge into my inner left wrist, twisted it violently and dragged it across the soft white flesh.

My arm split like butter.

As I surveyed the wound, blinking numbly, a thin stream of blood gushed from the gaping hole and a large lump of ragged flesh fell to the floor. I felt neither pain nor revulsion, only a stupefying and nullifying sense of shame, regret and wonder: how the fuck did this happen – did I really just do that? Wow, I fucking did, didn't I?

Then all hell broke loose. The barmaid began screaming hysterically and the nightclub became Technicolor with blood.

My blood.

If I was expecting sympathetic treatment at the hospital, I was to be sorely mistaken. Two paramedics sullenly dumped me onto a stretcher and wheeled me into a brightly lit, deserted room. A steady throbbing had begun to permeate the severed flesh in my arm and with each hot pulse came a needle-sharp stab of quivering pain. I closed my eyes against the cold, harsh light and gritted my teeth, forcing my drink-sodden brain to re-trace the bloody events that had led me to that stark cubicle.

When I opened them again, I was staring into the blank

face of a green-robed and stern-looking surgeon. He loomed over me, blocking out the naked bulb overhead, swaying and tutting as he examined my shattered, limply hanging wrist. As drunk as I was, I could sense that he was extremely pissed off with me and that, to him, I was just another drunken yob who'd had about ten too many and got what he deserved. His whole manner spoke of a brisk, detached clinical efficiency. With my embarrassment and shame ever increasing, I decided to adopt an attitude of meek subservience so as not to irritate him further.

'Clench and unclench your fist, then tell me if it hurts,' he demanded in a robotic tone.

'It stings a bit, doctor, that's all. I thought it'd be worse.'

'That's because of all the alcohol and adrenaline swirling around your body, young man – you ought to be in agony. It's a shame, really, as pain has its uses and teaches us not to do stupid things. It's a good thing, as it reminds us not to behave in foolish, selfish ways. Don't you agree?'

Eager to win the approval of this all-powerful authority figure now in charge of my recovery and desperately hoping not to appear the ungrateful dickhead he thought I was, I enthusiastically nodded along with all he said. I vainly, pathetically, tried to soften him and he quite rightly slapped me down hard, gruffly seizing my wrist in his blood-stained rubber mitt. The doctor then ordered me to look deeply into the raw wound. He said he wanted me to study it closely before he repaired it so that I'd always remember. As he thrust the gaping hole mere inches from my eyes, I forced myself to absorb every shredded lump of tattered flesh and tissue. I noted the thick black cord that remained mercifully untouched – a major artery, said the doctor, that if severed could have led to death. Absurdly, I was reminded of *Terminator*, when Arnold Schwarzenegger's murderous cyborg performs emergency surgery on his own mangled arm. I considered mentioning it to the doctor but didn't think he'd appreciate my thoughts.

My wrist was roughly stitched together with a minimum of local anaesthetic, which was no more than I deserved. I think he deliberately gave me just enough to kill any real pain, but not enough so that I was comfortable and didn't feel a thing. He made the exact right decision and played it well because sometimes in life one has to be cruel to be kind. If I had been in his shoes, I'd have done exactly the same.

The impulsive act of slashing my wrist in full public view was a grimly cathartic act for me. It was a bloody and symbolic statement about my place in the world, and how I saw things, back then, in 1989, as a broken-hearted 18 year old. I didn't know whether it would kill me and I didn't much care whether I lived or died, such was the state I was in. But somewhere in my conscious I knew that at that point in time I had to make some sort of physical expression, however drastic, that would serve as a lifelong marker to me, no matter what happened. I simply had to do something dramatic – to break me out of my spell – because things couldn't carry on as they were. Those who unfortunately witnessed it, or had to clean up my mess, probably viewed it as a confused cry for help or a clumsy suicide attempt – because it certainly looked that way from the outside. And while I'll never be able to understand it fully myself, the more time passes and the older I get, the stronger grows my realisation and certainty that it was a desperate act of warped defiance. The public meltdown, the act of extreme violence towards myself . . . it was a physical manifestation of how I felt inside. I had become a deeply troubled young man.

Physically, I would make a full recovery from my botched 'suicide attempt', but the mental scars remain. Before the incident I wore my watch on my right wrist; since that day, I deliberately wear it on my left. I am reminded of it every morning when I fasten my watch strap: glancing down, my eyes see a thick, jagged, angry red stripe that, like a misplaced zip, winds itself across my wrist.

At first I was embarrassed by it, but as time has worn on I've accepted it and – dare I say it – even become a little fond of it. I view it as a discreet tattoo, for my eyes only, which has great meaning to me. It's begun to fade now, but the memory lingers and serves as a sharp, significant and useful reminder: just because you once made a great mistake and behaved appallingly, it doesn't mean your whole life has to be that way. I believe in second chances and forgiveness when somebody's fallen by the wayside and is trying to pick themselves back up and do the right thing. My scar has taught me to respect the fact that no matter how much you've fucked up in the past, then provided your heart's in the right place and you're willing to put the work in, you can always fight back for another chance and try to do some good in your life.

I am a resolute atheist and this 'faith' has never been shaken, despite the premature death of my brother or indeed the things that I've seen and experienced in this life, especially during my military service. Yet I do sometimes find myself wondering about why two people – the policeman and my pal – had appeared exactly when I needed them to, in order to stop me from doing something stupid. I ponder on the things that I've achieved since then and I do ask myself what strange fate sent them to me in my darkest hours. If they hadn't flashed up, there's a good chance that I'd be in a decades-old grave now. I'm the sort of man that usually does what he says he is going to do.

I came across a quote from the great American writer Cormac McCarthy in his 1992 novel *All the Pretty Horses* that sums up my feelings perfectly, both then and now: 'Scars have the strange power to remind us that the past is real.' As I gaze at my damaged left hand, with its self-inflicted gash from one dark teenage night, and its half-missing middle finger and heavily scarred palm from a patrol gone wrong when I was a soldier on the streets of Northern Ireland, those words ring startlingly true in my heart.

The immediate aftermath of the wrist-slashing episode plunged me to rock bottom and forced me to make a radical re-evaluation of my life. I had publicly exposed my weaknesses and deepest fears, and my humiliation was such that I had to disappear for a few weeks. When I resurfaced, I tried not to notice the whispered sniggers, the finger-pointing and pitiful glances – though I did and each one of them served to deepen my shame. But as the weeks turned into months and my drinking pals came and went, off to either university or pastures new, I noticed that the chatter and gossip ceased. The long-rumoured incident – and the fleeting friends – faded from view.

In an ironic twist, I felt myself growing stronger mentally; I surprised myself that I had the apparent fortitude to bounce back from the personal crisis and brazen it out. When I was healing and still consumed by embarrassment, if anybody asked about it, and I could get away with it, I'd give them a bullshit story about having had an accident. But as my confidence returned, I grew strong enough to look a curious stranger in the eye and state simply that I'd been through a bad patch and had hurt myself but now I was OK. It took me a while, though.

I realised that a good deal of my problems were bound up in my restless and solitary nature: I was spending too much time in my lonely bedsit, broodingly staring at the walls or obsessively reading scores of books. If I was to truly make myself better, then I would have to seek out active pursuits that dissipated my energy and relieved the pressure that had been building in me like an angry volcano.

One of my favourite childhood pastimes was karate, but my premature family expulsion and unwanted excursion into bedsit land had seen it fall by the wayside. I returned to the art with a sudden and ferocious passion, training for many hours in local gyms and schools – basically wherever I could find a class that would tolerate me obsessively kicking and punching my way up and down their dojo (karate gym), carelessly mowing down unfortunates who strayed into my path. In my 20s, I would go on to gain a black belt and become a formidable fighter, but as an unstable teenager karate instead provided me with an essential sense of kinetic motion and purpose. I began fighting in karate tournaments and handily won most of the matches I fought, though I also frequently got disqualified due to my overly aggressive tactics. I found myself banished from several competitions due to my take-no-prisoners attitude on and off the mat. The rules stipulated that executing takedowns or using full contact strikes to the face were not allowed. Well, I was OK with that until I came up against someone a bit slippery or whom I would deem to be 'flash' – then I'd let my temper get the better of me and couldn't resist drawing blood and vanquishing their cocky arrogance.

My sensei (instructor) frequently counselled me on the need for calmness and self-control no matter how dire the circumstances. I agreed with all he said and tried to follow his wise advice, but ultimately he was wasting his time – back then, self-control and me were a combustible combination that mixed together like fire and petrol.

Years later, after many physical injuries, contest disqualifications and numerous scrapes with the police, I would realise how right he had been and begin to seek the calmness and removal of the inner ego that marks out all truly great fighters and masters of combat – be they professional soldiers or martial artists. It's an elusive prey that I'm still hunting today, and hope to be till the day I die: the beauty of the quest is that it never ends, as true perfection can never be attained.

I must confess, though, that it will always be a source of

great regret to me that I never achieved my full potential as a competitive karateka because I had all of the physical attributes at my fingertips and strived constantly to cultivate a 'warrior spirit' and samurai mentality. What I didn't have, though, was that all-important judgement, nor did I have self-confidence, self-belief, stability of mind and the ceaseless, unwavering self-discipline that marks out the great champions. My head was all over the place; I was living a nomadic lifestyle, flitting from bedsit to bedsit, merely trying to survive from day to day. I couldn't see a way to turn my undoubted physical potential into a professional martial-arts career because I was too busy trying to find a safe space in which to live and was too caught up in other things.

To have gone 'all the way' I would have needed a secure, stable base from which to launch and sustain myself – in an emotional sense as well as a physical one – and back then I simply didn't have it. I couldn't see a way to grasp it because I was too occupied in the daily struggle. I didn't have a grand vision; I was too easily distracted and my ambitions didn't dare stretch that far. It saddens me now because with the knowledge, experience and confidence that I have today, I can see that with a few minor tweaks to my lifestyle and core belief systems – well, I could have become a great champion. I could have been a contender. But I suppose all too many of us can say that, can't we? And history is history: you're judged on what you did, not on what you might have done.

I didn't become a great karate champion and I have nobody but myself to blame for that. I had my chance and I lacked the wisdom to take it. I'm a classic late developer: when I was young, I didn't have a fucking clue, then when I did have a clue, I'd grown too old, my life had speared in a new direction and it was too late. That is the cold reality of it.

It is crystal clear to me now, which is why I've gone on to try and develop whatever other talents I have to their maximum potential, both physically and mentally. But I confess regret over that missed karate career and where it might have led remains. I could have done so much more, but I sold myself short.

As a young martial artist, the chief attributes I had were speed and aggression, but unfortunately I didn't yet have the physical strength to back it up. I would often find that as I charged into a much bigger opponent I'd soon be flying backwards again – sent spinning like a skittle. Part of the problem was size: despite being as fit as the proverbial butcher's dog and not having an ounce of spare fat on me, I barely weighed ten stone. If I wanted to become a truly formidable fighter, I'd have to beef up considerably. At my sensei's suggestion I decided to do some extra work in the gym in an effort to build up my muscles and stamina.

The aptly named Olympic Gym became my second sanctuary. I continued with my punishing runs but now added serious weightlifting to the mix. In no time at all I was addicted and permanently energised by ferocious workouts. I discovered in an ironic but telling twist that many of the iron devotees with the greatest strength and determination had been picked on or badly bullied when younger. This struck a resonant chord with me and I found it immensely therapeutic to heave and clang those rusty weights. Previous resentments and failures merely became fuel to the fire and I began to grow ever stronger. With every rep I lifted, I felt as though I was banishing the ghosts of the past.

Much of my rapid, hard-won gains were down to the magical aura of the gym. It was an old-fashioned spit-and-sawdust type of place where only serious lifters trained, a real old-school *Rocky* gym that attracted the kinds of athletes that were searching for something primal, earthy and elemental in their training – something an overpriced health spa couldn't match. It was a safe space where you could unashamedly revel in the simple pleasures of trying to become a stronger man away from all the bullshit and pressures of daily life and work.

Here you could find comradeship, mutual respect, honesty, belly laughs and humour galore. It didn't matter if you were the biggest or weediest guy in the gym; the spiritual mantra was one of 'We're all here to make the best of ourselves and to hell with the world outside. So let's enjoy it.' Nobody was judging you and the only guy you were in competition with was yourself. There were no shiny chrome machines, fancy contraptions or plastic exercise bikes – just tons of well-used iron. It had a gritty, mystical atmosphere: this was a place of transformation, where the weak became strong.

The gym was situated under a bridge and beside a railway line; at first glance it appeared like some kind of medieval dungeon. But how wrong was that initial impression. Some of the happiest, most productive and character-building days of my life were had in that gym. It was a place where boys were turned into men and the weakest flesh was forged into steel.

The gym was run by a barrel-chested former Mr London from the 1960s named Ivor Markham and was owned by his great friend John Harrison – a fellow old-school powerhouse who was built to walk through mountains. Despite their advancing years, they both retained phenomenal strength and rock-like physiques; their attitudes to lifting, life and learning remain timelessly true to this day. They had a fighting spirit and unquenchable energy that you could smell as soon as you walked through the door and it infected the gym with a super-DNA that seemed to hang in the air, its mystical molecules lending a life and vitality that you could almost get drunk on. It was a place of health, a place of truth and a place of welcome.

The one cast-iron rule that both Ivor and John drilled into you as soon as you entered the Olympic's hallowed walls was that steroids were strictly off limits and anybody caught using them would face instant expulsion until such time as they had seen the error of their ways and got clean again – permanently. They had built their bodies, won their titles and founded their gym in a clean 'golden era' long before steroids polluted the scene and they were fiercely against them, constantly policing the gym with a watchful eye and cracking down hard on any offenders.

I became especially close to Ivor and loved listening to him wax lyrical about the golden age of bodybuilding and his adventures in the sport. Ivor was a true master of the 'iron game' and I sensed instinctively that the timeless wisdom of his lessons could be applied to everyday life, too. He was like a real-life 'Rocky' coach, being interested only in the essential and immutable truths of our existences – both in and out of the gym. I was incredibly impressed by the grace with which he carried himself and the vibrant aura he exuded, both in and out of the gym, and found him to be a calming and inspiring influence.

I trained with my great childhood friend Paul Clayton and between us the muscles soon began to stack on like armour plating. Paul would later go on to build an incredible life of his own, spending 15 years travelling the world as an English teacher and all-round adventurer, as well as building an all-natural body that looks like it came straight out of a *Conan the Barbarian* comic. His exploits would be worthy of a book themselves.

I couldn't have chosen a better man as a training partner because we were evenly matched physically and highly competitive towards each other, but in a natural, healthy and supportive way. Paul had the 'eye of the tiger' and I always knew that he'd push me to my limits and wouldn't let me slack off for an instant – and I'd be as relentlessly hard on him in return. I'll always be grateful to Paul for the strength he gave me, both inside and outside of the gym. If we hadn't teamed up together in those crucial early years, then I don't think either one of us would have achieved half as much in this life as we have. Forged by steel in that dusty old gym, our partnership was truly a meeting of minds.

After a year's hard training, I had expanded my chest and arms by a couple of inches and managed to pack on more than a stone of lean muscle. I was hardly King Kong, but these hard-fought gains in stature gave my battered self-esteem a welcome boost. I now understood that with hard and honest labour even someone like me could achieve success. It was like a revelation. For the first time, I realised any phantom childhood curses that had been placed in my head could be vanquished with effort and imagination.

What I could never have known was that the bodybuilding buzz would soon eclipse the karate high and help to tip me headfirst into the dizzying excessive culture of Blackpool's nightlife – a place where no rules applied and extreme aggression was a prerequisite. I did not yet know it, but it was at this point, with the sprouting of those first muscles and my sudden realisation that I was 'getting strong' and gaining confidence with it, that my journey into clubland truly began.

I was on my way.

The bright lights of Blackpool had me fixed firmly in their sights – a sniper zeroing in on fresh, glistening prey.

3

THUG DOORMEN

EVERY NIGHTCLUB, WHEREVER IT EXISTS IN THE WORLD, AND NO matter its popularity, enjoys only a finite amount of time when it is considered 'hot' and can enjoy the status of being the hippest and trendiest club in town. This is the honeymoon period, which if a club is lucky will last for perhaps three years before the inevitable decline sets in and the crowds begin to drift away, ever on the lookout for something 'new'. In the early 1990s, the place to be in Blackpool was Illusions nightclub.

Illusions was a club that catered strictly to the local clientele and that was the secret of its long and enduring run. In Blackpool, there are two kinds of clubs and pubs: those that admit large groups of rowdy holidaymakers (much to the locals' annoyance) and those that don't. And Illusions didn't. To reach the club, you had to venture down a scruffy side street onto which the rear of several nearby pubs backed. The dimly lit street was often littered with broken beer bottles, loitering drunks and troublesome clubbers. Perhaps the most notorious of these few alleyways was one that led onto the rear of an insanely loud gay club, with an extremely amorous and exhibitionist membership. Whenever a gay couple was spotted getting a bit carried away, a volley of abuse would be hurled from the punters making their way into Illusions – stinging insults that would often be returned tenfold, much to everyone's amusement. For the most part, it was only words that flew across the alley, but from time to time fists and boots did, too.

Once you had negotiated the chaotic queue for Illusions and managed to persuade the bouncers and assorted managers that you were sufficiently local and sober enough to be admitted, you crossed into a roped-off area and made your way down steep stairs that led into the crowded chaos below. Once inside, the belly of the club literally swallowed you up and as you fought your way to the bar the air became moist, sweaty even, with the promise of action to come.

The walls and floor of the club were decked out in shiny black marble, and a green-beamed laser light system, revolutionary at the time, snaked across the dance floor, reaching into every nook and cranny. The incredible light show pulsed in time to the music, a sea of hot white arms stretching out to catch its passing rays, while sweat-flecked hair was tossed backwards and forwards, bathing in the electric green glow.

Clubland was beginning to change and Illusions was at the cutting edge of this revolution. Disco music and a slow lingering dance at the end of the night were most definitely out; hardcore dance music, piano house and Madchester melodies were most definitely in. A typical greeting would be Shaun Ryder's less-than-dulcet tones blaring out the Happy Mondays' classic 'Step On' or Bizz Nizz beseeching 'Don't Miss the Party Line'. One of my favourites was The KLF not-so-subtly screaming obscenities across the floor in their 'Live at Trancentral' dance classic 'What Time is Love?' as the walls and floors pounded with energy.

The resident DJ and a real hot property in the Blackpool clubs at the time was Eddie G, a curly-haired black guy with a booming voice who always seemed to pitch it right and would hold the club in the palm of his hands. He commandeered his decks like a general and read the mood of the crowd like a composer conducting a dance symphony. Eddie G had a real charisma and presence about him that meant he was as much a part of the club as the fixtures and fittings; he was one of those guys who looked like he was born to be a DJ.

The compulsive beats had markedly differing effects on different individuals: for some, it would be a night-long trance; for others, a rush of high-energy whistling bliss. What I didn't fully realise at the time was that how you ended up, either aggressively drunk or deliriously happy, often depended on the drugs you had or hadn't ingested. Specifically Ecstasy.

This was all new to me, as I was still a little 'green' about these kinds of things – the only drugs I'd encountered before were the ones I'd seen Seamus taking back in his bedsit, the cannabis to mellow him out and the heroin to completely comatose him. These weren't 'club drugs' like Ecstasy or coke, which, as I wasn't a hardcore clubber, I knew very little about. Unlike the really hard stuff, these new club drugs seemed to electrify users, amping them up like exploding power sockets. Ecstasy was still very new back then and unless you were dealing or using it, it simply didn't enter your orbit. But the biggest clue of all was this: pints made people fight, but pills made people dance. I was learning.

I can say with compete certainty that I was not one of the trendy types who frequented Illusions: in fact, I was just about one of the saddest and scruffiest-looking clubbers you would ever have had the misfortune to bump into. On several occasions, the stony-faced doormen had turned me away and the manager had refused point-blank to issue me with a membership card, despite my offering to pay double the going rate. However, my persistence was beginning to pay off and the door staff's constant rejections had begun to soften. At first I had been greeted with an impassive glance and blank refusal – they barely seemed to acknowledge me as a human being – but as time passed the refusals came with a friendly grin and a slap on the shoulder.

Looking back on that time, I am immediately struck by the lonely, nomadic figure that I must have presented in that bright new world, aimlessly drifting in and out of clubs, alone, seeking some kind of adventure, wanting and needing to belong.

I had fallen into a series of drinking habits, training patterns and rowdy, risk-taking behaviour. Some were good – my karate workouts, for example – but others not so much. I was drinking too much and had begun to fall into that time old, perennially dangerous habit of wanting to 'test my strength', as so many restless young men do. I would get into scuffles and do stupid things like climb on top of bus shelters and parked vans or go to parties with complete strangers and potheads whom I barely knew.

My lifestyle was one big contradiction: in one sense, I was seeking health and vitality in the gym, but in another I was on the hunt for destructive pleasures in the nightclubs. Somehow I just about managed to hold it all together, walking the tightrope without quite falling off, but the near-misses were racking up. What I can see now is that my overall lifestyle – one of constantly seeking thrills, adrenaline rushes and new experiences – was, for better or worse, inexorably leading me in one direction: towards clubland.

On the good side of life, such as it was, I was working hard in a steady, 'respectable' job by day. During the weekday nights, I would spend hours exhausting myself, punching and kicking my way up and down the dojo, honing my skills and reflexes to a level of razor-sharp perfection and precision. After the karate lesson was over I would then jog home to loosen up my aching legs and help dissipate the adrenaline and lactic acid. Once home I would grab a quick shower and jump into bed with a good book for an hour's intensive reading, then it was lights out. And the same again the next day.

The 'routine', as I referred to it, not only got me through the dark days of my troubled youth that feature in this story but also became the foundation for the success and physical fitness that I have enjoyed ever since.

So, when did it all begin to go wrong, if I was sticking to such a great routine? Well, the answer to that question is very simple: it was my weekend 'routine'. It cancelled out the good stuff and soon began to fuck things up.

Despite leading an extremely disciplined, almost monk-like existence during the week, I had fallen into an addictive weekend habit of trawling drunkenly through various nightspots. Living slap-bang in the middle of Blackpool's notorious clubland proved to be a temptation I simply couldn't resist. My resolve would last until about 7 p.m. on a Friday night, when, in a fit of restless energy, I would grab my jacket and practically run out the front door – straight to the nearest pub. On most of these 'spontaneous' excursions I would be by myself, as my refusal to make plans for the weekend allowed me to continue the private fiction that I was 'staying in'.

It was on these disorganised and haphazard nights that I got my first exposure to the twilight world of Blackpool's bouncers. For the most part, they seemed like distant and remote figures, utterly isolated from the establishments they ruthlessly policed. But it wasn't a negative image of isolation that they projected – rather, a splendid one. Or at least that's how I initially saw it, gazing through naive, adolescent eyes. I envied them their apparent power, seeming independence from the crowd and utter self-control. In a pub or club packed with scores of screaming wild-eyed youths, they were the only ones who were totally aware of their surroundings and what was really going on.

I recognised a few of the faces from my time on the

martial-arts circuit and during my increasingly long outings to various local gyms, where I'd already spied a few of the town doormen weighing me up and eyeing me from a distance. The fact that I was training hard and visibly displaying a bit of strength, determination and character hadn't gone unnoticed, apparently, and this tenuous outside link meant I could approach them for a brief chat without suffering the humiliating fate that awaited many – the cold-shouldered brush-off. But nonetheless, I was always mindful of the social gap that separated us and even in my most drunken state I always took care never to cause them a physical problem or to overstep the boundaries of our casual acquaintance.

My first impression, and one that proved to be true, was that there were generally three distinct types of doorman. The first was a reasonable and friendly sort of bloke who could be approached in a 'normal' open manner, without any fears of undue offence being caused or accidentally triggering a psychotic over-reaction. I would term this type as a 'straight doorman'. This is the sort of doorman I would become. In my experience, the vast majority of 'ordinary' working doormen in Blackpool during the rave era, those employed by the main agencies or 'firms', were straight types – and still are, in fact.

Your typical straight doorman would have an average day job during the week that bored him senseless and left him feeling about as fulfilled as a Chinese sweatshop labourer. The pay would usually be crap, too. So, to counter this, he'd beef up a little down one of the gyms and get himself a job on the door at the weekends, with the aim of remaining straight – alas, not always possible in that world – and working his way up to a berth on a 'top door'. And then, once there, if so inclined, he'd give flesh to his weekend fantasies of fighting, fucking, after-hours partying and occasionally pretending to be a 'gangster' to impress a girl or ward off trouble from lager louts and football fans, all the while desperately trying to protect himself from the real gangsters, who might easily drag him into their lives and absorb him into their problems. The straight doorman had to nimbly balance on a tightrope, ever careful that his weekend 'nightclub' face didn't plunge him into the abyss.

On the upside, the rewards were more than worth the risk. He'd get to shag gorgeous girls that were clearly out of his league and wouldn't otherwise look twice at him if he wasn't 'on the door' and from time to time he'd get to smack fuck out of a gobby, obnoxious scumbag who thoroughly deserved it. An occasional black eye from a Saturday night ejection gone wrong or an uncomfortable, awkward encounter with a connected 'heavy' demanding free entry for him and his pals was a small price to pay for those guilty pleasures.

I'm aware my enthusiastic embrace of violence just described sounds like a contradiction in terms – just who is the real hooligan, the doorman or the punter? But, like I say, the straight doorman walks a fine line.

The second type of doorman is an utterly unapproachable out-and-out bullyboy – a 'thug doorman', as they are more commonly known. With the thug doorman, everything is about playing to the crowd and 'giving it large' – projecting an image of menace and fury. A thug doorman would draw a great big line in the sand and you crossed it at your peril, with retribution being swift, savage and completely over the top. He deliberately tried to cloak himself in a kind of glittery 'surface glamour' and affected an image of streetwise gravitas, which at first glance was very effective but when you looked deeper and got to know him personally often hid a rotten and nasty core.

The thug doormen were thankfully only ever in a small minority because inevitably they never lasted long: they'd routinely be sacked, locked up, unofficially blacklisted or battered. Many of them were expelled from the game altogether when new, increasingly tough licensing laws caught up with them and exposed their multiple previous convictions for violence and assault. Inevitably, they'd go overboard once too often and either their club manager or security firm would simply drop them from their rota and stop offering them work.

The third type, and unquestionably the most menacing, was the 'gangster doorman'. With these sorts, unless you were one of them, you weren't expected to ask questions or attempt to become over-friendly. Indeed, it would have been a pretty suicidal gesture to so much as hint at even-footing with them or becoming pally too quickly, as their tight circle was strictly invitation only. For the gangster doormen, the nightclub world and all of its associations was their full-time occupation; they didn't wear shirts and ties and they didn't have day jobs. They didn't work for the big security firms either but instead had their own private arrangements in certain places – and those shall remain nameless in this book. In reality, they were only a very small, select group that kept both themselves and their business completely private and locked off from outsiders – including the mainstream doormen and security firms. They vetted anybody that entered their orbit and only worked, associated and socialised with their own kind, for obvious reasons.

Even when I became, briefly, a clubland face in my own right, I never so much as nodded in their direction and studiously avoided conflict with them, as it wasn't what I'd got in the game for and I was only interested in having the odd tear-up and increased access to pretty girls. Others were less circumspect, though, or had bigger ambitions than me, and inevitably egos would collide and bad blood would be spilt, either in the clubs or out of them. I would describe them as being extremely severe when crossed but generally polite, distant and professional in a standoffish kind of way. Many of the punters in ordinary clubs were blissfully unaware of their existence because their paths rarely crossed and the gangster types, quite deliberately and wisely, tried to keep off the radar and out of trouble – again, for obvious reasons.

I explained to one of the friendlier straight doormen whom I'd seen at the gym that I was having trouble getting into Illusions and that no matter how respectfully I approached the doormen I was being continually fucked off. He listened to my story in a completely neutral fashion, nodding occasionally but otherwise regarding me with an impassive face, his meaty forearms crossed beneath his muscular, barrel-like chest forming an impenetrable barrier. At the end of our conversation he merely said he would have a word, but he wasn't making any promises.

It would prove to be a fateful conversation that would lead to a hilarious mishap and clumsy introduction to clubland that still causes me to cringe with embarrassment today.

I remember walking away feeling hugely impressed by the apparent power and influence a well-respected doorman could exert in the clubs. I never found out exactly what he said to the Illusions team, but I had a smile on my face a mile wide the next time I went there. Usually, I would languish at the back of the long queue, shuffling forward at an agonisingly slow pace, reasonably certain that when I did get to the front I'd be refused entry. But not this time.

As soon as I strolled into the dimly lit back alley, a burly-looking bouncer stepped onto the greasy cobbles and held his beefy hand aloft. I recognised him instantly as one of the club's most senior doormen.

'Fuck me,' I thought. 'Not already! I've only just turned the corner and he's barring me!' But I had got it completely wrong. As I slumped my shoulders and turned to walk away, he stepped out after me and called me by my name. I couldn't believe it – one of the most respected doormen of Illusions nightclub, after months of rejections, was now ushering me down the stairs as a VIP guest. He thrust a gold membership card into my hand, told me to behave myself and said that from now on I didn't have to queue to get in – I could just walk straight past.

With that one simple gesture, a nod of the head and a plastic gold card, clubland had grabbed me firmly by the balls. For the next four years of my life, it jealously possessed me.

I was keen to make a good impression with the door crew and was mindful of the doorman's friendly warning that I behave myself, so I decided to remain stone-cold sober and vowed to avoid trouble like the plague. Seeing that the club was absolutely heaving and it would take about half an hour to get served, I decided to take a quick leak first. In later years I would be able to buy my drinks instantly and wouldn't need to bother queuing up alongside everyone else, but my newfound status didn't yet reach that far, so I gingerly made my way to the toilets, still beaming from ear to ear, unable to believe that I'd been given a free VIP membership.

The girls' toilets were directly opposite the gents and, as a rowdy queue of scantily clad females formed a line, lecherous banter and flirtatious comments flew back and forth. The atmosphere was thick with sexual tension and highly charged testosterone. As the queue slowly inched forward, I allowed my mind to race ahead, imagining all manner of lurid possibilities and heated liaisons still to come. I had an unmistakable feeling that it was going to be a great night – one that I would never forget.

Classy club or not, after a couple of hours all nightclub toilets are the same – and Illusions was no exception. Such was the volume of customers the drains had begun to overflow and pools of stinking yellow piss crept along the step, leaking and spreading across the tiles. After what seemed like an eternity of waiting I stepped up to the urinal and emptied my bladder with a sigh of satisfied relief, enjoying the second best sensation that a man can have with his naked cock. Then, without thinking, as I was still zipping my trousers up, I stepped back and promptly flew several feet into the air. I barely managed to let out a muffled *'Fucking hell!'* before landing flat on my back in the middle of a giant piss puddle.

At first, there was a stunned silence, then followed an unstoppable wave of clapping, hooting and laughter. I had just provided every single person in that toilet with a story he could look back on and laugh about for years. The impact of landing had knocked the wind out of me and as I tried and failed to haul myself up I realised I had been badly hurt. There was an intense throbbing pain at the base of my spine, my head was ringing like it had been cracked with a lump hammer and I felt a growing nausea creeping into my gut and clouding my vision.

But perhaps worst of all was having to lie utterly immobile and helpless in that puddle of reeking, unbearably foul warm piss.

Once the laughter had died down and it became clear I was unable to move, one of the more sober types suggested helping me up. He was instantly howled down with an outraged chorus of 'Fuck that! I'm not touching him – he's covered in piss!'

I was still lying on the floor, blinking mutely at the ceiling, when none other than the self-same doorman who'd let me into the club in the first place arrived with an angry scowl on his flint-hard face. He berated me for ignoring his advice and expressed amazement that I'd managed to get 'comatose', as he put it, in the space of 20 minutes. My humiliation was by now complete and it took all of my strength to mumble that I hadn't even had one drink; I'd merely slipped and banged my head. Once he understood what had happened, he took on a more sympathetic tone and gently helped me to my feet. My dick was hanging out of my underwear and my trousers had fallen round my ankles – all in all, I was in a 'shit state', as we used to say in the army.

As my lucidity returned, I began to realise what had happened and why I was in such pain, barely able to move: when I had stepped off the platform, I'd slipped on the puddle of piss and flown into the air. As I hit the floor in an untidy heap, the base of my spine had struck the sharp edge of the step and the back of my head had bounced off the hard floor like a football. The senior doorman had to practically carry me up the stairs, redressing me all the way, as if I was a child. At the top of the stairs, looking none too happy, stood one of the club managers and the rest of the door team.

I tried to explain what had happened, offering a barely coherent apology that was roughly waved away. Seeing that I was having no success in explaining my predicament, and was coming across as just another drunken troublemaker, the doorman who'd helped me out took pity on me and spoke on my behalf. One of the other doormen suggested calling an ambulance, but the manager vetoed the idea, saying he didn't want his club gaining a reputation amongst the police as a trouble spot. He told the senior doorman to get me safely out of the club and lead me off down the alley, from where I could hopefully make my own way home.

The doorman carefully walked me out, before propping me up against a wall about 50 metres from the club entrance – just far enough away that I couldn't be categorised as one of their 'problems' – giving me a pat of commiseration on the shoulders, as if to say, 'Better luck next time.' As I sat there, utterly winded, I nodded him a brief thanks and concentrated on gathering my senses.

I lay propped up against that wall for over an hour, watching the December snowflakes fall to the ground, trying to ignore the pointed fingers and guffaws of laughter from Christmas revellers passing by. The perceived wisdom was that I was some foolish young lad who'd got carried away at a Christmas party and drunk himself into a state of frozen stupor. I didn't have the energy to protest or disagree – if only they had known the truth.

The snow continued to fall and I lay vacantly staring into space, trying to block out the dull, paralysing pain spreading through my back and legs. Eventually, I awoke from my trance and forced myself to my feet. I was covered in a fine layer of snowflakes and had begun to resemble a snowman. Shuffling off at the pace of an arthritic old man, I realised that if I didn't get home soon I'd be adding hypothermia to my list of woes.

I felt as though a red-hot poker had been rammed up my arse; every step I took jarred my spine into spasms of searing agony. I managed to lessen the pain by walking with one hand on the wall for support and taking twice as many steps as usual. Every now and again a particularly clumsy drunk would clatter into me or a well-meaning passer-by would clap me on the shoulder with hearty wishes that I get myself home safely and congratulations for having managed to get so expertly trashed. As I was in no fit state to protest, I'd either merely freeze and stare at the floor waiting for the pain or offer them a forced smile through gritted teeth in the vain hope they'd leave me alone and bugger off home themselves.

Never in all my life had I been so immensely grateful to be returning to my grotty little bedsit. As I fumbled with the ancient, rusted lock, I made a mental note not to drop my key on the floor – if I had done, there was no possible way I could have bent down to pick it up again.

Once inside, I carefully manoeuvred myself onto the bed and set myself down as if I was a plank of brittle wood – I lay still and straight, as if the slightest bend or creak would make me splinter and snap. I remained on that mouldy bed in that freezing flat for two solid days without moving, still dressed in my best nightclub clothes – a cheap jacket and tie combo from Burton that I thought made me look like a cutting-edge style king. The pain cancelled out all other bodily functions, save for sleep and air: I felt no urge to so much as cough or take a shit.

I knew a fair bit of physiology, thanks to my years of physical training, and I felt certain that I had slipped a disc or seriously damaged my spine. By the end of the week, the pain had barely improved and I knew a visit to the hospital was inevitable. I took a taxi that I could ill afford to the accident and emergency department and waited in yet another predictably massive queue.

Eventually, my name was called and I shuffled into a private cubicle, where an extremely attractive female doctor awaited me. As I told her my story, she let out a throaty giggle, before laying her hand on my shoulder, apologising for laughing – and asking me to drop my trousers. Under normal circumstances I'd have been worried about getting visibly aroused at such a request, but not this time. I was in so much pain she could have dropped her own trousers and I wouldn't have been able to respond. The only thing I could focus on was the giant invisible poker that was burning up my insides.

She pulled on a pair of sterile rubber gloves, manoeuvred me to the side of the bed and then sat down at an angle behind me. Whispering gently in my ear in a failed attempt to put me at ease, she asked me to lean forward slightly so she could guide her hand better. I then had the extremely disturbing sensation of the doctor's dainty index finger forcing its way into my back passage – where it stubbornly remained for what seemed like an eternity, wiggling this way and that. It was a surreal moment and I felt obliged to offer my apologies to the doctor for any mess she encountered 'down there', as I'd aborted a painful attempt to empty my bowels and had struggled greatly to keep myself clean.

She put me at ease with another throaty giggle and joked that she'd dealt with far bigger, smellier and messier backsides than mine – and some of their owners couldn't have cared less about the state of them, much less had the grace to apologise.

The doctor finally extracted herself and pulled off the rubber gloves with a loud snapping twang before deftly slinging them into a tin-topped bin marked 'human waste products'. As she washed her hands in the tiny steel sink, she told me I had badly bruised and cracked my coccyx bone, the tail-like spur that sits at the base of the spine. She said I was on the mend but would have to endure the pain for a while longer, as it was a notoriously slow bone to heal. If I had any sense, she added, I'd spend the entire week flat on my back in bed.

And so that was what I did for the entire Christmas week of 1989 and the last ever week of the 1980s: I lay down, slept and read. I also had a lot of time to think on a deeper level than I had ever done before about my hopes and dreams for the coming decade, asking myself where in my heart I truly wanted to be. I sensed that the 1990s would be a time of momentous personal change within my own life and that my rapidly approaching 20s would present a golden opportunity for me to take charge of my own destiny in a more assertive fashion.

I have always considered New Year to be of far greater significance than Christmas because to me it represents new beginnings and rebirth – out with the old and in with the new and all that good philosophical stuff, so the one night that I was determined not to miss out on was New Year's Eve itself. I had managed to get two tickets from one of my new doorman contacts for myself and a pal to attend a party at Shades nightclub – one of Blackpool's roughest and dirtiest dumps, but essentially – and conveniently – cheap. It was a wonderful night and there wasn't so much as a hint of trouble, which for that place was highly unusual and downright strange.

As the DJ played hit after hit from the 1980s, the crowd became unified and welded together in a celebration of a shared and suddenly nostalgic past – and a daunting unknown and optimistic future. Up to that point my feelings about the '80s had always been mixed and ambiguous – for me, they represented a dark decade of pain and rejection – but as the final countdown to the new decade began I experienced a hot wave of love for the good things of the past, such as my loving grandparents and wonderful brother, coupled with a bright and burning desire to embrace the years ahead.

So, for me at least, as I waved goodbye to the 1980s, I felt immense relief, coupled with burgeoning optimism and bright hope. I was saying farewell to my childhood and all of the trauma and sadness that came with it. And, in that magical, fleeting moment, as the New Year bells and whistles still rang in my ears, the bad things of the past were gone and forgotten, blown over my shoulders like smoke in the breeze – the demons banished.

It was 1990.

A shiny new decade had been born.

And I was at last a fully grown man in charge of my own destiny.

My New Year's resolution was to become intimately involved with the nightclub scene that continued to grip my balls like a jealous mistress.

Sure, I was seeking thrills, and the prospect of illicit action was also a motivator, but my dire financial situation was the biggest factor in pushing me towards after-hours employment. Hanging around the clubs was proving to be an expensive, addictive habit and I had to find a way to fund my excursions.

The daytime office job that I'd somehow managed to blag my way into barely covered my expenses and it was becoming an immense struggle to stay afloat. Though my interchangeable bedsits were little more than grungy crash pads, they nonetheless had to be paid for, and my active lifestyle meant I had to fund gym fees and karate lessons on top of everything else. I ended every week with pennies in my pocket and little more.

I got a harsh wake-up call when my bank manager called me in and threatened to cut off my permanently in-the-red overdraft unless I got a grip on my finances. A chill went through me as I belatedly realised that if I didn't have the means to pay my rent then I would be homeless and on the streets – cast out every bit as ruthlessly as Seamus had been.

I will never forget the cold fear that stabbed me like a knife as I walked out of that desperately awkward meeting, petrified that the axe might fall on my fragile yet hopeful existence at any instant.

Looking back, I'm glad it took place and happy that I embraced that fear, taking the warnings on board. Since then I have always been careful to pay for the essentials first and have applied a rigid discipline to my finances. But at the time I was shitting myself, of course – back then I didn't feel quite so sanguine about my perilous state!

The reality was that my barely minimum-wage job didn't cover my bills. Unless I reduced myself to a hermit-like existence of eating cold beans and shutting myself away – which frankly didn't appeal – I would have to get a second job. I thought about going back to supermarket shelf-stacking or even taking on some weekend factory shifts, but I soon realised that the perfect solution was staring me in the face.

I could kill two birds with one stone if I got a job in clubland: I'd be earning money *and* having fun at the same time in an environment I loved. I'd be a part of the action and wouldn't miss anything – which I certainly would doing nightshifts in a supermarket or working myself into the ground in a factory, too tired to even venture out once I'd finished. So, really, it was a no-brainer for me: it was clubland or bust.

I redoubled my efforts to find work and as I made acquaintances and friendships amongst the doormen, managers and bar staff, for the first time in many years I began to experience a sense of belonging. It was almost like finding a second family; however, the club was an inviting new home where I was unconditionally accepted for who I was – which contrasted sharply with the cruel rejections of my childhood.

I made a decision to start slowly and cautiously, getting to know first the bar staff, as they were generally more friendly and approachable, and then the doormen and local 'faces' – although that was a high-risk strategy and I'd have to tread carefully there.

What I was hoping for was an eventual job offer in a hot club – although this was easier said than done, as such places were always oversubscribed by desperately eager job hunters.

To start with at least, the only jobs I had in mind were either glass collecting or working behind the bar. The idea of becoming a doorman myself was only just fermenting in my mind because at that stage the harsh truth was I simply wasn't ready for it; I still looked a bit young. I was improving as a martial artist all the time and training harder than ever, which meant my physique was beginning to visibly bulge with hardened muscle, but, nonetheless, working the doors remained a goal for the future.

To get a job in one of the better clubs was all about word of mouth and whom you knew. The job interview didn't follow the traditional rules, where you presented yourself with a CV in a nice suit, said all the right things and hoped to get lucky; it was an altogether more informal and relaxed event. Jobs were given out on the personal recommendations and gut instincts of those already working in the clubs. To make sure my job hunting was successful, I would have to get to know the right people first – no matter how unpleasant or thuggish some of them turned out to be.

The only qualifications that mattered in clubland were whether you would fit in or not. Nobody gave a fuck about your interview patter or your shiny shoes. Nobody cared if you didn't have any GCSEs or had been turfed out of school. None of that trivial stuff mattered: you were taken solely at face value. Management didn't give a shit about the professional impression you gave at an interview either; they were only interested in the vibe you radiated when you were out and about: what mattered was whether or not they felt they could trust you.

If you were OK, then you were OK.

End of story.

Clubland was a nomadic world: new faces would constantly float in and out of it in a random and chaotic manner. And, as I would later go on to learn, everybody had a story to tell – and some of them were considerably worse than mine. Indeed, it was these collective and disordered pasts that united us: thanks to our fucked-up histories, most of us were inherently incapable of looking either too far backwards, forwards or within ourselves. We were only interested in one thing: the precious present – living for the here and now, in this very moment, this very second. And we didn't ever want the party to stop because when the music died and the lights faded out you were engulfed in a deafening silence and stillness – and then you were reminded of what you were running from.

The past.

This period of observation and learning from afar was one of immense personal value. From just standing back and watching, I learnt a great deal about how one was expected to behave within that dark and predatory world. There was a clear pecking order, and there was a right and a wrong way to manoeuvre yourself about the smoke-filled clubs. And unfailingly, whenever someone took a wrong turn and pissed off the wrong person, a swift and violent lesson would be brutally administered. I witnessed several disturbing incidents that to this day leave a nasty taste in my mouth, as the beatings dished out far surpassed the supposed 'crime' – often just a clumsy indiscretion the victim was accused of committing.

One incident that sticks forever in my mind concerned a young lad from Barnsley with whom I had struck up a fleeting acquaintance. 'Lee' had travelled down to Blackpool the previous summer in a noble attempt to break free from a grindingly dull and bitterly disappointing existence in his native Yorkshire. Like so many young men before him, myself included, he had felt the magnetic pull of Blackpool's bright lights, with all its gaudy and superficial surface glitter. He had fallen in love with the town during numerous childhood visits and it was as a starry-eyed and spotty adolescent that he made the fateful decision to make it his adult home.

For Lee, and the scores of young men like him who re-populate the holiday town every summer, the decision to move was an easy one. Lee had been kicked out of school at the age of 14 and seemed destined for an unfulfilling life, either sweating out mind-numbingly boring shifts in a procession of soot-filled factories or shovelling cement till his hands bled on a succession of wintry building sites. The jobs on offer in Blackpool were hardly much better, but, as Lee succinctly put it when we first met, 'If you're going to be in the shit, then you might as well be in the shit by the seaside.'

It was hard to argue with his logic and, instantly recognising each other as a kindred spirit, we struck up a haphazard and chaotic friendship. Like me, Lee had been trying to get that elusive first job working in the nightclubs, but after repeated knockbacks he'd been forced to accept work as a pot-washer in the steaming hot kitchens of a backstreet hotel. The job was about as unglamorous and depressing as it was possible for a job to be and at the end of a gruelling shift his aching forearms would be riddled with tender scalds and stinging cuts.

But here was the great thing about Lee – he never

complained. Whenever he was confronted with the bleak truth of his existence, he merely smiled and shrugged his shoulders in a 'couldn't give a shit' fashion. Some would call it grace under pressure; others, displaying the quiet dignity of a job well done – whatever it was, his cheerful and resilient attitude to what were tough circumstances, by any measure, impressed me immensely.

He didn't have a pot to piss in and often survived on little more than fresh air and sharp wits, but, as the Americans are fond of saying, he was just 'one hell of a classy guy'.

The one good thing about Lee's job was that it came with free accommodation and a steady supply of cheap beer. The hotel management provided him with a box-like room at the end of a dingy and mouse-infested corridor that housed all the hotel's live-in staff. Lee's room was so small it made my cramped bedsit look like the presidential suite of the London Hilton. But best of all, and the real reason why he stayed there, was the never-ending supply of free drinks supplied by the hotel's bar staff. On many a night we would find ourselves stumbling out of a seafront nightclub in the early hours and, like a couple of drunken sailors, steadily zigzagging back to Lee's hotel. Once safely inside Lee would liberate a bottle of whisky from the generously stocked cellar and the night's frivolities would continue.

We were both new to the town and trying to find our feet, without wishing to hurt either ourselves or anyone else; it was a period of youthful innocence and curiosity, but, unbeknown to us, we were also courting disaster by bringing undue attention to ourselves and antagonising the wrong people.

Our brief but precious friendship came to a bloody and violent end when Lee made a careless mistake that almost cost him his life.

We normally restricted our partying to the 'locals only' central clubs, but this one night, for some reason or another, we decided to visit the holidaymakers' end of town and ended up in a notoriously violent trouble spot, now long since gone, that the police had tried to close on several occasions. This was to prove a near fatal mistake.

We were becoming quite well known in the central nightclubs and, as we usually behaved ourselves and were seeking work, were building crucial bridges with the doormen and bar staff. We also knew all the important local connections and networks, such as who was going out with whom, which girls were off limits, which bouncers were dangerous and which individuals were unapproachable and untrustworthy. This local knowledge was incredibly useful to have because it meant we could enjoy a boisterous night out without getting battered or gaining unwanted attention from predatory eyes.

However, the little safety net that we had created didn't stretch to the noisy, jam-packed clubs that dealt solely with the rowdy holidaymaker crowds on wild weekend jaunts. The doormen who policed these establishments were invariably quicker to fight and more severe to deal with than their local-based central counterparts. In their defence, they had to be a bit rougher because the clientele they were dealing with were rougher; in general, the holidaymaker pubs and clubs attracted large gangs of aggressive revellers on drunken stag nights, bawdy hen nights or away-game football crowds. Whenever trouble kicked off, it would be in a sudden cascade of boots, fists, flying chairs and bottles, which the doormen would have to respond to in kind. The only problem was that some of these doormen didn't know when to switch the violence off and would deal with a couple of woozy teenagers – such as myself and Lee – in the same over-the-top manner in which they dealt with a gang of hardcore soccer hooligans. As we found to our cost – Lee especially.

I felt instantly uneasy in the club because the atmosphere had a palpable whiff of violence – a kind of unseen but heavily felt tension that even the least sensitive nose could detect. A lot of the bad energy was coming off the dozen or so doormen who routinely patrolled the dimly lit and increasingly claustrophobic space with jaws clenched tightly and beady eyes darting into every dark corner and crevice. Most of the doormen I knew from the town centre cultivated a serious image and a stony glare – but nothing like the ice-cold countenances of this miserable and moody bunch.

Sometimes you can tell straight away if the doormen are the sort who look for trouble, actively provoking fights, and that was the case with these guys. Instead of preventing conflict they looked like they were courting it. What made me feel particularly threatened was the fact that I didn't recognise a single one of them – and, in any case, they didn't look like the sort who were interested in making connections. They were giving off such a negative vibe that I started to feel increasingly paranoid and uncomfortable. The strange thing was, Lee seemed completely oblivious to the hostility; he wasn't picking up on it at all.

I noticed that Lee was in deep conversation with an extremely attractive blonde girl and, judging by the lustful look in his eyes, I could see that he wanted to take the liaison to the next stage. Not wanting to get in his way, and feeling that two's company and three's a crowd, I clapped him on the shoulder and volunteered to get the drinks in. He responded with a mischievous grin and told me to go the long way and take my time, which caused the girl to giggle and playfully poke his ribs. I left the young lovers to it and turned to struggle through the crowd towards the bar.

The bar was packed to the rafters and loud music reverberated from giant speakers bolted precariously to the ceiling. I was barely halfway to the bar, still trying to squeeze through the crowd, when I became vaguely aware of a disturbance where I had left Lee and the girl. I strained to see over the bobbing heads and tangled bodies of sweaty drinkers that hemmed me in, pressed shoulder to shoulder and cheek to beer-stained cheek.

Suddenly, over the muffled din of blaring house music and the blur of writhing bodies, I saw a series of crisp white shirts rushing to the corner and descending upon Lee. An angry-looking bouncer, with the big belly and bulky torso of a bloated bruiser, marched resolutely towards him. The guy didn't look healthy – in either mind or body – and in that one brief glance I could see that he intended to smash through his target like balsa wood. He was crashing into the gyrating bodies and barging people roughly aside; his flushed red face and expressionless black eyes focused solely upon Lee.

I heard a high-pitched scream and made out the sexy blonde girl clawing and screeching at the doorman's face. In the next instant I glimpsed Lee's shocked expression as he went down under an avalanche of powerful punches; in a sickening moment of clarity, I realised what was happening. I could see the fire-exit door being kicked open and Lee being dragged, kicking and screaming, through it, still with the same shocked and stupefied expression on his face. I rushed to where this was all happening but was too late. By the time I reached the corner, all that remained was the sobbing girl, her mascara running down her cheeks like black mud and her shoulders convulsing in hysterical sobs. I asked her what had happened and, without speaking, she just pointed mutely to the exit. As I turned to run outside, she grabbed my arm and blurted out an anguished apology – it was all her fault, she said, she was the fiancée of the enraged doorman.

I found Lee lying on the pavement outside the club, his face a mass of purple bruises, his lips shining crimson with blood. I could see he was in great pain, doubled over and coughing, quivering and shaking as the adrenaline and shock coursed through his veins. I laid my hand on his shoulder and his bloodied jaw grimaced and clenched. He looked like he had been run over by a herd of elephants. I had to stifle my own sense of revulsion, in fact, as I realised the black smudge on his cheek was the imprint of a boot.

At first Lee couldn't speak or walk, only quiver and grimace. I didn't know what to do, so I approached the doorway of the club (the same place where he had just been battered to within an inch of his life) and asked them to call an ambulance. I was met with a wall of stony silence – as I looked at the bruised and bleeding knuckles of the door staff, I understood why. I returned to the prone and crumpled form of Lee and asked him what he wanted me to do. He held out a trembling hand and gestured for me to help him to his feet. Between wheezing intakes of breath, he managed to mutter through gritted teeth: 'No fucking ambulances and no fucking police – just get me home.'

With Lee's panting and heaving body leaning heavily against me, I attempted to hail a taxi. His jaw was agape and leaking rivulets of blood across my shoulder, causing me to look as if I too had been battered. Cab after cab pulled up alongside us, took one disgusted glance, then sped off again into the busy night-time traffic in search of more sober clients. We eventually realised no one was going to help us so began the long, slow shuffle back to Lee's abode. For him, each step was bitterly painful: he didn't so much walk as stagger.

Cars sped past us and hooted their horns; some drivers wound their windows down and shouted mindless, misguided mickey-takes such as 'Fucking hell, lads! Must have been some night!' They all presumed that Lee's catatonic state was the result of being paralytically drunk, being unable to see his dripping face because it was either smothered into my shoulder or lolling crazily towards the floor. If he had been able to lift it to them, they would have seen that he wasn't drunk but beaten to a pulp.

As the welcome sight of the scruffy hotel loomed into view,

Lee began to recover some of his strength and started to walk unaided – save for my steadying hand, which gripped his elbow as he occasionally reeled towards me. Before we parted I asked him what his plans were for the next few days and when I would see him again – I was making a presumption that he'd need about a week off work to fully recover.

Lee thanked me for getting him home safely and told me to call round next week, by which time, he added, attempting a cheerful grin but abandoning it in pain, he'd be ready for another night out.

His eyes told a different story, however; they belied the manful attempt at humour in his words. I could tell that he had been psychologically wounded on a very deep level and that his usually buoyant self-confidence and chirpy humour had been cruelly shattered.

Surveying Lee's battered visage, I felt a growing sense of shame and guilt that I hadn't been able to help him in his time of need. I began to stammer out an apology. He listened silently and intently as I stated my sorrow at not being able to get to him in time. He then demonstrated his sheer class to me once again by waving away my words and assuring me an apology wasn't necessary; he knew I'd done my best, but it had all happened too quickly. As we shook hands and parted, I was careful not to squeeze his knuckles too tightly, not wanting to add to the considerable pain he was already feeling. We had both just learnt a harsh and primeval lesson at the hands of little more than Neanderthal thugs. I made a silent vow never to allow either myself or a friend to be placed in that dreadful situation again. And, for the first time, I felt a shiver of doubt about pursuing a place in clubland.

Lee had committed a completely innocent but at the same time catastrophic error: he had been seen chatting up the fiancée of an archetypal 'thug doorman'. To compound the error, he had attempted his romantic liaison in full view of all the doorman's friends and colleagues. Once he had been seen, a ferocious beating was totally unavoidable because the doorman would not want to lose face in front of his colleagues. Quite simply put, Lee was in the wrong place at the wrong time.

A week passed and I still hadn't seen Lee. I was beginning to feel increasingly concerned about him, so I decided to pay him a visit at the hotel. I wasn't too worried about him physically because, like me, he was young and strong, and when we parted he looked as though he was already well on the way to recovery. With a bit of restful peace and quiet, I could see no reason why he wouldn't be back to his old self after a week off. And yet I felt restless, for there had been an expression in his eyes of defeat and despondency that I had never seen before, despite the many scrapes we routinely got into. It was as if the beating had done more than just knock the stuffing out of him – it had taken away his vitality and lust for life, too.

My suspicions were confirmed when one of the bar staff at the hotel informed me that Lee had abruptly packed and left a few nights before. Without giving any notice or clue as to his intentions, he had simply stuffed his few belongings into an old suitcase and walked away. On his way out of the hotel he had told the barman he was travelling back to Barnsley to plot his next move – maybe London or Liverpool, but, either way, he was done with Blackpool for good.

I felt a wave of sadness and regret wash over me when I heard that Lee had left. Like two lost and weary souls, we had found each other at a particularly vulnerable time in our lives and we had gone on to share some crazy nights and wonderful times. But thanks to the nomadic lifestyles we were then leading, our friendship was never destined to be a lasting and permanent one, more of a temporary meeting of minds.

For Lee, the unexpected beating had forced him to reassess

the direction his life was taking and his place in Blackpool's turbulent clubland culture. I think he made a very wise and sensible decision to leave when he did. Wherever he is now, I'm sure he doesn't regret it. For him, it was the right time to leave town.

But it wasn't for me.

Not yet.

Lee drifted out of my life in the same breezy, unexpected manner in which he had drifted into it. I never did see him again. It bothered me for a long time that I hadn't been able to prevent his beating or help him more on that dreadful night when the violence exploded around us in a blinding flash and he was struck down with crippling speed. Whenever I think of him now, I try to focus only on the brief but special time we shared.

There is a desperately sad and inhumanely cruel sting to this tale. The story didn't reach its full conclusion until several years later, but it turned out the doorman who so needlessly and mercilessly bashed Lee up inevitably became a victim of his own violent nature and jealous love. And, once again, it was his blonde-haired fiancée who featured prominently in his troubles.

I became loosely acquainted with this individual during my own stint on the doors; it was clear that he didn't even remember the first time we had met. We didn't really speak much, as we never worked together, but as we moved in the same circles we inevitably bumped into each other from time to time and on those occasions we'd have a brief chat. Once you got to know him, he was usually OK with you, but he was definitely one of those you kept your distance from – and you knew never to look at his girlfriend in a certain way.

His volatile relationship with the glamorous blonde eventually broke up in extremely acrimonious circumstances, as so many clubland romances do, and this led to his tragic downfall. Such was his devastation and obsessive love for the girl that he killed himself shortly after in a particularly painful and grisly fashion, taking a massive drugs overdose, causing untreatable organ failure, then stabbing himself several times. The self-inflicted injuries were so severe that, despite the best of care, he simply couldn't recover from them. His death was a slow and lingering one, and I can only imagine what traumas and regrets must have danced around his mind as he lay waiting for the inevitable.

When I heard of his death, I felt a genuine sense of sadness and waste because even though he had committed a great wrong against Lee in the fury of his passion, he didn't deserve to die in that manner. In his time, he had been a violent, angry man, but clearly he was also capable of feeling great love because, you might say, he died of a broken heart.

If you spend a significant amount of time behind the scenes in clubland, you come across many such stories. There is often a terrible price to pay for living in an atmosphere of hedonistic excess, where sex, violence and perceived slights to status, whether real or imaginary, collide together in a combustible atmosphere. When you're living life at 100 mph, crashing becomes inevitable – and the consequences are more damaging than for those who dawdle along at a more sedate pace.

Lee walked away unscathed; the broken-hearted bouncer didn't.

4

THE HIT MAN AND HER

AFTER FRUITLESS MONTHS OF TRYING AND AN ENDLESS SERIES of knock-backs, my persistence finally paid off and I was offered an entry-level position in clubland.

The Palace was a huge seafront club on the outskirts of town that catered solely to the drunken masses of working-class tourists who descended upon Blackpool every weekend. I wouldn't normally have chosen to work in a holidaymakers' haven, but since it was the only place hiring, in reality I had little choice.

In its early days, the Palace had enjoyed a golden era when it was so successful and sought-after that it had managed the near impossible feat of pulling in locals and tourists at the same time. Soon after it was first built, the club became famous as one of the biggest and most cutting-edge in Europe; a genuinely iconic 'superclub' on a par with the Hacienda in Manchester or the Ministry of Sound in London, albeit catering to a radically different clientele. On a regular basis it would host the hugely successful *Hit Man and Her* show, starring Pete Waterman and Michaela Strachan. Thanks to this cult TV music show (which had become a beloved Saturday night ritual as it travelled up and down the country's biggest clubs), the Palace's hedonistic atmosphere and swaying crowds were beamed into the homes of millions of bored would-be clubbers and many of them ended up visiting the place themselves. If you were in your 20s in the late '80s or early '90s, then there's every chance you too stumbled in from the pub at midnight, fumbled with the remote control, flopped into your chair and gazed longingly at the screen, guzzling on greasy kebab 'meat', muttering in between mouthfuls of hot chilli, 'Fuck me, I wish I was there!' Or, more likely if you were male, 'I'd love to shag Michaela!'

For the solidly working-class, stubbornly beer-swilling, non-drug-taking and admirably unpretentious crowd that made the pilgrimage to the giant club, Pete had become an unabashed, embarrassingly cool 'dad-dancing' icon. Worshipped and lusted after in equal measure was a lean-limbed Strachan at the peak of her unobtainable beauty. Amongst the sweating hordes, the fantasy ending to a truly epic night – trumped only by the impossible dream of climaxing inside the big-eyed Michaela – was an on-air interview with the great Pete himself. He would be swaying awkwardly to the Happy Mondays whilst you jigged about with a basket of fried chicken in one hand and a pint of flat lager in the other, bigging yourself up to your mates back home.

But with the onset of the much-vaunted new 'rave era' the club had found itself labelled decidedly uncool amongst the self-appointed opinion-makers in the music press and it was struggling to survive against the backlash, becoming the butt of derision and jibes amongst the trendy media types, hardcore dance fans and student ravers. The local clientele began drifting away in droves, Pete Waterman and his celebrity crew stopped visiting and the club's fortunes seemed to be on the inevitable slide. In the past, clubbers from across Britain had felt compelled to visit the Palace because of its vast size and international reputation, but in a cruel stroke of irony those virtues that had previously served it so well had now begun to drag it down.

With the advent of the burgeoning dance decade – which the '90s became – regular clubbers were looking for a more intimate and uplifting experience in a purer space: they no longer wanted to rub shoulders with vast hordes of beer-bellied holidaymakers while they danced. Pete Waterman was out; Pete Tong was in.

Those of us involved in clubland could see people's habits and behaviour changing before our very eyes and the driving force for this change was becoming undeniably obvious: Ecstasy, and the emerging drug and dance culture.

The club was left with two painful choices: accept that the good times had come to an end and rapidly shut up shop (take the money and run), or let the club morph into something else entirely.

They chose the latter.

The locals were jettisoned, the trendy crowd was snubbed and the Palace embraced a revival as a gaudy Las Vegas style 'holidaymakers only' nightspot, revelling in a seedy reputation for cheap beer and easy sex. From that point on, the only locals or serious clubbers ever seen there were paid staff. And, as for the punters, well, they became an 'anything goes' sort of crowd.

Physically, the club was huge. It could easily cope with a 3,000-capacity crowd spread over its two floors. Although that limit had been set as the maximum official figure, the Palace frequently packed in as many as 4,000 punters, as the management had an unofficial policy of never turning anyone away, no matter how intoxicated they were. Whereas most clubs tried to discourage gangs of drunken lads from entering, at the Palace it was the complete opposite: they were welcomed with three-for-two offers and half-price drinks vouchers. The reason for this was simple: they were our core clientele and had often travelled hundreds of miles to visit us. By not letting them in, more fights would have been provoked on the door than would ever have occurred inside.

My job offer came in the form of a position on the glass-collecting team. Even though it was one of the hardest and least glamorous posts available, I was immensely grateful. From the grin that was permanently plastered across my face, you'd have thought I'd been accepted as a trainee astronaut.

As I climbed the steep stone steps that led to the club's entrance for the first time, I could feel myself becoming enamoured with the sense of history and occasion that the bright and noisy club radiated from its beer-stained walls. The nervous sensation in my gut told me I was on the verge of a great adventure.

I had arrived at the Palace at an unusual time. The club was still in a state of flux, struggling to cope with the transition from dance club to glorified holidaymakers' beer hall. Much of the old management team, doormen and bar staff were in the process of being replaced, as the owners felt that fresh blood would be more adaptable and accepting as the enforced changes took hold. It was a strange time to be starting a new job because the staff rota resembled a revolving door – you didn't know who would be next for the dreaded chop.

Despite the club clearly having seen better days, its size and celebrated history meant it was still an awe-inspiring place. As instructed, I arrived for my first night on duty two hours before the opening time of 9 p.m., dressed in a clean white shirt and immaculately ironed trousers – neither would stay in their pristine state for long. The club was already a hive of activity, as cleaners scrubbed the floors and polished tables and fresh-faced bar staff prepared the dozens of separate bars, ready for the nightly rush.

One thing I picked up on straight away was the pin-drop silence; it seemed unnatural given the level of frantic preparation that was going on. There was also an unmistakably hostile atmosphere, like a black cloud was threatening to noisily erupt at any moment. I was disturbed by this because at the interview

I had been led to believe that most of the club's teething problems were over and all the remaining staff were on sociable terms.

Feeling like an unwanted spare part and not quite knowing what to do with myself, I approached one of the barmen with the intention of finding out why things seemed so glum and menacing. Before I'd even had a chance to speak, he stopped me with a whispered: 'Don't fucking ask, but something's going down with one of the doormen.' He then nervously averted his eyes to the floor.

I wasn't an idiot, and didn't need to be told twice, so I returned silently to my seat to watch the drama unfold. There are times in life when you need to sit down, shut up and disappear – and this was one of them.

The silence was broken when a door crashed open and a huge beet-faced man stomped angrily towards the bar. He was muttering and cursing under his breath. As he gripped the chrome bar rail, his thick knuckles, flattened from punching too many drunken skulls, turned white. The doorman was clearly in a state of extreme agitation, his temper wound as tightly as a steel spring. I could see he was trying to calm himself by flexing his sausage-like fingers back and forth and attempting to breathe deeply, but he was failing miserably.

A moment later the same door swung open again, only this time with considerably less drama and force. One of the club's many junior managers peered warily across the empty dance floor, as if he was afraid of being ambushed by moving too quickly. He was a naturally exuberant cockney character whom I'd seen around town and chatted to briefly – I'll refer to him as 'Piers' – and I noted that the bright and breezy persona that he affected when he was out clubbing was in sharp contrast to the nervy one he was projecting now.

Despite being only about 25 years old, he was wily and well spoken and definitely had the slick aura of a nightclub veteran about him. By 21, he'd already made his way up north, first to Manchester and a stint in several major clubs there, and now Blackpool's 'Golden Mile' and its significantly less cool but nonetheless illustrious Palace superclub.

The club seemed to have countless trainee, assistant, deputy, acting and general managers and at times it was hard to figure out exactly who was who and what they supposedly did. Although Piers was only one of many, he was considered to be amongst the most experienced.

It was patently obvious he was trying to assess the mood of the red-faced hulk before daring to venture any further forward. The angry man raised his head and their eyes locked briefly before his gaze returned to the floor and he resumed his incoherent mumbling. Piers took this as his cue to approach the doorman – at least half-certain that he wasn't going to get beaten to a pulp.

At my interview, I had been told what a great big happy family the club's crew was and how much I'd enjoy working with them, so it was pretty bizarre, to say the least, to see one of the managers caught up in such a tense dispute. I began to wonder just what kind of a madhouse I had agreed to work in.

I wasn't looking forward to the prospect of seeing the doorman batter Piers senseless and was even trying to work out at which point human decency would mean I'd have to intervene and attempt to pull the hulking doorman off him – not an appealing scenario on your first night at work. But as I sat in tense silence, listening to their argument unfold, I was reassured violence wouldn't erupt right then.

The pissed-off doorman would go on to become a great ally of mine during my time at the Palace and he could always be relied on to provide back-up and laughs in spades; he was one of those larger-than-life characters that you loved working with because you knew you were guaranteed to have endless fun and scrapes. 'Brick' (not his real name) certainly lived up to his old-school bruiser image and weighed in at a whopping 18-plus stone. Dressed up in his dickey bow tie, white shirt and black suit, he was every inch the archetypal 'old-fashioned pub bouncer': big and burly, built like a bull-seal and with an attitude to match.

Brick was only in his 30s, but, like Piers, he looked at least a decade older. This is a strange phenomenon I would witness many times: anybody who worked in the clubs for any significant length of time often ended up looking prematurely old and burnt out. Working during the twilight hours under constantly glaring neon lights, mixed with jolts of adrenaline, seemed to suck the energy from the flesh like a blood-drained vampire. Clearly, living like a creature of the night for any length of time was bad for your health.

The root of the argument was that Brick hadn't been paid the correct wages for several weeks – a problem he had apparently repeatedly asked management to sort out. Brick was gesturing wildly with his hands and jerking his arms about all over the place, but Piers stood his ground, nodding solemnly and assuring him, once again, that his wages would be sorted out soon. Whenever Brick teetered on the verge of violent protest, Piers would expertly calm him down and repeat that the wages issues would be resolved shortly, as soon as the rarely seen general manager returned from his holiday.

According to Piers, the problem was down to senior management and the sudden turnover of a large chunk of the staff. The explanation sounded reasonable enough, but as the two protagonists ended the row and parted on awkward terms my common sense told me we hadn't heard the last of it.

From where I was sitting, it appeared that Piers had misjudged the situation – he had come across like a fast-talking salesman, using his patter and charm to outwit and placate the clumsier and less subtle Brick. Instead of stalling tactics and evasive language, what he should have offered was a heartfelt apology and sympathetic words. I'd noticed their omission and I was sure Brick was savvy enough to notice, too.

It is a very easy and common mistake to underestimate people – particularly when you usually come out on top yourself, as Piers no doubt did. At that stage, Brick clearly didn't feel it was appropriate to use force, though he was struggling against it; I could sense that his every instinct – each fibre of his being – was telling him it was the right way to go. When placed in a tight spot with his back to the wall, Brick's main tool of communication was physical coercion; whereas for Piers it was verbal negotiation – basically, he was expert at talking his way out of trouble with a combination of well-oiled and honeyed verse.

As Brick stalked past me with a sullen expression on his flushed face, still muttering to himself, I realised Piers had overplayed his card. As they parted, I noticed Brick looking bewildered, angry and confused; Piers, meanwhile, had allowed himself a wry grin and a subtle, knowing nod. Time would tell, but I was sure Piers had gravely misread the situation and would be paid back in spades later.

With Brick gone, Piers walked over to me and shook my hand, swiftly apologising for the tense scene I had just witnessed. He assured me it wasn't like that every night, saying, as the matter was now done and dusted, I should put it out of my mind and forget about it. I felt like saying, 'I wouldn't forget it quite so quickly if I was you,' but bit my lip and thought better of it.

Then Piers surprised me by telling me that it would be his last night on duty at the club so it was no longer his problem anyway. He'd been offered a better position in a big city bar that he simply couldn't turn down. I said I was sorry we wouldn't be working together, as I'd been looking forward to learning from him. He told me not to worry and assured me that there would always be someone around from whom I could learn the ropes if I wanted to progress. In later years I'd look back on how prophetic his words turned out to be – although the lessons I would learn in clubland extended far beyond the standard business variety.

As Piers was giving me a guided tour of the club and explaining what my duties would be, a never-ending stream of staff members began to arrive and the atmosphere became visibly charged. Piers finally led me into a cramped room behind the main bar and introduced me to my new colleagues on the 'glass team', as he referred to us. Stacked up haphazardly against the walls were dozens of white plastic milk-crate-like trays, each one of them filled to the brim with shiny, dripping-wet glasses. In the corner of the room was a huge metal conveyer belt littered with filthy, sticky glasses from the night before, being noisily dragged forward for a soapy scrub in the oversized, churning dishwasher. A collection of various coloured mops and buckets, full to the top with dank black water, completed the picture.

You would never have guessed from Piers's relaxed and confident persona that he'd been engaged in a heated stand-off with a burly bouncer only minutes before. Once the introductions had been made and my duties explained, he wrapped a welcoming arm around my shoulder and pulled me towards him in a warm embrace. In confidential tones, he stage whispered that I had picked a great first night to start work because once the club had closed a very special staff-only event would be taking place.

'It's my last night, Steve, and the big boss is away on holiday, so what he doesn't know won't fucking hurt him. We're going to have a little party. A lock-in and drink the place dry. And it's strictly staff only. Work hard and enjoy yourself, but the real fun starts at closing time.'

A loud whoop rose from the eager-eyed and energetic glass team and, despite not knowing any of them, I found myself exchanging high-fives and loud exclamations of 'Fucking yes!'

There was a constant stream of visitors to the glass room, as it had an ice machine that hot and sweaty staff members used to quench their thirst. Even before the giant club opened, the air was thick with heated expectation and nervous excitement. One way to calm yourself was to grab a half-pint glass, dip it in the ice machine and suck on the frozen cubes until they blissfully melted in your mouth.

It was interesting to note the differences in the types of individuals that worked in the Palace; just like in any other job or organisation, there was a clear pecking order within each group of employees.

The managers all seemed to have a wide-boy persona – they were the kind of fast-talking, slick 'lounge-lizards' who frequented bars. One step below them in the chain were the bar staff – invariably trendy young student types, studying at college or just taking a few years out from 'real life' before eventually returning to normality and looking for a proper job.

And at the very bottom of the pile were us, the glass collectors. The one distinguishing feature we all shared was that we were aimless drifters, our lifestyles seemingly without shape, structure or ambition. The 'glass lads', by and large, were barely literate schoolboy dropouts who had neither the inclination nor the patience required to function in a so-called normal job. I was an exception here in that I just about managed to hold down a 'nine-to-five' combined with a twilight life that gave me far more excitement and fulfilment. As far as I was concerned, my real life and my true work began as soon as I hit the club; the office routine and its petty distractions paled into insignificance. I became rapidly disconnected from my daylight world; soon only night-time types were my main associates.

The doormen were a breed apart, operating outside of the normal staff structure and seeming to occupy a space and identity that was uniquely their own – strictly separate from the rest of us. The doormen at the Palace weren't employed by a large security agency, unlike at most other clubs in Blackpool, but were privately hired by the club owners themselves.

The head doorman of the day was a bullet-headed ex-soldier who ran his team on almost military lines – in theory, the doormen had to answer to the club management first, but none of them would have dared dream of it. He was the man ultimately in charge of club security, no matter what the situation, and the first time you met him he made that crystal clear to you.

The head doorman prided himself on running a clean, highly professional and scrupulously fair door with iron discipline; if he felt one of 'his lads' was overstepping the mark, then he'd be as hard on the doorman concerned as he would an offending punter. It was good to know that a man of his calibre, maturity and supreme quality was watching your back. I could see straight away why management had put him in charge. As he himself was a straight doorman, he wouldn't tolerate any criminal types infiltrating his team and he worked hard to keep the gangster element out, making it clear on a regular basis to the management that if he ever turned up for a shift and found a bloke not to his liking wearing a dickey bow, then it'd be either him or the heavy leaving. He remained a comforting presence throughout my time at the Palace before eventually being poached to go and run another club door further afield.

When Piers introduced us, the head doorman's first words to me, which he uttered while looking Piers straight in the eye, were: 'Whenever any trouble kicks off, don't waste time going to the management and don't worry about sorting it yourself – just come straight to me. And if someone's fucking you about and making your job hard, the same goes. Straight to me or one of my lads and he's fucking out.'

It was very clear to me where the true balance of power lay within the club and, from the respectful expression in his eyes as the head doorman spoke, I knew Piers would never go against him once a decision had been made. I sensed an undercurrent of tension between the security team and Piers, and my common sense told me that it was likely a hangover from Brick's wages row.

I actually liked Piers and was grateful for the warm welcome he'd given me; he'd taken the time and trouble to introduce me to every single staff member – including the doormen. But there was no doubt that a confrontation was on the cards.

On that first night on duty, Piers dispensed a lot of good advice and clubland wisdom that he himself had picked up over many years. His helpful and genuine words saw me get off to a good start at the Palace – and they would benefit me in the years that lay ahead – but it struck me as profoundly odd that he remained blissfully unaware of his own plight. Judging from the tense atmosphere between him and the doormen, his day of reckoning was rapidly approaching and no amount of fast chat would prevent it.

The door team was an eclectic bunch. Their diverse personalities and body types had been carefully chosen to fulfil differing roles – each an essential ingredient within the club's security. You could have almost split the team down the middle to create two distinct entities: on the one hand, 'bouncers' in the old-fashioned sense, and on the other, 'doormen' in more modern parlance.

The traditional-looking 'burly bouncer' stereotypes tended to be well over six feet tall and weighed in excess of 16 stone; the fact that a lot of it was pure blubber didn't matter – they looked intimidating in a penguin suit and had a notable deterrent effect, which is what they were employed for, after all. They provided a lot of highly visible 'beef' and because of their great size were good at controlling and 'leaning on' a rowdy crowd or a troublesome individual. If I could cite a perfect example of this breed, it would undoubtedly be Brick, the extremely pissed off and perennially underpaid bouncer in perma-conflict with Piers.

The bouncers conformed to the 1980s archetypal 'oversized bruiser' image. In an earlier era, pub pavements were replete with such men, jealously guarding their own little piece of turf. They undoubtedly still played an important role in clubland, and they always will, but this was the 1990s and the trend of using such confrontational types was already in steep decline. Among the huge bouncers of that time, the ones who couldn't get past the 'cracking heads' phase were now finding themselves increasingly sidetracked and underemployed, like dusty relics of a bygone but once glorious dinosaur age.

There was a clear difference between the 'bouncers' and the 'doormen', although officially they performed the same job. And this is where the doormen came in, fulfilling an emerging and developing role that required a newer and altogether different style of nightclub policing. The doormen tended to be a bit smaller, leaner and fitter – and decidedly more diplomatic in their approach to problems. I recognised many of these types from my time on the martial-arts circuit and my daily visits to the local gyms. In the same compulsive way that the old-school bouncers drank endless pints of beer and smoked scores of cigarettes, there existed an equally obsessive devotion to physical fitness amongst the doormen. A lot of them were very heavily into martial arts and combat sports, and an equal number were fanatical bodybuilders and general fitness freaks.

There was also a smattering of ex-military types that the club had gone to great pains to recruit, and although these individuals more closely resembled the doorman type than the bouncer, they kept themselves to themselves and adopted a posture of aloof detachment. You could spot the military guys a mile away because they were invariably ferociously fit in appearance; they also clearly took great pride in looking the part and remaining icily calm and ultra-professional at all times.

In all my time working in the clubs, I never once saw an ex-soldier lose his rag and initiate a confrontation – but when things did kick off, they were unfailingly vicious and highly effective opponents. Once they had emotionally committed themselves to a course of violent action, they didn't hold back and would not stop until their adversary was literally bleeding on the carpet or slumped unconscious. I used to struggle to understand how such outwardly benign and endlessly patient men could suddenly explode with such shocking violence. In later years, when I became a frontline infantry soldier myself, I finally understood how they could mentally detach themselves from the harsh consequences of their actions. But that's a story about a different kind of violence and it doesn't belong in this book.

As the summer holiday season hadn't yet begun, the gigantic club wasn't quite as packed as I had been led to believe it would be. But nonetheless it was pretty damn full and, as a first-time glass collector in a multi-thousand capacity nightspot, I found it backbreaking work. By the end of the night, my previously pristine white shirt resembled a filthy dishcloth that had been doused in a bucket of sweat and cheap ale. There wasn't one square centimetre on my body that wasn't covered in a thin film of sticky spirits, beer splashes and an assortment of cigarette burns and make-up smudges.

But I had loved every second of it.

As the doors closed on the last punters, I felt a sense of sadness and regret that the night had ended. Or so I thought . . .

The Palace had a strict policy that no staff were allowed to drink while on duty, but as the general manager was away on holiday and had no way of knowing what we'd been up to in his absence – and it was Piers's last night – the rulebook had been cheerfully chucked out of the window. Quite a few of the staff were already noticeably merry, which wasn't surprising when you considered the access to free booze they had. Under normal circumstances we were allowed as many free soft drinks as we wanted, both on and off duty, but we could only purchase alcohol, at a 25 per cent discounted rate, after the club had closed.

Over the course of the night I'd witnessed all manner of staff repeatedly strolling over to the bar and pouring themselves large measures of spirits and pints of lager. Piers couldn't have cared less and, in any case, he seemed to be guzzling it down, too. I'd had a fair few gulps myself, but I had packed it in once I'd begun to feel tipsy, as I didn't want to make a fool of myself on my first night. I expressed amazement to a barman that we could get away with raiding the stock in such a blatant manner, but he replied that as the club sold so many thousands of drinks nobody batted an eyelid at the staff enjoying freebies – just so long as it was only the occasional one-off, we took care not to do it in front of senior management and we didn't take it too far.

We were all eager for the party to begin, so everyone joined in giving the club a quick clean-up, including the DJs, managers and doormen. This was a show of generosity that was only repeated whenever a party was in the offing – cleaning up was a truly shitty job. Once the cigarette butts had been picked up and the bar restocked with clean glasses and full bottles, we flopped wearily into our seats and the DJ popped a CD into his decks. Suddenly the club was alive with dizzying sound and lights again, but we were all so tired most of us were content to merely loll back lazily, sipping on our free drinks and bantering away. As the new boy, the others mercilessly took the piss out of me as well.

To begin with at least, the atmosphere was calm and chilled out, and I can remember feeling a joyous sense of privilege at being accepted by the group and becoming part of their world. Whichever way I looked, I could see only happy faces. Likewise, wherever I turned my head, I could hear only the sound of laughter and companionship. It didn't matter if it was the young barmaids giggling and flirting with the managers or the sweat-soaked glass collectors sharing a filthy joke with the doormen, everybody seemed to be having a good time.

The sensation I remember feeling at the time was quiet contentment; it felt like I had innocently discovered a new world. But sadly my warm, peaceful feelings were about to be shattered, as the night took a cruel and unexpected twist.

As it was his last night, Piers had been particularly boisterous and on razor-sharp form. He had been cracking jokes all evening and was now on his feet, making a farewell speech that was filled with expletives and had us all roaring with laughter.

When Piers had finished, the head doorman strode over to him and gave him a manly, bear-like hug, then pumped his hand and wished him well. Then he said, as it was getting late, he was off home to bed. He shouted a noisy farewell to the rest of the staff and, as always, jokingly cautioned 'his lads' to behave themselves and have a safe journey home before bounding off into the night. At his departure, a few of the doormen – and in particular one extremely large individual – appeared to visibly relax, as if the green light for playtime had been switched on, which was natural given how tight a leash the team were kept on and how professionally the door was run. Although none of us yet knew it, the head doorman's early exit would prove to be very bad news for Piers indeed: had he stayed, the unfortunate accident that followed would never have been allowed to happen.

I hadn't really had a chance to get to know Piers properly, but from his polished performance I could see he was a man who felt he was on top of the world, brimming with self-confidence, wit and certainty. Unfortunately for Piers, somebody else had noticed it too and, unlike the rest of us, he bore him no affection and little goodwill.

Brick had been silent for most of the night and had drunk very little, which I would learn later was highly unusual for him. Whilst the rest of us had been laughing at Piers's misty-eyed reminiscences and hilarious tales of his life at the Palace, Brick had been staring at him intently and silently brooding. Truth be told, I don't think there was anything much that Piers could have done about getting Brick's wages backdated as swiftly as he wanted them other than do his very best, as he'd already promised; as he had said several times, wages weren't his department and he was only a junior. But unfortunately for him, in the absence of the general manager, he'd become the unconcerned face of management and the symbol for Brick's ire.

The expression on Brick's face was one of calm, quiet resolution – as if he had long ago decided on the course of action he was going to take and was now just biding his time, waiting for the opportunity to present itself. As Piers was halfway through one of his clubland tales, I noticed Brick leaning into the squared shoulder of one of his beefier colleagues and whispering in his ear. There was a slight pause before his friend gave a curt nod and indicated that they should rise from their chairs.

Brick and his pal rose and casually made their way over to where Piers was chatting. They positioned themselves either side of him, utterly dwarfing his diminutive figure, and each placed a heavy hand on one of his shoulders. Piers abruptly stopped his story midstream and smiled hesitantly, exclaiming, 'All right, guys, who set this up and what the fuck is going on?' He spoke in a tone of bewildered amusement because, like the rest of us, he assumed some kind of practical joke was afoot.

Piers was indeed about to become the victim of a 'practical joke'—but it certainly wasn't of the variety that he was expecting. A mischievous twinkle creased Brick's eyes as he beamed down at the hapless Piers. Everybody else had noted it too and began slow-clapping their hands and hurling jocular insults at Piers. The atmosphere was still warm and playful, and nothing appeared to be untoward, but I had a sickening sense that Brick had at last found his moment to settle his grievances with his smooth-tongued nemesis.

What disturbed me about Brick was just how genuine his cheesy grin appeared to be. But it was a perversion of a grin; it had such an appearance of satisfied intent about it, it reminded me of the look of a hunter who has finally bagged an elusive prey. None of my new colleagues seemed to have picked up on it, probably because they were all pissed, but at the last moment I could see a dawning realisation spread across Piers's slumped shoulders.

All of a sudden, he knew he was fucked.

With one hand firmly gripping Piers's puny arm and another clamped tightly across his bony shoulder, Brick bent down to gleefully stage whisper into his ear: 'I just wanted to wish you well in your new job, Piers, and to say . . . Wheeey!'

With a speed that belied their great size, the two doormen abruptly jerked Piers off his feet and held his sparse frame aloft. He began to thrash about furiously, demanding to be put down in an increasingly agitated voice. But his words and struggles were all to no avail. His burly assailants merely tightened their punishing grip and frog-marched him towards the glass room.

At this stage, the noisy subjugation still had the air of a practical joke about it – albeit an exceptionally rough and crude one – but that was about to change. Piers seemed to sense he could get hurt and heightened his struggles and protestations.

Despite his small size, he put up an impressive fight. Brick was going red in the face and had to utilise all of his extra weight (about eight stone of it) to keep Piers under control. He shouted to one of his colleagues to rush and get the blue ice-bin, as he felt Piers was getting a bit overexcited and needed cooling off.

Seconds later the dreaded blue bin was being wheeled out of the glass room and manoeuvred towards Piers like a shopping trolley that refuses to travel in a straight line. The blue bin was a large ice bucket on wheels that was continually stocked full of ice and wheeled around the bars to fill the dozens of smaller silver ice buckets that the bar staff used. By the end of the night, much of the ice inside had melted so it was more like an ice-cold pool of water.

Unfortunately for Piers, when half full of ice there was still enough room in the bin to stick a man inside it. On frequent occasions during my time at the Palace a glass collector or barman would find himself stuffed inside it, to emerge soaking wet, teeth chattering and vowing vengeance on his multiple assailants. But on those occasions it was merely considered a harmless joke, as indeed it was – a childish prank that enlivened the night and gave everyone a laugh. What was about to happen to Piers was something altogether different, but on the surface along the same lines.

With the help of his fellow 'prankster', Brick tore the clothes from Piers's body. As soon as he was stripped naked, Piers was roughly dumped into the freezing ice bucket and forcibly held down by Brick and his pal so that he couldn't jump out. Several doormen then ran into the glass room and returned with silver ice buckets filled to the brim with glistening cubes, which were then dumped onto the furiously protesting Piers. After a minute or so all that could be seen of Piers was his greying face and his mop of wet hair, as he was pinned down under the considerable weight of Brick's shovel-like hands and thick forearms.

When the cold grew too much for Brick's hands to bear, he lifted his arms from Piers's shoulders and hopped about laughing and gesturing wildly at the shivering form beneath him, trying to shake the blood back into his own freezing fingers. Seeing his opportunity, Piers burst clumsily from the ice and managed to half-roll, half-collapse over the side of the blue bin, which tumbled noisily onto the floor. Hundreds of melting ice cubes and a vast pool of cold water crept onto the tiles, forming a mini lake on the club's dance floor. In the middle of this spreading puddle lay the sprawled and prostrate form of the half-frozen, shivering Piers.

The severe cold had numbed Piers's senses and slowed down his reactions to the point where he was barely aware of what was going on around him – the fact that he was also extremely drunk didn't help matters. He tried repeatedly to rise to his feet but kept slipping in the pool of iced water, unable to find his balance. Brick, in the guise of being helpful, loudly volunteered to help him to his feet but announced in his best stage voice that he had no intention of getting soaked and slipping in the puddle like Piers. Instead he grabbed a discarded broom handle from the glass room and strolled over to where Piers lay, extending the handle towards him, telling him to grab hold of it so he could be dragged from the water. Piers groggily reached for the hovering handle but repeatedly missed it as the giggling Brick withdrew it at the last second, giving him a 'playful' dig in the ribs at the same time.

This ridiculous scenario played out for few moments until Brick, like a bored child toying with a doll, grew tired of it and finished the game with his own *pièce de résistance*. As Piers made one last grasp for the broom handle, crawling to his knees, Brick managed to somehow accidentally drop it on Piers's skinny arm, sinking him into the puddle once again. He clutched his arm to his chest and rolled onto his back, clenching his eyes shut tightly, dizzily shaking his head. Brick then grabbed hold of one of Piers's ankles, all the while whooping with playful laughter, and helpfully dragged him out of the puddle, Piers's head juddering over the wet tiles as he went.

Brick stood looking down at Piers's form, soaked and crumpled, with a faint smile playing on his lips before spinning on his feet, theatrically taking a bow and coolly returning to his seat amongst his cheering and clapping friends. He looked serenely calm and relaxed – like a man who had just resolved a long-standing upset or cleared his conscience of some bothersome unfinished business and all was now right in his world.

Piers gingerly returned to his seat and allowed one of the more sympathetic bar girls to wrap a large towel around his shivering shoulders and fetch him some dry clothes from the staff room. He looked bewildered and confused – like a man who has suffered a sudden shocking turnaround and has no idea how it occurred. All of the wit and patter had been knocked out of him. The only words he spoke to Brick were: 'Thanks for hurting my arm, mate.'

Brick didn't answer, merely nodding his head and bowing slightly, with an enigmatic and disturbingly gracious grin. The message he conveyed, in that single ambivalent gesture, was both stark and subtle in its simplicity.

Even though it didn't affect me personally, I had learnt an essential lesson about survival in clubland: 'Be careful how you deal with people'.

The party soon petered out and people began drifting off home. In truth, many of those who witnessed the incident missed the significance of it entirely and simply chose to write it off, rightly or wrongly, as harmless horseplay – just one of those silly little mishaps that occurs when you're drunk and a moment of playfulness gets out of hand. Sometimes it was easier that way, and as far as all of us were concerned no ill will or injury was intended: indeed, who could be so cynical as to suggest such a thing? But the few of us who'd witnessed the earlier arguments over wrongly paid wages and so knew of the underlying tensions perhaps took a different view.

There was never any question of the police being called because the whole water-ducking had appeared like boisterous fun. The bruises and hurt to both arm and ego would heal soon enough and by the following week the air would be cleared and all would be forgotten – or so the logic went.

At any rate, another unspoken clubland rule was that the police were only ever called when something really serious had happened which couldn't be dealt with in-house – the last thing a nightclub wanted was the kind of attention that could lead to the loss of its licence. So I learnt another very simple truth that night: what goes on in the club stays in the club. End of.

5

'WATCH MY BACK'

THE HARSH NATURE OF PIERS'S DEPARTURE FROM THE PALACE disturbed me. I was struck by how quickly and unexpectedly an occasion of innocent celebration had stumbled into something dark and threatening. Piers's 'accidentally' damaged arm, alongside the vicious beating that Lee had endured on our excursion to the rough end of town, served as grim reminders to me that in clubland strength was king and you must never drop your guard – because that was when you'd get battered. It was such a hyper-masculine environment that any sign of physical weakness was immediately pounced upon as a chance to settle old scores or 'test skills'. An inadvertent slip-up represented a welcome opportunity where violence could be mercilessly applied. I made a mental note never to fall into such complacency and to try and make sure that I never found myself on the wrong end of that predatory equation the deeper I became involved in clubland.

Reprisals came in many forms – the wild gang attack such as Lee had fallen victim to or the apparent accident that befell Piers – but the end result was always the same: bloodshed and injury. Either way, you were fucked.

As I began my second shift at the Palace, I forced myself to remember these lessons and to patrol the floors of the vast nightclub as if I had eyes in the back of my head.

A few weeks after Piers's departure, the general manager finally returned from his long holiday and gathered us all together for a team talk before the night began. As with all the management-grade staff at the Palace, the GM was perched precariously on the merry-go-round of hiring and firing and crashing and burning: it was a never-ending cycle. There was no permanence or conventional job security whatsoever within management; they all seemed to inhabit some kind of dysfunctional, transient twilight world where they were quite literally here today, gone tomorrow.

The GM of the moment and temporary king of the club was a tall, slim man with darkly ringed eyes, a permanent tan and a nervous, twitchy manner that hinted at too many late nights, too many soft drugs and generally too much of everything. He possessed the same propensity for fast patter and slick banter as Piers – a characteristic of the nightclub veteran and a trait I would wearily become very familiar with.

The 'current GM', as he was referred to, made a grovelling apology of sorts to the doormen and promised there'd be no more wage disputes now that he was back in charge. I noticed he glanced around warily when he was saying this, only to be met with a silent baleful stare and a solemn nod from a certain individual very familiar to Piers. Brick graciously accepted the GM's stuttering assurances whilst blowing smoke rings in the air and drumming his giant fingers contentedly on the table-top, his shirt sleeves rolled up for maximum effect, exposing his oversized forearms and hairy, yob-choking wrists.

Once the meeting was over, the customary pre-opening buzz returned to the club and the usual high-octane rush to prepare the bars for money-jangling, till-ringing business began in earnest. I found the faintly chemical aroma of alcohol mixed with freshly disinfected carpets and tables to be intoxicating: it registered in my senses as a promise of action to come.

Like hospitals, nightclubs have an extremely distinctive smell: once you've been immersed in it for a couple of years, you never forget it. But unlike in hospitals, the nightclub smell was to me uniquely invigorating and pleasant. Somehow it just seemed right.

The smell was at its best when you were just about to open the doors and everything was pristine. Just like in a hospital, first there was the whiff of powerful industrial-strength detergent – that's what we used to clean the sticky bars and frankly stinking toilets – but there was something else there, a magic ingredient, if you like, that sweetened the atmosphere and made it somewhat glorious: a perfume that emanated from the sealed bottles and chrome shot dispensers on the bars.

It was a combination of strong spirits: vodka and Pernod, blackcurrant and lime. On top of this was the musky smell that hung in the atmosphere and never left the club – no matter how much the carpet was shampooed or the bar shelves scrubbed. This scent – of cigar hoops long since blown, perfumes long since washed off and sexual encounters long since consummated – was the elusive special ingredient. It was the smell of the club's history and its strength was a measure of how many magical nights had been celebrated within its walls.

In the Palace, this smell clung to your clothes it was so pungent and if you inhaled it deeply enough it made you feel like dancing on the tables – even when the club was as silent and deserted as a graveyard at midnight, with its own eerie breeze blowing through. Glasses tinkling or leaves rustling, the effect was the same. The club was haunted with magic and atmosphere.

As I began stacking the bars full of dripping wet glasses, I noticed the GM eyeing me suspiciously, as if deep in thought, his fingers rubbing the designer stubble on his chin, kept at a precise length in an effort to look *Miami Vice* 'cool' – which didn't quite work in the '90s. I immediately thought I'd upset him by not working hard enough or perhaps putting the glasses away on the wrong shelves, so I rolled up my shirtsleeves some more and started tidying at a manic pace. Although he seemed to have the same happy-go-lucky personality as Piers, the GM seemed a bit edgier and more watchful, and as I was the new boy I was anxious not to make a bad impression.

A common trait that some club managers and top doormen shared was a streak of arrogance, an almost adolescent need to constantly reinforce their presence as top dog within their designated spot of clubland turf. I wondered if the GM was one of those insecure, needy types who couldn't resist revelling in his status and rubbing it in at every opportunity, playing childish mind games with the newcomers until they kowtowed to his need for validation and acknowledged how cool he was.

Every time I raised my eyes from the bar I could see him looking at me as though he was checking me out and after ten minutes of this I began to grow increasingly embarrassed. I wondered if he was some kind of opportunist homosexual who had mistakenly viewed me as fresh meat and a chance for exploitation. Then it crossed my mind I was about to be subjected to one of those absurd initiation ceremonies that some clubs insisted on – being dunked in an ice bucket or something similarly stupid. But my instincts told me to keep quiet. I was a fast learner and the one lesson I never forgot was this: if in doubt, just shut the fuck up and observe the situation closely.

Finally, the GM strode over and tapped me on the shoulder. He was no longer eyeballing me and seemed back to his usual uber-smooth, cocky, friendly self. I attempted awkward small talk, but he spoke over me in a typical 'I'm the boss' fashion. He then complimented me on my work ethic and big arms, quizzing me on my gym habits and asking how often I worked out. He then insisted I flex my biceps for him. I was a bit taken aback by the conversation and was acutely embarrassed, wondering where it was all heading and what the point of it was. But I tensed my bicep anyway and he muttered to himself: 'You know, I've just had a fucking brilliant idea. I'll pair you up with Zenon and stick you in a vest and shorts.'

I was by now completely confused and started nervously wondering just who this mysterious 'Zenon' character was. The GM read the worry in my eyes and burst out laughing, then placed a reassuring but assumptive hand on my shoulder. Zenon was his best glass collector by a mile, he said, and he needed someone to partner him as he went about his rounds. The 'glass boys' always worked in pairs – one holding the tray, the other filling it – and it turned out that Zenon was so physically fit and strong that none of the other lads could keep up with him: they couldn't lift the trays he stacked and just trailed in his wake as he cut a path through the crowds with his mammoth load. However, the GM reckoned I'd be up to the task and promised to introduce us as soon as he arrived.

That was, he added, if I thought I was up to the task.

I don't know if he had done it deliberately or not, but his comments about Zenon's supposed superior fitness had already piqued my curiosity and stirred my competitive instincts. As the clock wound down to his arrival, I found myself pining to meet him so I could formulate my own opinion. The GM seemed to think Zenon was some kind of superman, whereas I was convincing myself his judgement was merely skewed.

An hour later a boisterous Zenon Malkuch strolled into the club like he owned the place, the GM beaming happily alongside him, like a proud coach leading out his best prize fighter. As he made his way to us, he greeted the doormen, the bar staff and my fellow glass collectors with a high-five in between bouts of raucous laughter. And for that moment at least, as he sucked up all the energy in the room, time seemed to stand still. I had to concede that the GM's glowing assessment of Zenon's indefatigable energy was utterly spot on: the guy was like a magnet.

Without exception, Zenon was one of the most charismatic and physically impressive men I had ever met. In the prime of his youth, when he walked into a room he lit it up like a megawatt light bulb; the sheer physical energy and vitality of his presence had the power to lift the blackest of moods. Throughout my life I've been lucky enough to work alongside some outstanding individuals, including elite soldiers from within the Royal Green Jackets and the SAS, and without hesitation I would place Zenon at the very top of that list – a man amongst men. Within seconds of meeting him, you sensed that beneath the relaxed and jaunty exterior lay an inherently gifted and capable man who possessed both the capacity and the will to get things done.

The first thing that struck me about Zenon was his incredibly thick Slavic accent, which I could barely understand. As he introduced himself in indecipherable, guttural tones, it was hard not to laugh. I wondered if he was deliberately exaggerating it as a piss-take and having a laugh at my expense (something I'd learn he'd do when he was feeling mischievous), but he wasn't and he really did speak like that. As Zenon continued babbling away, I mutely grinned and nodded my head as if I understood what he was saying.

I managed to pick up the odd word here and there and, like a grinning lapdog already fallen under his charge's spell, the GM beamed with pride, helpfully filling in the gaps whenever Zenon took a pause or managed to stop roaring with laughter at his own absurdly impossible-to-understand jokes.

Still only 20 years old, he'd come over to Britain from Poland with his mother as a teenager, when she'd fled the Eastern Bloc and managed to escape from the yoke of Communism that strangled 1980s Poland like a rusted and rotten garrote.

The second thing I noticed was the decidedly threatening

aura that he projected, which wasn't consciously put on but entirely accidental. God, or whoever decides these things, had seen fit to bless Zenon with a face that looked as though it had been carved out of cold steel and a physique that resembled a block of granite stone. He had a shock of brilliant blond hair that flopped onto his brows and the sort of deeply set turquoise eyes that you can see from across a busy street, boring into you even from a casual glance – what we ex-soldiers call the 'thousand yard stare'.

But what was truly outstanding about Zenon was his rock-hewn physique: he resembled a professional bodybuilder rather than a glass collector and, had I not known otherwise, I'd have sworn he was a seasoned bouncer. He wasn't particularly tall, at barely six foot, but the sheer muscularity he possessed had to be seen to be believed. Massive thighs burst out of his shorts and his forearms resembled Popeye's, while his shoulders seemed to start somewhere behind his ears and sloped downwards like a steep mountainside. As he shook my hand in his powerful grip, I noticed that the muscles above his wrists flared like a bunch of tightly coiled bananas, criss-crossed with a map of lean, tanned veins and taut sinews.

I could see straight away why the GM had insisted that we pair up: both of us were muscular and fit and shared similar, albeit strikingly different, appearances. Neither one of us was good-looking in the conventional sense, but taken together we definitely had something a little bit different that made us stand out from the crowd.

Having now met Zenon, I didn't kid myself about who would be the real head-turner: despite being very fit, I was physically no match for him. At that point in time, he was far broader and infinitely stronger than me – or pretty much anyone anywhere, for that matter.

In addition to his massive physique, Zenon had been blessed (or cursed, depending on which way you looked at it) with an intimidating and unusually tough-looking face. He had the stern countenance of a KGB hit man, and even when he was laughing and relaxed his razor-sharp contours and hawk-like profile never seemed to soften or lose their hard edge. The great irony of this, as I would later learn, was that Zenon had the temperament of a big, soft teddy bear. He was an improbably gentle man. He ambled around like an ever-genial Terminator who would simply laugh off the most grievous of insults and wounding of challenges like barely-there gnats that weren't worth swatting. The term 'gentle giant' was coined to describe men like him.

Even more surprisingly, his sandblasted physique and fearsome appearance contained another startling contradiction: despite looking like a Soviet assassin, he hadn't spent so much as a day in the gym and had never lifted weights. For some bizarre reason, nature had sculpted him that way.

My first reaction to Zenon's freakish genetic good fortune was one of 'some people have all the luck'. But as he told me his story in faltering and broken English my envy softened and I realised just how wrong my first impression of his apparently lustrous and glowing good health had been. For Zenon had not only been blessed – he had also been cruelly cursed.

Zenon had a particularly aggressive form of Type-1 diabetes. He injected himself with insulin between four and six times a day and had to constantly watch what he ate, monitoring his blood sugar levels and often lapsing into dangerous hypo comas. Indeed, this might have been one possible explanation for his phenomenal size; for certain individuals, the daily doses of insulin can cause accelerated muscle growth – so much so that some professional bodybuilders, without diabetes, even choose to use it. It is perhaps the one positive side effect to what can be a crippling and immensely upsetting disease, but, as Zenon frequently stated, he'd have gladly swapped his bulging muscles for a skinnier, diabetes-free body and a pancreas that worked, freeing him from the cruel burden of the never-ending needles.

Sometimes you get a feel for a person and find yourself being instinctively drawn to them. So it was for me with Zenon. As he told me of his illness and his struggle to adjust to life in Britain, his piercing blue eyes bored into me. Beneath them I detected a genuine warmth and sincerity. Zenon confessed that he was having great difficulty learning the English language, as he had received barely any schooling and wasn't a particularly keen student, his youthful energies having been spent on plotting his escape from a then Communist Poland. He loved and missed his home country greatly, but he detested its government and its loathsome ideology, which he felt had robbed him of his teenage years and precious freedoms before forcing him to flee.

He'd been working at the Palace as a full-time glass collector for two years and admitted that he'd put little effort into improving his vocabulary, preferring instead to rely on grunts and gestures. I told him that it showed and he must stick with it and try to improve – otherwise he'd be communicating in sign language forever and would never learn. At that, he belly laughed and slapped me heartily on the shoulder, almost knocking me off my feet.

Zenon was a man with only good intentions and his readiness to laugh at himself and the absurdity of his situation endeared him to me further. I've always been drawn to people with a thirst for adventure and a twinkle in their eye; in Zenon, I felt I had found a kindred spirit who shared my values and philosophies about how life should be lived. He wouldn't disappoint me.

At the risk of sounding like a big-headed bastard – oh fuck it, I am! – the idea of pairing me with Zenon was to help foster the image of the Palace as a sexy, young, vibrant club.

It worked well because we stood out from the start and got a lot of female attention straight away. It wasn't that we were particularly handsome or charming; it had more to do with the fact we were in half-decent shape and not mind-numbingly drunk like many of the male customers.

We immediately hit it off and treated our jobs like a workout at the gym, bouncing off each other's energy. Thanks to our extra strength and competitive spark, we could pile our crates twice as high as our skinny co-workers, which in itself got us attention as we made our way through the crowds, attitudes buzzing and brawny arms bulging for all to see. In no time at all, we had become the club's resident muscle-men glass collectors.

I had never in my life enjoyed much luck with girls, so you can imagine how immensely I appreciated my new status – I was like a kid in a sweet shop who's been given the green light to eat till he's sick. To say I gorged would be an understatement. If we saw a particularly attractive bunch of girls, we would amble over to their table and bend over, innocently stretching across for empty glasses. Sure enough, a few seconds later a wandering hand would pinch our bums or begin to creep up our legs. We would laugh along at the joke and playfully pretend to be offended, but nine times out of ten we'd end the night in a deserted fire escape having our wicked way.

I like to kid myself that it was my good looks and charming personality that attracted these girls, but deep down I know it was no such thing; it was purely the job and nothing else. I soon began to appreciate the power of working in a popular nightclub, even at the lowest level.

Quite often even the most hardcore party animal leads a relatively boring, uneventful, soul-sapping life. I know this because that was me back then. I lived for the weekend and nothing else, then it was Friday-night millionaire time. If you're just an average-looking, cheerful face that clubbers see every weekend when they are at their happiest, then pretty soon you become a fanciable face and someone they want to know. I think perhaps it's because you begin to be associated in their minds with 'good times' and their favourite place. Put it this way; seeing your favourite barman or glass collector when you're pissed up and having a blast on a Saturday night produces the opposite effect to seeing your po-faced boss on a miserable Monday morning.

Whatever. I enjoyed the effects and took full advantage.

I was always happy to be grafting in the Palace over a weekend, and although it was incredibly hard work, it never actually felt like work. Unlike my regular job, which had the effect of putting me to sleep, at the Palace having a bit of spark and rebellion about you was actually encouraged by management. Having been dragged onto the dance floor more than a few times by a gaggle of over-excited girls, management decided that it was an opportunity to liven things up by allowing Zenon and me to dance as well. So, as long as the glasses got cleared away, we were practically ordered to dance at will. We even began devising our own silly little routines for our signature tunes: 'Doin' the Do' by Betty Boo and 'Step On' by the Happy Mondays.

Looking back, I suppose we often looked stupid – ridiculous even – but the crucial difference was that customers weren't laughing at us but with us, and we were making a name for ourselves and getting noticed by all the right people.

If any punters managed to upset the glass team, then we had myriad ingenious tricks up our sleeves to gain revenge. Perhaps the crudest was devised by 'Billy', a rough, monosyllabic Glaswegian who had drifted down to Blackpool in search of bar work in time-honoured Celtic fashion. Billy was fine with the punters until they upset him or began to take the piss, and then he would use a disgusting but curiously apt way to gain revenge: the glass-switching trick, or the 'free whisky', as he christened it. He only ever bestowed this dubious honour on his nastiest and most offensive customers (not that that makes it excusable in any way) and, I have to confess, at the time it seemed funny to me, albeit in a sick kind of way.

The 'free whisky' involved Billy casually sauntering up to a table of offenders who had treated him like dirt and at an opportune moment when their attention was diverted – perhaps by a fellow glass collector, if he agreed the offence was genuine – he would subtly place a 'free whisky' on their table, or swap a genuine drink for one of his golden specials. If they noticed him, he smiled dumbly and surreptitiously left the 'gift' behind. Nobody ever really noticed what he was doing or caught on, as he discreetly melted away into the crowd, but it was always a blast to see his tormentors' faces as they realised they were in fact drinking pure piss. It certainly sobered them up quickly.

Eventually the management heard about Billy's antics after he urinated in one glass too many. The management wasn't too happy at having to calm down a hysterical customer screaming about 'filthy bastards' to the entire club. Billy was instantly given the axe. Before he left he managed to sneak into management's office and, in his own inimitable style, left a memorable 'leaving present' on a desk – a lurid pile of steaming shit with a cherry artfully stuck in it. Still, at least he didn't bother to sprinkle it with any peanuts. That was typical Billy.

For obvious reasons, he was a man we all tried not to upset.

I was having so much fun at the Palace that time flew by in a neon-streaked blur. Zenon and I had set out to be the fastest and most 'up for anything' glass-collecting team in Blackpool and we had got there at blitzkrieg speed. We had secured the female attention for which our young cocks ached, but along with it came another type we could do without: specifically the attentions of aggrieved and jealous male punters who felt compelled to take us down a peg or two. Several times at the end of the night we found ourselves fighting with spurned rivals, drunken bullyboys or possessive boyfriends who didn't like their girlfriends – real or imaginary – chatting to us.

I learned early on – occasionally to my cost – how devious and manipulative some of the most beautiful women can be – how they could use you as pawns in their own mind-fuck love games by flirting with you outrageously in order to wind up their jealous boyfriends.

I'll never forget the time a stunningly exotic blonde almost got me into a fight with her Godzilla-like boyfriend (of whom I only learned as he was about to launch his first haymaker in my direction). Zenon swiftly darted in at the decisive moment and stared him down with his own massive muscularity. I'd spent half the night brushing up against this lush temptress and every time we touched we engaged in an intense, sexually charged staring game. Wherever I went in the club, her eyes scoped me out and I could feel her lusty gaze boring into my back, her pillowed lips pursed as she challenged me with her tilted chin and jaunty stare.

The looming hulk next to her didn't even register – until he stomped over and demanded that I stop staring at his 'cock-teasing bitch of a fiancée', as he put it, who was apparently always fucking winding him up and flirting with pricks like me!

To say I was mortified is an understatement.

When I glanced over at her again to confirm the giant's story, she merely cocked her head with a malicious grin and defiantly gave him the finger. She then sashayed out of the club with an arrogant scowl on her face and not a trace of remorse – en route squeezing my backside and breezily apologising to me for dragging me into 'their shit'. I actually felt sorry for the big guy and offered him an apology before he stormed out after her like a maddened hound on the scent of an evasive, tormenting fox.

Zenon and I never looked for these confrontations, but if and when it got heavy we dealt with them in the same manner: swiftly and physically. I learnt a very valuable lesson during the months we spent working together that would serve me well in the coming years: a large drunken man, however powerful he thinks he is, often lacks the stamina or conditioning to overcome a fit and sober opponent. We would usually win a midnight scrap easily, not because we were hard men – which we weren't – but because the aggressor was either too drunk or too fat to make an impression on us.

It was during these clumsy and chaotic early rumbles at the Palace, long before we became recognised doormen in our own right, that we learnt the critical importance of that oft-repeated bouncer's mantra 'watch my back'. We always did – and we never let each other down. Wherever Zenon went in the club, if someone threatened him or took a swing in his direction, I was always on standby, watching his back – and vice versa. If you ganged up against one of us, then you fought both of us. It was as simple as that.

A few of the scuffles we'd been involved in had also caught the attention of the club bouncers, whom we had helped out on those occasions when they found themselves outnumbered. In door work, a premium is placed on the quality of 'bottle' – the ability and willingness to get stuck in when the situation calls for it and the blood and snot is beginning to fly. To their minds, Zenon and I had displayed bottle and were therefore worthy of respect and consideration. One or two of the senior doormen began to sound us out about working the doors and what our future clubland ambitions were, beyond the glass team.

There is generally a strict pecking order in clubland and separate cliques form around each group. Glass collecting is considered bottom of the heap, while working the doors is nearer the top. Neither one of us had considered switching to door work yet, so this was very flattering attention indeed. It wasn't that we didn't think we could do the job, it was just that we were having a great time on the glasses and, for the time being, hadn't looked beyond that. It felt a little premature. Nevertheless a seed had been planted in our minds.

Reluctantly, we decided to carry on with the glasses, as we didn't feel quite ready for the responsibility of 'the door', but at the same time we vowed to observe the profession from afar and learn as much about it as we could. Now it was no longer a question of *if*, but *when* we stepped up.

The advantages of glass collecting as opposed to door and bar work were that you could really get out amongst the crowd and mix and chat. When you are on the door, you have to maintain a professional distance and adopt an air of detachment for much of the time. While behind the bar, you are simply too busy to stop and chat, such is the urgency and weight of the throbbing masses. I had helped out behind the bar a few times and absolutely loathed it: the place was so insanely busy you felt under constant siege from the crowd. You would stand behind your own small section of bar and serve only that area, but it was impossible to keep a sense of order because all of the customers had been waiting for ages and were becoming agitated. You couldn't win. There was a never-ending chorus of pissed-off punters shouting 'Me next' or 'I've been here longest'. But the tips could be very rewarding – sometimes I would wave my tip jar in the air and shout, 'Who's next to be served?' I would end the night with as much as £20 in tips – a shiny pint glass half-full with coins and a few damp banknotes.

Working the bar was no match for the buzz of being on the glass team, however: although you made more money, the perks were far fewer.

Zenon and I made a big effort to ingratiate ourselves with the DJs, as they could often tip a bit of sunshine our way, giving us shout-outs in return for keeping them topped up with free drinks from our pals on the bar. We always responded promptly to their calls for refreshment and would get a 'big me up' on the mike for 'Blackpool's top glass men'.

Another pleasant duty that we bagged was going out on the streets at night doing promotional work, trying to get punters into the club. This involved handing out cut-price tickets and flyers, as well as trading insults and banter with opposing nightclub crews battling for space with us on the pavements. Promotions were also a great way to meet girls: we would often surreptitiously go into rival pubs and clubs, dishing out free tickets to gangs of good-lookers, scoring a quick snog and a crafty feel-up along the way. We'd get crumpled up phone numbers and smudged-lipstick promises to meet up later, which, being the perfect gentlemen we were, we felt duty-bound to honour as best we could. Our cocks and our clear consciences demanded nothing less.

Happy days, indeed. Minimum-wage jobs didn't get any better than this. And, come to think of it, nor did many high-paying ones.

One of the best things about joining the nightclub community was that you gained free entry wherever you went and became a recognised face among your peers in other clubs. Girls seemed to find it particularly impressive that you could breeze past a long queue and a friendly doorman would let you in for free, then once inside a barman pal would serve you straight away, chucking in a free shot for good measure. Of course, you would be expected to return the favour when it was their night off and they became VIP guests at your place of work.

Zenon and I continued to study the doormen, making enquiries as to what the job was really like. We were hearing good things. The money was approximately double what we were earning on the glasses and it was for a lot less work. The doormen would generally be treated with a lot more respect, both from punters and management, and they seemed to have as much pull – if not more – with the girls.

Doing the glasses was fine if you wanted to pull a 19-year-old girl or a budding nightclub queen, but working the doors seemed to attract older, classier women who were that bit more mature, being well into their 20s and fit as fuck. The more we compared the two jobs, the more door work started to look a lot more appealing. Zenon and I had forged a formidable reputation as good scrappers within the club, which, combined with our muscular physiques, meant we were constantly being asked why we weren't on the door making good money like everybody else and enjoying the perks. It felt like a decision was being forced upon us.

It was time to make the move.

I had by now turned 20 and had under my belt a full year's experience on the glass team. It had been tremendous fun and had provided me with that all-important introduction to working life in the clubs – but it was also starting to get tiresome.

Glass collecting in a 4,000-capacity space was no easy task; in fact, it was backbreaking work. In our partnership, Zenon and I had prided ourselves on being the fastest, strongest and most efficient team in Blackpool – but after a year our little adventure was becoming stale in the small universe of the Palace. It was a case of 'Been there, done that', as the saying goes.

We cleared approximately double what most lads could manage in the same time, so effectively we grafted twice as hard. At the end of the night, we would be absolutely shattered and drenched in rank sweat and sticky beer. The stench of stale alcohol and smoke seemed to permeate every pore and hair on our bodies, and our arms would be singed with tiny cuts and cigarette burns from careless punters. The club would close at 2 a.m., but we'd not finish cleaning up until 4 a.m., such was the state of the place. At the end of the night, the club looked like a bomb had gone off – broken bottles, discarded lipstick, fag butts and champagne corks all jostled for space on the party-scarred floor. Shards of glass studded the carpet like a minefield of diamonds, clinging to the soles of your shoes and crunching underfoot wherever you stepped.

As we tore into this mess, I couldn't help but glance at the ice-cool bouncers who would be lounging around, quaffing freebie staff drinks with an attractive stay-behind customer they'd picked up, before slipping off home for an undoubted shag of their lives. They appeared serenely calm, unruffled and in enviably good spirits. We, on the other hand, felt like we had been rolled in cigarette ash and shoved head first down a rubbish chute.

The decision was made: fuck this shit, we were going on the door.

Not long after this, we requested a meeting with management and told them of our plans. They weren't best pleased at the prospect of losing their two best glass collectors and informed us we could forget about our ever working on the Palace door. In our naivety, we had expected a smooth transition, just presuming it would be sorted out with a quick change of uniform. We were wrong.

In his usual helpful and totally straight style, the head doorman said he would have a word with management on our behalf and see if he could get it sorted – even if only on a trial basis – but to our surprise he couldn't. It seemed the harder we pushed, the harder the top brass dug their heels in. We were only ever going to be glass collectors at that club, nothing else; we were simply too good at our jobs.

The head doorman explained to us that unlike the majority of nightclubs in Blackpool the Palace operated what was known in the trade as a 'closed door' – essentially a door team that is employed directly by the club owners themselves to work solely for that club. An 'agency door' is a club door that is run by doormen who are supplied by a security firm whose staff are invariably sent to work at either specific or random clubs. He told us to apply directly to one of the main agencies that supplied doormen in Blackpool and that if we had any problems he'd put a good word in for us. We hoped that by seizing the initiative and going straight to one of the bigger firms ourselves we'd be able to find work quickly.

A week later I found myself climbing some rickety stairs to the offices of 'Premium Security', a firm that controlled many of the club doors in Blackpool. I felt a sense of foreboding as I awaited my interview with the boss, whom I'll call 'Pete Milton', but these were not my usual pre-interview nerves. I knew at the back of my mind that if I were offered employment I would be entering a twilight world of frontline violence where danger lurked in every shadow.

'Fuck it, I'll be OK,' I told myself. But even as I muttered the words a chorus of conflicting doubts ran down my tingling spine. Becoming a doorman would involve taking a significant personal risk . . . but then again, wasn't life supposed to be all about taking risks? Wasn't that how you succeeded? Weren't we meant to face down uncertainty? Didn't we grow stronger that way?

'Fuck it,' I muttered again.

A gruff voice called me in. The decision had been made.

I had been briefed well on Pete Milton and knew what to expect before I even saw him. As I walked in, he didn't rise or offer me his hand but gestured to me with a stern nod to sit down opposite him. Dark eyes bored into me – he didn't bother to disguise the fact I was being weighed up. Pete was a bald, shiny-headed, tank-like figure who seemed to hover somewhere around middle age but with a hungry gleam of energy about him that knocked years off. In his younger days, he'd been a professional rugby player and his tough-looking visage bore the scars of this previous sporting life – a fighter's nose and thick brows matted with scar tissue long-since healed, giving way to his piercing eyes set beneath. I wondered if a few of the nicks had been acquired off the playing field during his own bouncer days.

When he spoke, his deep voice had a slight nasal quality that resonated with authority – a by-product of a decade's worth of heavy tackles that only seemed to have strengthened his 'clubland king' aura. He radiated streetwise gravitas and I got the distinct impression that he could still go a few rounds if he had to.

Pete recognised me from the Palace, a door he was considering adding to his organisation if he could broker the right deal. His questions were direct and probing, and all to do with why it was I felt I could control a rowdy door at a mere 20 years old, with very little prior experience to boot. He pointed out that I was not the biggest of blokes, despite my marble-like muscles and obvious conditioning.

I detailed my background in martial arts and described the scrapes I'd been involved in at the Palace – all of which he brushed aside with a shrug and a laugh. He told me he'd give me a chance, not because of my background, which I could see didn't impress him in the least – nor should it have done, really – but simply because I had had the balls to ask him straight. If I could do the job, then fine. If not, well, we'd soon find out, wouldn't we?

With the interview over, he finally shook my hand and ushered me out of the door.

Pete Milton had impressed me immensely on every level and I, in turn, wanted to impress him. He was a self-made man with a well-deserved reputation for running a top-notch, highly efficient and totally straight operation. He had built his security business from nothing and it was now such a glowing success that even the police and his many would-be rivals had to pay him a begrudging respect and concede that his set-up was second to none. I vowed I would not let him down on the doors and would do my very best wherever he placed me, whether it was on the outskirts of town or slap-bang in the middle of the Golden Mile chaos. Zenon had his interview after me and received the same no-bullshit, straight-up treatment.

The only bad news was that Zenon and I would not be working together – or at least not to start with. Pete explained to us that downtown we were known primarily as glass collectors, a perception we'd be wise to get rid of as quickly as possible because it could create problems on the door. By separating us, he felt it would speed up our acceptance, by the punters we now had to police, as genuine doormen in our own right.

So our days as the Palace's musclemen glass collectors and resident pranksters were now at an end. And the dynamic duo was no more – for now. We couldn't argue with Pete's logic and knew in our hearts that he was right, so reluctantly we accepted the temporary dissolution of our partnership.

Zenon and I actually felt quite sad as we handed in our notice to the Palace management. Somehow it all felt like the end of an era. At the same time, it was the beginning of a new and infinitely more exciting chapter in our lives.

We were doormen now.

6

DRAWING BLOOD

NOT LONG AFTER MY INTERVIEW, ONE OF PETE'S ASSOCIATES RANG me. When he told me to report for duty at a large hotel bar on the promenade, I wasn't quite sure I had heard him right and queried his instructions. Surely he didn't mean the big family hotel on the beach? But yes, he did.

I had harboured secret fantasies of being immediately placed in a heaving club bang in the centre of town where I'd be assured plenty of action – with either my fists or my dick, preferably both. In comparison, the gig I was being offered sounded more like a stint in a pensioners' hall.

As I started to protest, Pete came on the line and, in his own inimitable style, began to 'educate' me about the facts of life. In no uncertain terms, he told me that, as I was still very much an unknown quantity as a doorman, he wasn't about to put me into one of his best clubs, especially when there was a long list of highly experienced, well-proven and capable men in front of me. All doormen aspired to work on a top door, but you had to prove yourself elsewhere first to earn that right because competition was fierce. That was how the system worked.

Pete ended the conversation in his usual blunt style by telling me I could always go back to washing glasses and cleaning tables at the Palace if I didn't like it and thought I knew better. Suitably educated – and chastised – I told him it would, of course, be a great pleasure to work at the hotel bar.

Unlike today, where a strict licensing and vetting system operates, back in the early '90s the clubland security industry was almost completely unregulated. Consequently, you got a harsher mix of men who worked the doors than is allowed today – a tiny minority of whom were hardened criminal types with serious records for violence who usually ended up on private doors and avoided working for straight agencies like Pete's. A slightly larger minority again were basically old-fashioned thugs and 'bruisers' who somehow slipped through the system despite regular tear-ups with punters and repeated visits to magistrates' courts for almost daily low-level charges of assault and public disorder, etc. But the vast majority in Blackpool were simply local lads who liked a bit of rough and tumble over the weekend; I like to think that I fell into this latter category.

I already knew a lot of the lads from my time at the Palace, others I had met in various gyms as we slaved away, pumping iron, or locked horns on the martial-arts circuit – a trail that many of us followed, always looking for that elusive 'fighter's edge'.

Gyms have always been a fertile recruiting ground for bouncers, as they abound with beefy young lads eager to test their strength and establish a reputation. If I am honest, there was a little bit of that stereotype in me as well. As you got stronger, you began to feel that it would be a shameful waste not to use your muscles in a 'manly' way or at least to earn you some money for all the sweat-drenched hard work that you'd put into gaining them in the first place. A coveted place on a top door, with an abundance of opportunities for physical 'expression' of all sorts, seemed like a just reward for all the blood, sweat and tears you'd expended along the way.

117

But, as with so many things that start off with innocent albeit mischievous intentions, you walk a fine line and the environment can be both seductive and corrupting. Some of the lads get too caught up in the 'glamorous' clubland lifestyle and start believing in their own infallibility and bullshit. They then end up crossing the line from 'weekend warrior' and part-time wannabe stud to full-time aspiring gangster, becoming entrapped in a web of spiralling risks and violence that it's hard to break free from without leaving behind precious chunks of your life, liberty and flesh. Others become obsessed with the He-Man image and start bloating their bodies with excessive doses of mind-altering, powerful anabolic steroids, a previously healthy interest in fitness becoming a poisonous journey into something altogether darker and more dangerous where 'roid rage' and mania await.

So, before I'd even set foot on my first door, I'd educated myself and made it my business to find out about the temptations and pitfalls. My goal was simply to enjoy myself, crack a few deserving heads, coin in some cash and bang a few willing chicks. But, above all else, I was determined not to become another of Blackpool's crime statistics – as either victim or perpetrator.

Shallow and unworthy goals? Hell, yeah! I embraced them then and I make no apologies for them now. I was 20 years old, horrendously immature and on the door in Blackpool, for God's sake. At that stage in my life, I was supposed to be stupid: there would have been something wrong with me if I hadn't been.

I bought myself a second-hand sturdy black suit from a charity shop for my first day on duty. The white shirt and black dickey bow were brand new and, as I put them on, I felt strangely self-conscious and uncertain. I found myself dwelling on the seriousness of what I was about to undertake and for the umpteenth time ran through in my mind all of the reasons why I felt able to do this job. Standing in front of a full-length mirror, I analysed my appearance as a customer would, then compared this with my own biased perceptions. As I stared at my fresh, unmarked face, with its clear eyes and distinctively average stature, I knew that I would face physical challenges and gauntlets that others wouldn't: an obviously bigger man than I would be able to ward off trouble with a glare, while an older man would carry more natural authority and gravitas. I didn't have that air of somebody who had 'been around a bit' and was painfully devoid of its protective glow.

A sober and streetwise punter would look at me and see a fit, stocky, keen and fast adversary to be avoided. But what would a drunken yob see, or a drug addict high on speed, or a 17-stone football hooligan? The answer: a distinctly unimpressive fresh-faced lad barely out of his teens trying to tell him what to do; a 5 ft 8 in. borderline short-arse with a few pumped-up muscles and oversized arms that needed taking down a peg or two – preferably by kicking the fuck out of.

The best visual deterrent to trouble that I had was my powerful build, but unfortunately much of my muscle was hidden under my new suit. As I didn't have a naturally big frame – and was indeed a bit of a short-arse – it would go unnoticed. When I was glass collecting, would-be aggressors would often clock my muscles and think twice – but now that they weren't on obvious display, they wouldn't think at all.

'Well, Steven, you wanted the job and it's too late to start worrying now,' I told myself, still looking in the mirror.

I had been wrong to tag the hotel bar an 'old fogeys' joint', especially as it was a bank holiday weekend and half of Scotland seemed to have arrived in town to celebrate. As I walked into the bar and introduced myself to the manager, I could see that he was a little taken aback by my youth, although he was too polite to say it. He asked me if I was sure I could do the job and I replied with false, jaunty confidence that I wouldn't be there if I couldn't. He nodded sceptically and gave a slight sigh before leading me to the porch entrance to the bar for a briefing. I listened intently as he told me the criteria for entry and what he expected from me in the event of trouble. The streets were absolutely heaving with drunken revellers and I could already see trouble ahead if they landed on my doorstep. Once the manager had finished talking, I asked him when my partner would be turning up. My chin practically hit the floor when he told me this was a solo door and I would be working on my own.

'Fucking hell' was my stunned reply – but by then he had already gone.

Standing by myself in that scruffy porch, which opened onto an always quiet, dirty side street off the promenade, I began to understand why Pete insisted on new employees proving themselves first. The way the entrance was situated, I realised that I could be involved in a full-on brawl right in the doorway and none of the drunken revellers streaming across the beachfront would even see it; in fact, unless a passer-by literally walked right past the doorway and glanced inside its deep-set porch, my struggles would be invisible. And even though it had been described to me as a 'hotel bar', it was actually a pretty rough pub grafted onto the back of a hotel that catered to local holiday trade workers on their nights off, as well as groups of rowdy tourists.

Pete regarded doors like this one as 'training doors', where a newcomer would find out if he was up to the job. I have to admit that his philosophy was both a wise and an effective one: your physical courage was tested by your being alone, but more importantly your mental limits were stretched by the pressure. If you are by yourself, then no matter how capable you think you are, you remain only one man – and one man alone cannot fight a crowd. Consequently, you had to really learn how to talk to people, calm them down, humour them, defuse tense stand-offs and negotiate with them without losing authority or face. It was actually a brilliant training ground for life itself, as all of your mental limits and abilities were tested and stretched, far more than your physical ones. You were forced into becoming an effective diplomat and by extension a much better doorman – and wiser person, too.

That first day on duty I realised I had better learn fast. I made sure that everyone who entered the bar was greeted with a cheery hello and a bit of humorous banter. If it were practical to do so, I would hold open the door for them and give a friendly nod; nice little touches that gave the impression I was a friendly guy and this was an OK pub. Whenever a barman came outside for a chat or a cigarette, I would grill him about who the local troublemakers were, how past doormen had behaved, and any previous problems they'd had and tips on how to deal with them. I learnt that by getting the staff on your side before trouble starts, you would have an effective ally beside you when it inevitably did.

Knowledge is power, and forewarned is forearmed.

Surprisingly for my first day on the job, we had no trouble whatsoever. As my shift came to a close, I felt a growing confidence in my abilities. I had learnt a heck of a lot about how the pub ran and the local area, but more importantly I had made some contacts amongst the staff and locals and had hopefully made a good first impression. Of course, I knew the real test would be how I reacted when anything physical went off – but for now that particular problem hadn't reared its ugly head. I surprised myself by really enjoying the responsibility of the job. I felt honour-bound to show the wary manager that he need have no worries with me – he was going to get the first-class professional service that he was paying good money for.

I walked to work on a bright Sunday morning with an eager

spring in my step, looking forward to getting back to my own scruffy porch space and the illicit promises of new adventures it held. It already felt like my own little patch of concrete, my tiny sod of clubland turf, and it comforted and contented me. If nothing else, I was merely grateful to be working on the door. I knew I was in for a long, stressful shift, as it was traditionally the busiest day of the bank holiday weekend. The fact that I was on double-time pay cheered me up, though. Surprisingly, once again there was no real trouble throughout the day: the most I had to do was talk down a few hotheads, beer-goggled peacocks banging chests and arguing amongst themselves over mating rights with the kind of women that really weren't worth arguing about. But, other than that amusing diversion, there was nothing more.

I found myself relishing the diplomatic side of the job (which, looking back, isn't surprising, I suppose, when you consider that in future years I became a conflict resolution counsellor and participated in peace-building sessions with former members of the IRA, UVF and other enemy combatant groups). Our clientele were generally middle-aged and consequently far more open to reasoned argument than hot-headed youngsters. I also discovered that if you treat people with respect and goodwill, allowing them to keep their dignity no matter how tense, stressed or fraught the situation is, then most of the time they will respond in kind. But I knew that diplomacy and tact would only get me so far . . . and sure enough, my luck dramatically ran out in head-crashing fashion that night.

Despite my best efforts at being friendly and professional, there was one customer who was just not responding; in fact, as he eyeballed me relentlessly that night, I could see he was building up his courage for an attack. A self-styled 'hard man', he clearly thought he was the proverbial dog's bollocks and existed in a deluded state of social superiority – so much so that whenever he came in he would ignore my greetings and give me dirty looks of dripping contempt. Physically, I didn't assess him as much of a threat, but I noted that he had the distinct air of a 'tool man' and I worried that he might pull a blade on me if things got nasty. He was in his 30s, tall and rawboned skinny, with an expression of arrogance permanently etched on his pinched, rat-like features. I had even stopped holding the door open for him because my wariness of him was such that I didn't want to give him an opening to attack me while I had one hand otherwise engaged: I adjusted my body language when he slinked past like a sneaky, pox-ridden rodent lest he launch a surprise attack. My sixth sense screamed at me to keep an eye on him wherever he went, as I was sure he was going to test me.

At 11 p.m. that Sunday night, he turned up steaming drunk with a burly accomplice, complete with tear-drop tattooed cheeks, rotting teeth and whisky-spittle breath. His pal was a particularly aggressive, grossly unpleasant Scot who was bleeding from his fat potato nose and sporting a ripe black eye that wept with a rancid yellow discharge. Of the two, I judged the Scot to be the designated fighter and the main threat, as his skinny pal stood a good bit behind him, wearing his customary sarcastic grin and playing the wind-up role.

I wasn't happy about the Scot's bulky presence in my doorway, crowding the tight space. Though he was clearly a veteran druggie, replete with customary sores, he hadn't yet entered the 'wasting away' stage and had managed to hang on to his chunky build. I felt as naked and vulnerable as a man in a cage with an agitated chimpanzee about to go schizoid while its quiet but menacing mate licks its chops, waiting to pick up the pieces. It was a stand-off before any one of us had even uttered a word – and each of us knew it.

I told the pair of them in a voice that I struggled to calm that they could not enter the bar in their current states. I tried to stay professional, even apologising to them for not being able to let them in – a courtesy the cunts didn't deserve and instantly spat back in my face.

As I knew they would, they protested vigorously and loudly, building up courage and justification for the beating coming my way. I knew the drill: they were painting themselves as the innocent party and I the unreasonable one, then they would argue with me for a while longer before battering me senseless for being 'unreasonable'. By now, the bar staff had heard the commotion and came outside to investigate, albeit from a wary distance. I felt extremely nervous and I'm sure the yobs detected my fears. New life and new blood is always at its most vulnerable during its first confrontation: they felt strong and were relishing extracting 'respect' at my young skull's expense.

In the space of a few seconds, I ran through my options and analysed my doubts.

First, I knew that this confrontation was going to get physical and bloody and that no amount of diplomacy could avert it; in fact, my diplomacy seemed to be making me appear weak in their eyes, heating their blood up even further. Second, I didn't want this fight to happen, but the other two most certainly did. What was really worrying me, however, was the state of the Jock's face: it was literally dripping with blood and I didn't fancy repeatedly ramming my fist into it, however pleasurable that might be. I wasn't bothered about injuring him further (in fact, I would have enjoyed it tremendously, viewing it as morally just) but was worried for myself in case he had some communicable disease. The idea of possibly catching hepatitis off this drunken, drug-addled prick didn't appeal to me in the least.

But I knew what I had to do.

As the Jock was in mid-sentence issuing yet another threat, I stepped forward into his personal space, taking him by surprise. A split-second later I kicked him as hard as I could in the balls with a heavy front snap-kick. He doubled over in a quiet, slow-motion wheeze and looked up at me in stunned surprise. Fearful that my first kick hadn't done the job, I stepped forward and repeated it, my shoe sinking deep into soft blubber before finally finding bone. I think I knocked the wind out of him because all of the aggression inside him suddenly deflated: like a popped slug, he half-toppled, half-slid down the tiled wall. Without a word, he slowly picked himself up, meekly held up his hands and staggered back away from the entrance, his small pig-like eyes rapidly blinking and watering with shock and hurt – bizarrely, as if he were the victim.

His stupid pal, who I knew had egged him on and caused the whole damned thing to happen, just stood there, open-mouthed, gawping like a fish. I made no effort to strike him, not wanting to push my luck any further against the two of them, no matter how much my blood was up and I fancied my chances. I needed to maintain complete self-control – of my mind, my body and the situation, because it was still 'live' and dangerous, and they could easily have regrouped once their shock wore off and begun a messy but effective attack. So I just gave him a look that conveyed my feelings – that I was willing to fight for my life and, if necessary, take the pair of them down with me – and thankfully he, too, backed away.

I was deeply offended – albeit also very relieved – by how quickly and cynically the pathetic specimens switched into passive victim mode and abandoned whatever scraps of dubious honour they had. It was as if they thought I was utterly stupid: did they think I was going to forget the inconvenient fact that if I hadn't resisted them and struck out in self-defence then they'd have half-killed me? If I hadn't managed to overpower the fat man, then the pair of them would have gleefully used my head as a football, melted away into the night and laughed about it afterwards – with me left lying on the floor like a car wreck.

As the two of them slinked off in search of easier prey, I remember wishing that the next time they picked a fight with an innocent man he'd finish off what I'd started and knock the living daylights out of them, so much so the bastards woke up in hospital beds, as they so thoroughly deserved, eating massive doses of humble pie till they puked on it and repented. I somehow doubted it would happen, though, and the law of the jungle being what it is, they'd pick their victim more carefully next time and repay him with added interest for the beating they'd planned to put on me. As I saw it, my successful defence would mean that another man suffered in my place at their bestial hands.

Once I was certain they'd retreated for good, I let out a huge sigh of relief and leant trembling against the wall. All of a sudden I felt pale, weak and clammy as the adrenaline left my body and my hormones shut down, my body and my equilibrium fighting to rebalance themselves.

The manager came over and congratulated me for sending the two idiots packing; he said they had pulled the same trick on previous doormen but that I was the first one to finish them off. I felt good that I hadn't let them intimidate me and had done my job well. The locals had seen me in action and now they knew I wasn't just a nice guy trying to talk my way out of trouble because I lacked the courage or ability to fight. I had survived my first true test on the doors.

But the overwhelming feeling I had was one of immense relief that I hadn't had to punch that rotten, bleeding pox-like face. God only knows what diseases or infections such a specimen could have been harbouring – to this day, I remain grateful that I didn't have to find out.

The troublesome pair had made one of the oldest and biggest mistakes in the book by grossly underestimating their opponent's abilities, while at the same time woefully overestimating their own. I always make an effort to respect people: you never know what is going through somebody's mind if you teeter into the conflict zone or what personal background and skills they might have. For example, had my kicks failed to stop the Jock then my next move would have been to grab him by the hair and smash his face into the wall; once he was down I would have made sure he stayed there with a well-aimed strategic stamp, freeing me up to deal with the expected assault from his similarly misguided friend. And as the situation would have been one of self-defence and survival, I would have been morally and legally justified to carry out such a severe but completely necessary counter-attack. To protect my life, I would have had to at the very least temporarily disable one of them – preferably the stronger one first – in order to fight off the other and have a chance of surviving.

Do you think that in their tiny drunken minds they would ever have imagined that as I was trying to avoid fighting with them and to calm them down, I was simultaneously planning my ultra-aggressive defence?

The answer has got to be no – which perfectly illustrates my point: everybody (especially potential opponents) should be treated with human decency, diplomacy, and a wary and watchful respect. And this aggressive defence posture especially applies when dealing with the cowardly sorts who 'tag team' you and ambush in packs, getting others to back them up and do their dirty work for them. Unlike in Hollywood films, it is no easy task to ward off two or more men and it's not always the most skilful fighter who wins, but the one who is willing to use the most aggression. In the real world, cold aggression backed up by skilful application wins fights full stop. And notice that I put aggression first and describe it as cold; it must be controlled, and focused like a surgeon's scalpel, lest it be wasted and lost in the mêlée.

I learnt this lesson several times during my time on the doors. On one occasion I was ambushed after I had turned away two steaming drunk 'steroid boys' demanding entry. They were clearly looking for trouble, so after about five minutes of angry pleading they simply abandoned all niceties and went for me. It is no fun trying to wrestle off an 18-stone steroid abuser who's high on testosterone whilst his baboon-like pal is piling in the punches to your kidneys and ribs at the same time. In my mind, they have forfeited all human decency by attacking you in a pair, so you must give them no quarter and defend your life. If I hadn't been so enraged at the cowardice of their double assault and fought back with equal vigour, then I doubt I would have survived it. Luckily, when they realised that if I went down then at least one of them was coming with me, they gave up the ghost and scarpered.

One of the most disappointing things about human nature that you learn on the doors is that while there aren't many men who are willing to stand and fight alone, there are sadly all too many who are willing to take you on in pairs and packs.

Zenon was still a big part of my life and we spent most of our time off duty together. He'd frequently pop by the hotel bar on his way into work and we'd exchange a story or two or I'd go round to his house. There were always interesting people there, usually from Poland, who were either living or holidaying in England. They always had incredible tales to tell about fleeing persecution and evading the secret police in Communist Poland, and every time I visited I felt like I was getting a history lesson. I never wanted to leave.

A frequent houseguest was Zenon's bear-like cousin Marian Hreska, known as 'Polish George', for obvious reasons, who came to England before Zenon and helped pave the way for his arrival in the late '80s. Marian opened the door for Zenon to work at the Palace, as it was where he got his first job when he came to England. After the fall of Communism, Marian went back to Poland and became a self-made industrialist. His was an amazing journey – it was a hell of a long way from cleaning glasses in the Palace nightclub and working as an occasional bouncer, as he was when I first met him.

Much as I was grateful to be working at the hotel bar, I still yearned for the bright lights of the town centre; it was tough for a young man to be surrounded by middle-aged faces all weekend: the opportunities for action – of both varieties – were few and far between.

Zenon had been luckier than me and one of his first gigs was on the door of a hot new 'superclub' called Heaven & Hell that had opened in town and was even challenging the Palace for supremacy. The club management had put out a call for especially large and beefy doormen, as they wanted to quash any trouble from the off. Whilst I didn't fit that description, Zenon certainly did – his KGB hit-man appearance was just the thing they were looking for; in fact, he'd only got bigger since we'd switched over to the doors because he was now pumping iron with me three times a week in the gym.

Just as I'd suspected, Zenon's steel glare and girder-like arms deterred trouble before it even started. But not everybody was unwilling to try their luck and he had inevitably found himself falling victim to hilariously cowardly 'hit and run' attacks – some of which were laugh-out-loud funny.

He once had to tell off a drunken lout for putting his hands up girls' skirts on the dance floor and generally behaving like a disrespectful prick. It was the man's birthday and his pals frantically reassured Zenon that he'd just got carried away because he was drunk and he meant no real harm – they'd make sure he behaved himself from now on. Being sometimes too soft natured, he agreed that the guy could stay in. A few hours later he found himself alone on the front door briefly when none other than the loose-handed miscreant and his tanked-up pals were leaving. One by one they shook his hand and thanked him for letting them stay in; when it got to the troublesome one's turn, he shook Zenon's hand, said 'Cheers, mate, see you later,' and turned as if to walk away – then suddenly he whirled back around and landed a head-butt smack on Zenon's nose.

Zenon staggered back, seeing stars, and almost fell over as the offenders ran off down the street. What they hadn't realised was that Zenon saw exactly which bar they'd disappeared into and he sent a radio message to his pals on the door to make sure that they let them in and discreetly encircled them, pending his arrival. Twenty minutes later a cleaned-up but silently seething Zenon strode into the packed bar and grinningly confronted his tormentor, who promptly dropped to his knees in front of his cowering pals and begged for forgiveness. Zenon hauled him to his feet and the discussion was continued in the fire escape, on a one-to-one basis. I think it's safe to say that by discussion's end he saw more stars that night than Zenon had and returned home with the bigger headache.

Still at the Heaven & Hell, when a major battle erupted at the bar he stumbled into a rumble with a gang of Lancashire-based gypsies, one of whom was a boastful sort who claimed to be a bare-knuckle boxing champion – though he still felt the need to wear a steel knuckleduster when the fight broke out. He managed to land a clean punch straight on one of the doormen, leaving perfect indentation marks on his forehead and sending him reeling. When he ran at Zenon and tried the same trick, Zenon was ready for him and it didn't come off quite so well. Zenon ducked under his charge and knocked the gypsy off his feet with a haymaker of his own. He dragged him careering down the steep stairs and flung him hard onto the pavement. The so-called champion was badly dazed and had to be carried home with his arms draped over his friends' shoulders, his mouth dripping drool.

That wasn't the end of it, however; he arrived at the club entrance drunk a week later, demanding to be let at 'that Polish twat' so he could knock him out and teach him a lesson. He turned up a few more times, making a nuisance of himself and issuing threats, but never once actually doing anything about it.

At one point, he even goaded that he'd be willing to fight Zenon for several thousand pounds on 'gypsy ground' and under 'gypsy rules'. Zenon just laughed at him and said he'd seen the so-called gypsy rules in action with the sneaky knuckleduster business, so if he ever wanted a real fight then he knew where he could find him and they could do it for free. Other than that, he told the gypsy, could he kindly fuck off back to his caravan because he was tired of his bullshit and couldn't be bothered with it any more. Typically, as with most braggarts, the gypsy disappeared, taking his intimidation tactics and 'guilty secret' knuckleduster with him.

In the meantime, it appeared that things might finally be looking up for me, as word got back to Pete and his associates about my seeing off the couple of yobs, so now in their eyes I was at least half-proven as a doorman.

Pete ran his firm with two of his best former doormen, whom he'd promoted to act as his minders and office managers. Either one of these sturdy figures would drop off your wages on a Friday night from what looked exactly like an unmarked police car. If you had a problem, then that was your chance to air it. By now, I had been at the hotel bar for a few months and I felt I had learnt enough to move on to a bigger pub. It was a pleasant enough place and rarely attracted trouble, but working by myself was proving to be a lonely existence. Plus, at the back of my mind I was worried about the two scumbags I'd seen off ambushing me in a gang attack, as I'd frequently see them prowling and scowling on nearby streets, casting threatening looks my way, trying to build up their courage for a repeat run.

I had a chat to one of Pete's men and he agreed to put me on the door of a busier pub, where I would at least have somebody to talk to. The Palace had given me the false impression of a doorman's job as one of non-stop action and excitement; I was finding out that the grim reality of the job (unless you were on a 'hot door'), just like being a professional soldier, was 90 per cent sheer boredom and 10 per cent pure adrenaline. In their own strange way, the quiet moments could be more draining than the tense ones because you had to be on your guard and mentally alert all of the time. In addition, standing, hardly moving for hours on end, meant that your legs soon began to tire and ache.

The following week I was pleased to learn I had been transferred to the 'Kennel' pub (not its real name) in the holidaymakers' end of town. I wasn't yet back in the centre, but this was definitely a step in the right direction. I would be working with two other highly experienced doormen and was told to consider myself very much the junior partner. The pub itself was a solidly unpretentious working-class place that catered solely to local tourist trade workers, but at the weekends it got a few holidaymakers in, too. My two fellow bouncers were both in their 30s and were devoted family men: 'Big Roy' from Scotland and 'Fergal' from Ireland.

There is a large Celtic subculture in Blackpool that many of the locals are completely unaware of unless they work in the tourist trade. Young men travel to Blackpool seeking seasonal work and often settle there, raising their families and continuing to work in the service industry. Roy and Fergal were typical examples.

As soon as they saw how keen I was, they made it clear that all they were interested in was running 'a nice quiet door' and avoiding trouble. I respected that they made this clear to me from the start and I told them I wanted the same. They had done the whole 'angry young man' bit years ago, they said, and had now grown up and moved on. Both men worked together as joiners during the day, and their only purpose in working the doors was to put bread on the table and feed their families. Although very experienced, they were about as far removed from the gangster-doorman type as you could get: they were totally straight.

It was good to have someone to talk to while on duty and the pub had a tatty but cosy feel to it that made working less of a chore. There were quite a few oddball locals and we soon had a great piss-taking banter going on that warmed the mood. I used my time there to learn as much as I could about being a doorman and bled Roy and Fergal's knowledge dry. Both guys had been in the security game a long time; often I would just stand back and observe their handling of a heated situation, only getting involved if they waved me over or it looked like a 'kick-off' was imminent. It was a real education and I felt that working on the doors was giving me a broader perspective on life than any other job possibly could: I had to interact with all kinds of different characters and was learning about human nature all the time.

Roy had a particularly moving story to tell and the fact that he was still alive, thriving and functioning ably, impressed me as a great personal victory. As a child, he had suffered serious deprivation and tough setbacks, which had tipped him into youth crime. He ended up doing a spell in a borstal and still bore the scars of his cruel and inhumane treatment there – hot spoon burns, jagged knife scars and crooked, homemade tattoos all vied for space on his brawny arms.

Fergal, too, had some heartbreaking tales to tell; much of his youth had been spent in Ireland until the escalating Troubles prompted him to move to England.

I respected these guys for surviving and standing tall. They were great examples of men doing their best and displaying courage in the face of adversity. They were easy to work with because I admired them.

Things were going well and whenever trouble broke out the three of us could usually put a lid on it without too much claret being spilt. It was a well-run door with a solid crew and a great place to learn your trade, away from the prying eyes and pressure cooker atmosphere of the town centre.

It was a piece of appalling bad luck and a near-death tragedy that led to the break-up of our happy team. The injection of an explosive ingredient triggered a dramatic shift in our dynamics.

Once we had closed for the night Roy and Fergal often liked to go to a seafront bar to unwind for an hour or two before heading home for the night. I never went along because I recognised this was their private time together, as close friends and colleagues who went back a long way and had been through much. Instead I'd either amble along the seafront and soak up the Golden Mile Technicolor ambience or go and see Zenon wherever he was working.

On this particularly fateful night, Roy went alone and ended up getting stabbed. It's a sad and unavoidable fact of life for a doorman that you will make many enemies for just doing your job properly; in fact, the better and fairer you are, treating all customers the same (including the arrogant and nasty ones who think they're 'special'), then the more enemies you'll tend to make. Roy had the misfortune to encounter a yobbo he had been forced to bar from the pub many months before. For his troubles, he ended up with a six-inch blade in his back and almost bled to death.

Roy had emergency surgery that night and was told to forget about working the doors again for the rest of that year. I didn't find out the full story until the next day at work. Fergal was absolutely distraught, his eyes filling with tears as he told me how good and kind a friend Roy had been to him. He was visibly consumed with guilt and furious with himself for not having been there. I tried in vain to reassure him there was nothing he could have done to prevent it, as it was just one of those things – a classic case of a good man being in the wrong place at the wrong time.

The immediate problem we now faced was how to get a suitable replacement for the injured Roy. This was no easy task, as the replacement would have to possess the same qualities as Roy. Neither Fergal nor I were big blokes, so the other guy would have to be, in order to preserve the balance of the team. You cannot have three small guys working on a door together, as they will attract trouble, no matter how capable or diplomatic they are. You always need to have at least one big guy to physically deter yobs, if only on a visual level. It always makes sense to employ a couple of 'biggies' on a door because their mere presence can often quash trouble before it starts.

Fergal was a physically strong man, but he was more of a diplomat, whereas I was in effect a young apprentice. Roy had been the quiet big guy in the background, a constant and reassuring presence. We needed someone like Roy to restore the completeness of the team.

The man we got was just about as physically imposing as it was possible to be, but unfortunately he had a very different disposition to Roy and the way he dealt with problems showed none of Roy's judgement or sensitivity.

'Tonka' (not his real name) was a well-known doorman in the Leeds area – perhaps a bit too well known. Tonka was cagey about his reasons for coming to Blackpool and, given his reputation, we thought it wise not to press him. The first time I saw him walk into the pub I did a double-take, as did most of the customers. He was a seriously big guy; years of obsessive bodybuilding had given him a physique that looked like it could punch through walls. At 5 ft 10 in., he wore 16 stone of rhino-grade muscle that plated his bones. He was like the Hulk's younger brother. He carried it off well and had a preternaturally solid appearance that didn't seem bloated or overworked at all – just loaded with powerful tonnage. I noticed he had scarred, spade-like hands that looked as if they had done a lot of manual work. I was sure they had been exercised on more than a few heads, too.

Thanks to my own experience in the 'iron game', I had learnt quickly to spot the bloaters who had got addicted to steroids and pushed their bodies way beyond their limits; lightweights masquerading as heavyweights and struggling to cart it all round, monstrously morphed and chemically compromised. Such men often puff like pensioners when walking up stairs and possess truly pathetic stamina; they are strong and explosive in a fight for about one minute, then weaken rapidly, after which they usually get battered senseless by a man barely half their size. When you're on the door, it's better to be a lean, mean and clean 13 stone or so – able to rock and roll for however many rounds a fight lasts – than 18 stone, puffed up on gear and unable to do anything other than perform a one-time shot-put-style hurl onto the pavement. If the punter gets up and comes back at you, you've got a problem.

But Tonka was the polar opposite and this certainly didn't apply to him; he looked like he was born to be huge, a sort of white Mike Tyson and every bit as menacing. Contrary to his fierce appearance, however, he proved to be an affable and humorous man, completely at ease with himself, devoid of arrogance and comfortable in his own skin – because he knew better than anybody that with the latent power he'd got in that steel-trap body he had nothing to prove.

Once we had been introduced, it felt like we had known each other for years and we were soon ripping the piss out of one another. Always wanting to learn something from an old hand, I immediately started asking him for tips on training, nutrition, door work and self-defence. I think Tonka was flattered at my interest and genuine respect for him and he soon became another mentor to me.

But mentors can come in many guises and some bring bad lessons as well as good; Tonka was somewhere in between. I felt a little flutter when he advised me to stand well clear of him if it ever kicked off badly, as it wouldn't best please him if I got involved prematurely and he was liable to turn on me. The thing about Tonka was he loved to finish fights – conclusively and on his own terms. I would soon find out that Tonka's great downfall was his uncontrollable temper if he felt slighted or insulted; he couldn't bear to be 'fucked off', as he put it. And although he had a reasonable amount of patience and humour, if he felt he was being mocked or ignored then his over-reaction could be lethal. One of our customers found this out – at an almost terrible price.

The bane of any doorman's life is drinking-up time. People just don't want to leave the pub at the end of the night and go home, no matter how firmly or nicely you ask them. Fifteen minutes after last orders we usually asked politely for people to finish their drinks. Thirty minutes after last orders we aimed to have the pub emptied and closed up – then we could start to relax. On this particular night, we had an American visitor in the pub and he seemed to be struggling with the whole concept of 'drinking up'. Several times Tonka asked him nicely and each time he got withering sarcasm in return. Finally, after 45 minutes of cajoling, near pleading and increasingly strained requests, the American agreed to leave.

On his way out, he made the fatal mistake of tossing a challenge in the quietly seething Tonka's direction. I just stood there and shook my head at his remark, which was grossly offensive and totally uncalled for. The guy was a very tall, lean-looking type who appeared to be pretty fit and perhaps a bit handy too, but he was clearly no match for Tonka – yet he insisted on goading him.

Tonka, who, to be fair, had shown endless patience to the surly miscreant, followed him outside, muttering to himself in agitation and surprise. I felt sick at what happened next.

The guy actually got into Tonka's face, completely invading

his personal space, and insulted him again. Tonka just stood there staring at him, not moving back an inch. Unbelievably, the Yank began to laugh slowly, as if he were addressing some kind of illiterate hillbilly not worthy of his attention. Once he'd stopped laughing, he stepped even closer to Tonka and half-raised his hand, as if to feign a punch or wind one up. Whether he was going to give Tonka a cheeky slap in a sucker-punch attack or simply a patronising pat on the head, we'll never know. Either seems likely, but Tonka didn't wait to find out.

Smack!

Tonka punched him with a heavy left hook full on the jaw. It was a peach-perfect punch, clearly practised many times in the ring and on heavy bags. The Yank's knees buckled instantly and his eyes began closing as he toppled backwards like a tree, already unconscious mid-flight.

Crack!

The back of his head clattered onto the concrete so hard it actually bounced back up. For a few seconds, we all just stood there, staring in silent shock. I had never before seen anybody so catastrophically hurt from just one punch; he was out cold before he'd even hit the floor. Both friends and foes alike formed a midnight tableau of dead silence round his spread-eagled, crumpled body. His pals eventually snapped to and moved around him, attempting to rouse him, as the rest of us just stared in stunned disbelief. Hoping and praying that the incident was over and that the Yank would soon awaken, we all trudged back inside and the door was hurriedly locked.

The landlord poured us a few pints and we downed them with sick bellies, ashen lips and trembling hands. You could have literally cut the air with a knife; none of us wanted to be the first to speak.

A few minutes later came the banging on the door that we had all dreaded but knew was inevitable. Fergal motioned a seemingly unperturbed Tonka to sit down and went out to deal with it. The tension in the pub was becoming unbearable. A few seconds later, Fergal reappeared and said they couldn't wake the Yank up. The landlord's face drained of colour and he looked on the verge of vomiting: to have a customer lying on your doorstep mortally injured must be the stuff of a publican's nightmares. All of us trooped outside except for Tonka, whose face now betrayed the first faint frowns of doubt.

Fergal made an effort to sit the Yank up, but he was completely comatose and clearly beyond help. If it hadn't been so serious, it would have actually been funny watching Fergal's ludicrous but well-meant efforts at first aid. It was obvious to us all that the Yank was in a bad way – the kind of bad way that needs a doctor – but Fergal seemed to think that talking to him, slapping his cheeks and helpfully dragging him to his feet would somehow miraculously revive him. The landlord soon took charge and snapped at one of us to call an ambulance. Fergal again protested that 'a bit more fresh air' would bring him round, but he was angrily brushed off: the situation had gone way beyond what could be dealt with 'in-house'. I felt completely useless, as at that point in my life I'd undergone no medical training whatsoever and hadn't a clue what to do. (Ironically, several years later I'd be a fully qualified Regimental Medic, serving as an infantry soldier in Northern Ireland's infamous 'bandit country' of South Armagh on an operational tour with the British Army. I'd receive praise for treating a deeply unconscious policeman in a similarly comatose state after our security patrol fell victim to a murderous hit-and-run driver. But back then, in that blood-freezing moment on a Blackpool pavement, I'm embarrassed to say that I was about as much use as tits on a fish.)

Finally, an ambulance and police car drew up.

The paramedics dived into action and supplied speedy first aid, showing us up for the clumsy amateurs that we were.

Within minutes the casualty had an oxygen mask strapped on and was rushed to hospital with blue lights blazing. When they took him away, he was still out cold.

The policeman called Tonka outside and asked him if he knew anything about the incident. Tonka shrugged his massive shoulders in reply and casually sauntered back into the pub, trying and failing miserably to look unconcerned by the trauma, as if by pretending it wasn't a big deal it would all magically disappear. I could see that the policeman wasn't buying it: his eyes drilled sceptically into Tonka's back.

As a group, he asked us if we had anything to add and in unison we solemnly shook our heads, somebody mumbling that we couldn't be sure exactly what had happened at this stage and still felt a little confused. I felt like shit nodding along to this but thought it was the best thing to do – for now. My reasoning told me there was no point incriminating Tonka, as we didn't yet know how it would turn out. All we could do in the meantime was simply hope and pray that the Yank would be OK. If it turned out he wasn't, then the whole story would have to come out – but then and only then.

For the moment, I reasoned, whatever happened to Tonka made no difference whatsoever to the recovery of the stricken Yank and that's where all the focus of our prayers and wishes should be. To my astonishment, none of the American's friends were willing to say anything to the policeman either and immediately tried to downplay events and get rid of him, as if they felt that his presence was only heightening the drama and prolonging a night out from hell that they simply wanted to forget – once they got their injured pal fixed up.

They had witnessed both their pal's outrageous insults and Tonka's devastating riposte first hand, which made me wonder if the Yank had some previous form for this sort of thing: you find it's often the case with provocative sorts – which might explain his friends' obvious haste to dismiss the policeman. But the truth is I don't think that any of us knew what to do for the best, such was our confusion and shock, other than hope that the Yank would wake up. Whatever happened later we'd worry about then.

Going home that night I streamed through the pounding fog in my head and tried to come to some sort of resolution about what had happened and why. My main concern was that the Yank pulled through with no permanent damage. He didn't deserve to get hurt like that – but how could he have been so stupid as to provoke Tonka? The guy seemed to have no common sense and a practically suicidal death wish. Most people realise that if you pull a tiger's tale and it starts to growl at you it's time to back off, but the careless Yank clearly thought otherwise.

I felt for Tonka, too: after intense provocation, he had hit the Yank only once and then walked away, never intending to do him such harm. To his credit, he didn't kick him when he was down or beat him any further (as a truly crazed thug would have done) but chose to leave it at that. To him, it was a simple one-punch punishment that was intended to leave the Yank with nothing more than bit of wounded pride and a bruised ego for his insults and troubles.

But, by a stroke of unbelievable bad luck, the Yank's head had struck the pavement – compounding the punch – and it threatened to morph into something tragic. If things worsened, then Tonka could be looking at a potential manslaughter charge. Even worse, the American could be looking at the end of his life.

The next weekend I was relieved to hear that the Yank had pulled through; although he had a bruised skull where he'd banged his head on the pavement, he would be completely fine. Brilliant, wonderful, stupendous news. Tonka was incredibly relieved, as indeed we all were. The only topic of conversation that day was the previous weekend's incident. Tonka confessed that had the guy deteriorated any further he would have gone to the police voluntarily and told them the whole story. I could tell that after a week's sober reflection he was genuinely shaken up by it and filled with remorse. Tonka wasn't a bad guy – he wasn't what you would call a 'thug doorman' or a bullyboy – but this incident went a long way towards calming him down and gave him a tremendous scare. Previously he hadn't realised just how dangerous his own strength was, but now he was all too aware of it. From now on, unless it was the gravest of situations, he'd be pulling his punches a bit more and working on his diplomatic skills instead of his punchbag.

The Yank had learnt his lesson as well. Two of his contrite pals came in to see Tonka and tell him that as there were no serious or lasting injuries – sore head and bruised ego aside – no charges would be pressed. They'd firmly told the policeman that they wanted no further action taken and as far as they were concerned the incident was completely over with, done and dusted, and already put behind them. They couldn't have made it any clearer that they didn't want any further conflict and I could tell by their guilt-ridden expressions that they were mortified that they'd egged their pal on and let the situation get so dangerously out of control. They had had ample time to pull him away and calm things down, and as true friends that's what they should have done when he'd begun squaring up to Tonka. On behalf of their pal they said they wanted to apologise for all the trouble that had been caused.

Sitting up in his sick bed with the headache to end all headaches, the Yank had had plenty of time to reflect on his own bad behaviour and decided to call it quits. It was a wise decision and I think the right one. Tonka had been wrong to wallop him as hard as he did and shouldn't have risen to the bait, but equally it has to be said the Yank had behaved in a stupid, deeply provocative way and had paid the price for it. Most probably he'd been as belligerent and offensive to others in the past and had got away with it – but not this time. I think they were both chastened by the incident and learnt something from it, walking away wiser and more mature men.

However, despite the outcome, this incident was too serious to be swept under the carpet. Tonka had always made some customers nervous and now that the rumour mill was in motion it made for an awkward atmosphere in the pub. You can't just knock a customer spark out like that, no matter what the circumstances, and expect to go straight back to work as if nothing's happened. The landlord told Tonka that even though all concerned had shaken hands and exchanged genuine apologies, he would have to transfer to a different pub just to be on the safe side and to ensure peace and harmony. To soften the blow, he agreed to give Tonka a glowing reference and said that he could continue working there until he'd sorted out another spot on a different door. Tonka knew how the business worked and left the pub a few weeks later, with no hard feelings. In no time at all he was in demand at many of the top nightclubs, where his reputation as a fearsome 'trouble-sorter' served him well.

At the time, the incident shook me up badly, though as time has passed I've realised that it wasn't quite as dramatic or desperate as I at first thought. In the final analysis, all that happened is that one man picked a fight with another, got knocked out by a single punch, got taken away in an ambulance and had to spend a night in hospital. The next day he turned out to be completely fine.

This sort of incident happened every weekend in nightclubs up and down the country in the 1990s. In fact, it still does today. And, like then, most of the time it turns out to be no big deal at all. But occasionally it doesn't.

143

The incident will always stay with me as one of those razor-sharp reminders of how all of a sudden, with lightning speed, an 'innocent', hasty decision or minor careless blunder can lead to the gravest consequences imaginable.

It was one of those awful moments when it could have gone either way.

I thank God it went the right way.

7

MARTIAL-ARTS MYTHS

TONKA'S DEVASTATING PUNCHES ALWAYS DID THE BUSINESS. HIS whole body was an object lesson in how to generate heft, power and crushing knockout blows. To the uninitiated, he was a frightening beast to be around, but if you could take the best lessons from his worst excesses and leave the bad bits out – such as the TNT temper – then you'd have something special. Tonka was a big believer in maximising muscular strength, then cranking it up with one or two reliable fight-winning blows and a bone-breaking grip of steel. As he often growled to me in his inimitably blunt, plain-speaking Yorkshire-bass style, 'It's no fun tryin' t' get out of a headlock when a guy can bench press 300 lbs and's tryin' t' fuckin' strangle y'. Thee wants t' make sure thee's n the right end o' that equation and not the wrong' n' – so slap on a few pounds, gain some fuckin' beef and get some fuckin' leverage.'

I recognised that I had shortcomings in these areas and immediately set about putting them right. The first area I worked on was body weight: although I had a wiry, flexible strength, at 11 stone I would struggle mightily to make an impact on a truly large man with several stone of genuine muscle (not fat) on me, no matter how superior my conditioning and skills were. Thanks to my smaller frame, I would never be able to carry as much bulk as Tonka, but I recognised that I could still add some valuable extra poundage, improve myself physically and tip the balance in my favour.

Over the course of the next year and a half I added two stone of lean muscle to my frame by cutting back on my running and doubling my weights routine and food intake. At times I'd push myself so hard in the gym that the sinews in my arms seemed to howl aloud in pain, while my ever-full belly struggled to keep down the pounds of protein that I forced it to digest. It was a period of agonising but intensely satisfying and rewarding pain and sacrifice – for the pain was the forced hurt of a positive growth that represented a physical rebirth of sorts.

I think much of the weight came on quickly because at 20 years old your muscles haven't finished growing and you can naturally accelerate the process way beyond what you'd achieve if you began training later in life. It starts getting harder to add weight once you get past 25 because in every sense of the word you have completely stopped growing: your muscles, bones, tissues and tendons. It's still possible, but a big chunk of your natural growth potential has forever gone. Funnily enough, you can still get vastly stronger and make big strides in terms of power well into middle age, but aside from a few lean pounds and a general 'hardening' and maturing of the muscles you don't really get much bigger. It's one of the weird vagaries of the human body when you train it beyond a certain point: at first you get bigger and stronger together apace, then you cease getting bigger but continue getting stronger, all in the same tight space.

Once I achieved my target weight of 13 stone I concentrated on just doing enough to maintain it, switching back from an intense, super-concentrated style of bodybuilding to more explosive cardio and pure strength work. I chose not to get any bigger because I instinctively realised that I'd reached a peak state and had found an optimum fighting weight – adding any more would have just slowed me down and hampered my all-important endurance, agility and balance.

Following Tonka's stern advice, the second area I went to work on was developing a few effective strikes. Whenever you get dragged into a confrontation, you need to know that you have something you can rely on and perform well: a few tricks up your sleeve for when times are hard and things get dirty or you need a reliable back-up plan to knock your attackers out or stop them dead in their tracks.

I will shatter a few martial-arts myths here because I think it's about time that these endlessly propagated, dangerously deluded sacred cows were dumped in the bin of failed combat moves where they belong, along with the ludicrous Hollywood-style 'fantasy fighting' that perpetuates them. And I say this not as some fat-bellied, self-styled martial-arts 'guru' who's never had a real fight in his life, preferring instead to pontificate on his own particular brand of bullshit whilst hiding behind his rank, but as someone who's found out the hard way, by bleeding and being beaten up, what *really* works. My knowledge comes from not only traditional 'safe' study in pristine gyms and dojos with polished floors but also practical experience on beer-soaked pavements and within one of the British Army's most decorated infantry units – quite literally at the razor's edge.

When I began working on the doors, I was already an experienced martial artist, with five years of very hard karate training behind me. Without wishing to sound big-headed, I was also way above average black-belt standard, largely thanks to my extreme conditioning and the warrior mindset that I always tried to cultivate. I thought this would give me a substantial advantage when it came to coping with violence, but I was wrong.

In karate, you are offered dozens of different techniques to ward off an attacker. All of these are taught in a pleasant learning environment and practised on compliant and disciplined fellow karateka. The presumption in training is that you will always have a nice open space to fight in, be wearing comfortable, loose clothing and have ample time to select your defence. The reality I observed was that even in this kind of tightly controlled, falsely policed 'ideal' fighting environment only a few of the most athletic and agile karateka could usefully apply the skills they had been taught. And to make it worse, these tended only to be the naturally gifted 'street fighter' types. From a self-defence perspective, most students were simply wasting their time and reinforcing dangerous delusions about their own 'abilities'.

So what chance would they ever have in a pub fight, rolling around on a glass-strewn floor with a lunatic trying to re-mould their head with a bar stool? Shamefully, none! And the only lesson they'd learn would be a bitter and humiliating defeat at the hands of some moronic thug with no skills or training whatsoever – unless you count caving in the heads of rival football fans at weekends and ambushing carefully selected victims less savage than themselves.

Almost without exception 90 per cent of fights go to the floor after the first few punches are thrown. Once on the floor it becomes a dirty, sweaty, bloody test of strength, grit, endurance and grappling skills. Karate and most other striking-based martial arts are virtually useless in such desperate circumstances. The main problem is that you have too many techniques to choose from, which can cause paralysis, indecision and fatal hesitation. In contrast, the most brutally effective pub fighters act on primal gut instinct. They don't worry about skills until they are trying to strangle you or tear your face off.

During my first year on the door, I learnt this lesson the hard way. It pissed me off – and humbled me – but, more importantly, it made me go away and think about my weaknesses. It was a wake-up call to the law of the jungle, life in the animal kingdom, a brutal belief system that most bullies subscribe to, be they corporate bruisers or politically correct drones in shirts and ties hiding behind surface respectability, or beer-bellied football hooligans in scarves and boots 'giving it large' after a few pints and a meat pie.

I hadn't yet lost a fight on the door, but it was the strength I'd gained weightlifting, the physical conditioning and my never-say-die attitude that had saved me. Not the karate.

It was depressing to acknowledge this fact, but once I'd accepted it I could begin to put it right. I agreed completely with Tonka's assertion that the best way to win a fight was to strike back hard with a couple of dazing blows, then use superior strength, aggression and technical skill to tie your attacker up and wrestle him out of the door. The only caveat to this is that even though you need to know how to fight on the floor at all costs, you also need to avoid actually doing it; it's there merely as an emergency back-up in case you do go down and is not to be regarded as an efficient solution in the first instance. The reason for this is that if you're preoccupied applying your 'ground game' in a pub fight, then your opponent's pals are going to be busy applying their 'stools and boots' game to the back of your head.

The question was: how do I apply karate to the situation?

In a tournament, I could apply multiple strikes at will, but I had to narrow this down to just two useable pub strikes. So I settled on my old favourite, a heavy front-kick to the groin, followed up by a boxing-style head punch, headlock and possible takedown if the occasion called for it and it was safe (i.e. there were no yobbo pals around to assault me if we went to the floor). This combination – which only used one solitary karate technique (the front-kick) was simple and would work well in a close environment, provided the conditions were right.

My next choice for those rare and luxurious occasions when

I had distance and timing on my side was a roundhouse kick to the neck/head area followed up by falling onto my opponent and using my momentum to wrestle him out of the door.

And that was it. These two techniques I practised in the dojo countless times – often on a heavy bag and dressed in shoes and trousers – until they became second nature. The karate training hadn't been a complete waste of time, but after all those years and, eventually, a hard-won black belt it only amounted to two practical techniques, the front and roundhouse kicks. Those I'd chosen were highly effective, however, thanks to the shock effect they had when they hit home properly.

Over the years these strikes would serve me well, but not always. To get the maximum benefit, they were best used against a charging or stationary attacker, but without appropriate spacing they were useless. Against a particularly big man, they would only slow down his approach rather than stop him, giving me time to compose myself and plant my feet. When both strategies failed, it was all about blood and snot and who wanted it most. I recount these points here not to slag off karate but to open readers' eyes, tear off the blinkers and show what it can and cannot do.

I have a genuine respect and love for karate as a means of self-improvement and I admire how it can build discipline, focus and martial spirit in alert and willing minds; but at the same time I disapprove of it because I feel that it peddles false hope to vulnerable students and ultimately sells them a dangerous deception. I suppose you could say that it is conning them with a big but well-intentioned lie: learn this and you can defend yourself. Which would be fine if we were talking about tennis, cricket or squash – but the lie that is karate can get somebody killed if they fall for the mythical spell that it sells. Karate bills itself as an effective self-defence system when it is no such thing – quite the opposite, in fact, for the vast majority – and that, in the final analysis, concerns me greatly.

I feel it's a confidence trick, however honourably applied. And it's a shame that so many good people have fallen for it – senior instructors and genuine grand masters included. They have spent years mastering a fundamentally flawed self-defence system that ultimately doesn't work. In my experience its lessons pale into insignificance when battle-tested and objectively and honestly compared to other martial arts. For all the 'skill' that they believe they have gained, on the battlefield of real life it is physically redundant, despite the enduring power of the romantic myth that it can 'save you' from all kinds of dire situations. The brutal truth is, it can't.

You only realise how weak karate is as a self-defence system when you try to use it in real life or begin to study a more effective and well-rounded martial art. I'm not exaggerating when I say that I learnt more in five days of Krav Maga training (how to break-fall, elbow strike and hip-throw) than I did in five years of intensive karate training. That was a depressing and humbling blow for my ego to absorb, but I am glad I accepted it because otherwise I might never have broken free of the karate dogma and would still be blind to its faults today.

Forget what you see in the movies because 90 per cent of it is sheer bullshit, what with all the flying kicks and ridiculous mid-air acrobatics. The grim reality is that even if you were athletic enough to be able to perform such absurd moves – and only about 1 per cent of the population are – you'd never have enough space, your opponent would see them coming a mile away and you'd utterly exhaust yourself within minutes, no matter how fit you were. To kick a suited and booted muscular leg into a live, resisting opponent uses up masses of precious energy that you can ill afford to lose: once you're rolling around in the broken glass with a drunken bear of a man desperately trying to choke you, Hollywood-style fighting will be the last thing on your mind. It will simply be about survival and trying to avoid having your ears bitten off. This is the unglamorous reality of pub fights.

If I am asked today to recommend a style of martial art to anyone, I always say do a few years of a hard-striking art like Thai boxing, backed up by an effective battle-proven system such as Krav Maga in order to learn how to deflect and counter powerfully. If you have the ability and dedication, I recommend you achieve black-belt standard because then you'll have a strong and effective base to work from and it won't desert you in your hour of need.

Krav Maga is a particularly devastating military self-defence system that originated within Israeli Special Forces units and is now taught to security experts worldwide. I first learned of it during my time in the army at private training sessions with like-minded souls who had either served in overseas units or were fellow martial-arts nuts. And one thing that I can assure you of is this: if the military uses it, that guarantees it works. When it comes to fighting, they have no time for frivolous bullshit, as their lives depend on it.

One must never forget that in many ways military service in a 'teeth arm' (i.e. a combat unit, such as the infantry) is perhaps the purest and most primal example of the martial arts in action that can be found. The word 'martial' is defined in the Collins dictionary as 'characteristic of war' and if that's not a valid description of the true nature of martial arts then I don't know what is. I certainly regard my own military journey as an essential part of my development as a martial artist and a man. In my view, a modern-day professional soldier should aspire to be the living embodiment of the martial arts: a twenty-first-century Samurai warrior, with an assault rifle instead of a sword, but the same fighting spirit nonetheless.

Krav is a martial art of last resort that assumes no quarter and focuses purely on disarming, disabling and, if necessary, destroying your opponent. Every possible scenario is catered for in as far as it can be, so unlike karate you'll train for combat with armed opponents against a backdrop of presumed injuries, restrictive clothing and multiple assailants. It's no use being able to do fancy karate kicks in 'angry white pyjamas' if you don't know how to take a pistol off a guy, force a knife from an attacker's hand or break free from an attempted rear choke-hold. No martial art can guarantee to get you out of these life-and-death situations, but what Krav can give you is a genuine chance, which is a lot more than can be said for the nonsensical bullshit taught in many dojos, where you'll only learn one useful kick that can actually be used in combat – and even then only in ideal circumstances.

Once you know how to strike, then consider learning judo or jiu jitsu, which will teach you how to grapple on the floor to a high level in order to overcome a far stronger opponent. Mix the two together, combined with fitness and a fierce warrior mindset, and you've covered all the bases as far as you possibly can. What we've seen from the 1990s onwards is a long overdue evolution in understanding what's required to put an opponent down and what isn't – what's real and what's fanciful nonsense, basically – coupled with vastly increased knowledge within the security industries, military community and martial-arts world.

Two historic developments launched this revolution.

The first was the rise to prominence of Reality Martial Arts from within the military. Reality Martial Arts exploded onto the scene in the 1990s, with the implosion of the Eastern Bloc and the collapse of Communism, the brutal Bosnian wars, the continuing ruthless professionalisation of the Israeli Army and the export of brutal but effective fighting methods from Russian soldiers who'd served in Chechnya. Mix all of these toxic ingredients, battle-tested and deadly, together, chuck in a vastly expanded market in mercenary soldiers and suddenly 'retired' elite instructors, and you have a worldwide cadre of self-defence experts. Or, to put it more accurately, professional killing machines who can snap a man's bones as easily as a jobsworth stirs tea and issues fines.

The second was the surge in popularity of Mixed Martial Arts (MMA) sports fighting within the Ultimate Fighting Championship (UFC). The UFC and its famed Octagon fighting ring is slowly but surely eclipsing professional boxing, exposing its inherent weaknesses and choking the life out of the sport like a relentless anaconda feasting on a hapless sow. While there's no disputing that a great boxer with fast hands will always be a threat and must be respected, there's also no denying that if his punching platform is removed and he has no back-up skills or 'ground game' to speak of, then he becomes an even greater threat to himself.

What we've learnt is that boxing's effectiveness is greatly reduced once you remove the generously padded gloves because the fighters can no longer risk punching with full knock-out power lest they break fragile hands on inconveniently hard chins, sharp noses and bony foreheads. These are problems utterly alien to the cosseted boxer, spoilt and pampered as he is with the gloved-up luxury that allows him to throw all kinds of suicidal and carelessly aimed 'bombs' anywhere to an opponent's head.

The Victorian-era bare-knuckle boxers who were famed for going 50 rounds or more and fighting for hours rarely employed full power. As brutal as those fights were – and as skilled as those warriors must have been – they had to conserve their energy and pull their carefully aimed shots lest their hands be broken, too. The reality is that not even a fully taped and gloved-up boxer could fight for 50-plus rounds at full power in the finest mitts available without severely damaging his hands.

It's ironic, but the UFC has exposed one cruel and undeniable truth: boxers struggle to punch safely – let alone fight – without thick gloves and are incredibly vulnerable once they are taken to the ground (which they inevitably are). Ninety per cent of MMA fights are won with jiu jitsu, wrestling, grappling moves and good old-fashioned brute strength. It's worth noting, too, that even with the gloves on, boxers have a worrying habit of breaking their hands, which would soon render them at a massive disadvantage in a brawl, whether in the Octagon, on the cobbles or in the back room of a pub.

I can state with complete confidence that even a lightweight UFC champion, such as the famed grappler and Brazilian jiu jitsu black belt B.J. Penn, could utterly destroy a massive heavyweight boxer within a few bone-crunching, arm-twisting, ligament-tearing minutes, just so long as he avoided the big one-punch knockout shot. For B.J., it'd be a simple case of shooting at the hips to take the big guy down, whilst at the same time keeping his vulnerable chin nicely tucked in to avoid any big punches or to catch them harmlessly on top of his thick, notoriously hand-breaking forehead. (In fact, we're all blessed with such a forehead and any punch from an ungloved boxer will probably hurt him a lot more than it'll hurt us.) Next up, B.J. could apply a clinical rear-naked choke-hold or bone-crushing arm-bar. And then it's 'Goodnight, champ. Tap out, choke out or snap out, it's up to you, and I ain't bothered either way because it's happening, brother.'

Of course, what an even greater-sized UFC fighter, such as the fearsome former heavyweight champion Brock Lesnar, could do to a pure boxer doesn't even bear thinking about: it'd be like feeding a careless zebra to a ravenous lion. And as I pointed out earlier, that works for the pub and street, too. Indeed this exact scenario was played out in 2010 when the legendary former heavyweight UFC champion Randy Couture, despite being past his peak at 48 years old and long since retired, took on and utterly destroyed the much younger former heavyweight boxing champion James Toney in a fight that was frankly embarrassing. Toney, great boxer and tremendous champion that he was, flopped hopelessly about the ring like a fish out of water, dribbling and drowning on the sand.

I'm not stating any of this to disparage or discredit the well-proven combat sport of boxing, for which I've got enduring respect and love, but merely to point out that in this age of truly 'complete fighters' you need to be able to do a lot more than punch like a mule when padded up with protective gloves on. No matter how hard or fast your shots are, sooner or later you'll be on your back and then it's a whole new ball game, with different skill sets required. The wisest boxers with the most street-smarts will adapt to the new ways and learn how to grapple on the floor, kicking, kneeing and elbowing as powerfully as they can punch. And as for those who won't – well, let's hope for their sakes that they never have to find out the limitations of a one-shot style, no matter how great they are.

The one exception to the above are the true 'street fighter'-type boxers who you know instinctively would have still been great fighters even without their professional training, thanks to their natural ability, warrior mindset and physical make-up. I'm talking about men such as Mike Tyson, Marvin Hagler, Evander Holyfield and Joe Frazier: the type of men who remain lethal simply because nature intended them to be that way. When you're on the door, you should always watch out for these raw diamonds, trained or otherwise, because you tangle with them at your own peril and unless you've put in some very serious training of your own you will most likely lose.

Despite the years of formal training I've received, I always try to remind myself that sometimes nature can be the greatest trainer of all. A tiger doesn't get any special training, but it's still pretty deadly, isn't it?

The existence of such men makes it even more imperative that we mere mortals who haven't been so physically blessed make an even bigger effort to close the gap – because it *can* be countered and defeated. And the only way this can be done is in the dedicated pursuit of the even greater martial skills that cannot be gifted by nature, only mastered by hard and relentless practice.

As Jigoro Kano, the legendary jiu jitsu master and inventor of Kodokan Judo, advises us: 'To become truly undefeatable one should not rely on one's strength; for when one meets a stronger opponent one will surely be beaten.' I cannot think of any wiser or timelier advice to offer an aspiring doorman or martial artist.

My only regret is that I only discovered how beneficial the right kinds of martial-arts training can be long after I'd ceased working the doors: had I learnt all this earlier it would have saved me many a black eye and bruised fist.

But better late than never. I've always been a late developer and believe that it doesn't matter when you learn, just so long as you eventually do – and that once you start, you don't stop until the final breath leaves your body.

But I digress.

I remained at the Kennel for another six months. It was a good place to learn the trade and make some new pals, but if I am honest it was starting to feel a bit claustrophobic. I felt I had gained as much knowledge as I could there and was itching to get into the town centre, where all the real fun happened and to sample some of the action that my good pal Zenon was getting. The Kennel was like the hotel bar in that it was a pretty middle-aged sort of place. As a youngster, I passionately yearned for the bright lights.

The problem was, breaking into the town centre clubs was extremely hard if you weren't well established on the door scene. I was slowly getting a good reputation as a decent doorman, but it still wasn't enough to get me into town.

Another problem was that the town centre crowd viewed working the holidaymaker type of pubs as strictly second division. They, of course, saw themselves as first division. What I needed was a bit of luck or perhaps to meet someone with the inside track on the best clubs.

I was about to do just that.

We had a succession of random doormen once Tonka left us. The landlord, fearful of making the same mistake again, wanted to try out as many blokes as possible before settling on a calmer replacement. So, for the time being, Fergal and I formed the permanent main team, plus whoever turned up for the weekend.

Unbeknown to me, I was about to meet somebody who would change my life, colour it with joy and catapult me into the very world I had been seeking. Sometimes in life you find yourself standing next to a stranger and for no apparent reason you feel uncannily drawn to them; it's almost like déjà vu, as your senses spark into life and tell you that you've just encountered a soulmate of sorts and have already bonded, despite the fact that neither one of you has uttered a word. It could be a lover, a friend or a business partner – you just don't know – but you'll know when it happens because you walk away with that person's presence imprinted on your mind like a tattoo. It's happened to me several times in my life – probably because I'm an intensely curious and natural 'seeker' of all things new – and each time the person's become significant to me and tinged our time together with joy.

And so it was with 'Callum' (not his real name).

I was standing at the edge of the Illusions dance floor one Thursday night, it being the only night I had the chance to go out myself, gripping the chrome railing, when he came and stood beside me. He seemed strangely aloof, yet was oddly mirroring my body language as we stared silently into the teeming throng of skinny white arms drawing shapes in time to pounding dance tunes. He was working on the Illusions door but seemed detached from the regular crew because of his age and his apparent newness to the town; I'd never seen him in Blackpool before. We never said so much as a word to each other that night, but for the next two years we'd be bonded like glue. Callum would play an instrumental role in my life: he'd become a major father figure to me when I desperately needed one and help mould me into a half-decent doorman who could 'get the job done'.

He stood out from the regular door crowd because of his middle-aged but fresh and ruddy appearance. Most doormen are in their late 20s or 30s, but Callum appeared at least a decade older and in fact was already well past the dreaded 40 mark. He looked anything but old and worn out; instead he carried in him a lust for life that fizzed with radiant energy and charisma. He was 6 feet tall and solidly built, with a deep chest and broad sloping shoulders, and he had the weathered features of a man who has seen – and enjoyed – a lot of life. We had a brief introduction a few nights later and I was struck by how deeply wrinkled yet curiously handsome he was up close. The lines suited him and enriched his 'aura' with character and a touch of wisdom.

Callum really looked like he'd been around a bit – and indeed he had: part Irish gypsy, he had the jet-black hair, bronzed skin and twinkling, burnt-blue eyes synonymous with that race. A gruff Birmingham accent pitched with warmth, honest mischief and what I can only describe as a curiously heartfelt goodness completed the picture. He was quite simply a very special man.

As I stood on the door of the Kennel a few weeks later, my spirits soared as I saw Callum energetically striding up, his mega-watt smile beaming from a hundred yards out. He bounded up the steps, warmly pumped my hand and told me that as a favour to Pete he would be working the door with me that weekend, even though he was due a few days off. I smiled to myself that this was fate: it was meant to be. I was chuffed to bits.

Callum was strictly a town centre man, so I would get the chance to catch up on all of the gossip. He told me he was a roofer by trade and had moved up north from Birmingham to make a fresh start. I didn't probe too much, but I already knew from my own enquiries that he had just completed a 'five stretch' in jail for serious drug offences. It is a measure of how immature and foolish I was back then that I was actually rather impressed that he had been in the nick. Nowadays, of course, despite being brilliant at his job and not in the least bit thug-like, Callum wouldn't get licensed to work on the doors because of his criminal record and various scrapes with the law – which ironically would be a great loss to the profession because he was so bloody good at it. But back then it was a different age. And I was a different person.

So, there we were, standing shoulder to shoulder, eager to form a new alliance. We hit it off instantly and soon had a great natural rapport going. It was as if we'd known each other for years. Callum had a certain roguish charm and I noted he used it on customers to great effect. Most of his jokes were self-deprecating, incredibly rude, grossly offensive or at his own expense – but somehow he always got away with it. His devilish insults always worked on the rowdy punters and calmed any tensions. I noted how the punters would shake his hand and pat his shoulder on the way out, promising to return soon and earning an instant riposte from Callum – cue more laughter. This was Callum's great secret to running a quiet door: he would use wit and humour to play the fool, but in actual fact he was anything but. A more streetwise, shrewd operator I had yet to meet.

The shifts flew by and we parted on warm terms. I was sad to see him go, as it had been the best weekend I'd had in years:

non-stop laughter, piss-taking and tall tales. I doubted I would see Callum on the door at the Kennel again because he was a cut above, but I sensed that I had just made a good friend and, crucially, an ally. My instincts proved right.

Callum began dropping by the pub periodically for a chat; often he was on his way to work in the town centre and promised to put a word in for me, or he'd be driving back from a roofing job in his battered old Sherpa van, covered in dents, rust and cement. I was flattered that a senior bloke like Callum would take the time to chat to me and show even the faintest interest in my career, as I was still regarded as a new face in town.

In time, Callum opened up to me about the details of his prison sentence. He had picked up a consignment of drugs from a ship in port and as he was about to drive away he was arrested in a police raid. The entire gang had been caught up in an undercover police sting, so from the moment he'd agreed to the deal, long before he'd turned the key in the ignition, he'd been doomed and on his way to prison. The drugs weren't his – thank God – but he was being paid to transport them. At his trial the judge had described him as 'a small cog in a big wheel' and sent him down with a purse of his lips and a bang of his hammer.

He lost three stone of flab and a personal fortune whilst inside and vowed to go straight on his release – or as near as dammit that a man like Callum can. That was the reason he had moved to Blackpool – to absent himself from his old gang and the temptations of the same old easy money. As he told me about the luxurious lifestyle he had loved and lost, I got the feeling that he was sincere. It was a hell of a step down to go from a detached house in Midlands suburbia, with a new sports car in the driveway, to a cramped prison cell, then a rundown Blackpool terrace, but he had handled the loss with grace and humility, and I admired him all the more for it. He confessed to me that he still intended to get involved in small-scale 'scams' from time to time, but he never wanted to go near drugs again because of the associated long jail sentences and the inherent dangers of the 'drug game'. He knew of guys who'd been utterly ruined and lived in fear for their lives because not only had they been arrested but their criminal masters were demanding that they cover the cost of the seized drugs as well – often an impossibly large sum that they had no hope of raising, by fair means or foul.

Callum actually earned a pretty good living from his roofing business. He was a hard grafter: whenever I saw him he would be covered in paint, wood chips and dried cement. This, combined with his door money, meant he was able to stay reasonably straight and keep away from the serious stuff.

I have always believed in giving genuinely deserving people a second chance and so it was with Callum. I accepted his friendship in the generous spirit it was offered, but I also made it clear to him that if I ever suspected he was involved in drugs again then I would drop him like a hot potato – not because of any moral objections I had but purely for my own safety and survival.

My own feelings on drugs have never really altered: I was, am and always will be against their abuse. When you have to start popping pills and snorting powder to have a good time, it all starts to get a bit sad and desperate – not to mention risky and expensive. Working in clubland, I was constantly exposed to drugs, but seeing their effects close up was a massive dampener: it actually turned me off them as opposed to turning me on.

I admit that, like many of my generation, I briefly experimented with soft drugs, but all that amounted to was a few joints and a couple of Es. Hardly the crime of the century. In my youth, my poison was always a bellyful of beer and a few generous shots of vodka.

From bitter experience on the ragged frontline of society, I know for sure that you'll never stop certain kinds of people taking certain types of drugs; there will always be that person who seeks them out, getting horrendously addicted and their unfortunate family in all kinds of agonising trouble. Similarly, you'll never stop the most remorseless and predatory kinds of twilight dwellers from preying on vulnerable individuals, feeding the addiction and making it ten times worse. I've seen it happen too many times and I've watched the innocent and hopeful faces pinch and wither. It's wretched, it's tragic and it's vicious. It is also an eternal cycle of decaying life, truth and reality.

We're never going to eradicate the drug problem, but I think we can make it better – because, fuck it, we can't make it any worse, can we? I think we should consider legalising the drug business, taxing it, cleaning it up, government regulating it and making it as safe as we possibly can – just like we've done with alcohol, one of the most destructive drugs of all. So maybe we should drop the endlessly repetitive, ultimately futile, redundant, colossally wasteful, cripplingly expensive and self-serving politico-driven 'war on drugs' and start doing something a bit more useful to control and limit the problem. In my opinion, we're not going to solve it any other way – and certainly not by quasi-military judicial force, however well intentioned.

I wasn't used to laying down the law for the terms of a friendship, but as Callum had proven himself to be a bit of a rascal in the past I felt it wise to. Callum accepted and respected my position, so we never had any need to raise the drugs issue again. Anyway, Callum had some good news for me – and a proposition.

Pete had offered him a position on one of the best doors in Blackpool – the 'Varsity'. Callum said he would accept and asked if he could bring one extra 'bod' with him, whom he felt he could trust. The only question now was: did I want the job?

Did I ever? To say I was over the moon would be an understatement. In only a matter of months I had gone from working on the door at an old fogeys' bar to one of the hottest clubs around. What a result.

The Varsity was a large bar situated on the corner of a huge amusement arcade. It was right next door to another fun pub called 'Charlie's' and between them they had Blackpool's nightlife sewn up. I would be working as part of a six-man door team in a bang up-to-date, state-of-the-art fun pub. The best part was that the bar closed at 1 a.m., which meant I could go on to another nightclub for the last hour as a customer. The Varsity had a brilliant DJ called 'Dan T', whom I knew from my Palace days, and he was guaranteed to get the place rocking.

On my first night on duty, I was introduced to the rest of the door team. We were a mix of backgrounds, types and ages, and on balance I felt we had a good squad. We were fortunate to have Charlie's right next door, so if anything got too big for us to handle on our own then we could get instant, boot-rushing back-up.

The club was in a state of flux, as it had just undergone major re-branding with a complete refit. A new manager had also been installed to oversee it all. Everything was brand new, from the door team (the one exception being an experienced doorman, 'Chaz') right down to the glass collectors and cleaners. Initially, there was some uncertainty about who exactly would be the head doorman, as it had been a rushed and chaotic re-opening and recruitment exercise, and the management wanted to try out a few senior blokes working together first – such as Callum and Chaz – before deciding who would get the top spot permanently.

Straight away this caused tension, as inevitably the two best qualified blokes were butting horns from the word go. Chaz was a veteran of the doors and had served a spell as a doorman in the Varsity's previous incarnation under the old management team, so he knew many of the locals and understandably felt he should become head doorman. Such a smooth transition for Chaz was never going to happen, though, especially not when Callum made it abundantly clear that he felt the top spot should be his and he set about vigorously, repeatedly and aggressively proving it

Chaz had been a decent fighter in his youth and still packed a punch. During his early years on the doors, he had been a real enforcer and his nose, messily splayed flat, attested to his lion-hearted spirit and willingness to get stuck in. But he was now mistakenly – and to his great cost – surrendering himself to the effects of creeping middle age and an ever-advancing beer gut. Louts who only a few years previously would have tiptoed around him or withered under his harsh glare were beginning to get braver, tossing insults and potshots at him. It seemed like Chaz was letting slip all his authority on the door.

He was a lovely guy with a great personality who didn't deserve all that was being heaped on him by the endless challenges and draining face-offs, but at the time I felt it didn't have to be that way – he could have still turned it around. But he chose to let himself go. He had grown too comfortable in his position and let complacency creep in. Faced with the vitality and sheer force of Callum (who, ironically, was substantially older), his life on the door only got harder.

Other notables were the truly giant 'Big Sam' (an amusing thing about working the doors was that almost everybody ended up with a sobriquet that began with the prefix big/old/fat/Glasgow/Scouse/Cockney or similar followed by their name. It could get confusing at times, as you could have two Big Sams or Cockney Petes working on the same door). At

6 ft 7 in. and built to match, Big Sam was a virtual mega-deterrent to trouble. Sam's signature move was a quite awesome 'elephant charge' through the crowd whilst gripping an unruly punter or two under his octopus-like arms. As he barrelled through the club with his unfortunate victim, customers would bounce off his mountainous shoulders, the dance floor parting like the Red Sea.

We called him the 'Moses of Bouncers' and reckoned that when they did a remake of *The Ten Commandments* he'd be a dead cert to get Charlton Heston's starring role; the only difference was Sam wouldn't need the godly staff to work his sea-parting magic.

We also had without doubt the oldest active doorman in Blackpool in 'Para Bob'. At an unbelievable 50-plus years old, he was a fanatically fit ex-army sergeant who still loved to fight and prided himself on his undoubted ability to 'put the gobby ones out'. He was forever joking, half-seriously I think, that he could still 'out-run, out-fuck and out-punch' any youngster around. Bob had served in the famed Parachute Regiment and he proudly wore his silver Pegasus wings and regimental tie with his dark-blue doorman's blazer. Coupled with his shaved head and 'anything goes' grin, they were a great icebreaker and deterrent, particularly with inquisitive squaddies, with whom he'd swap ferocious banter and war stories. If ever we had trouble with a gang of drunken soldiers, it was often Bob who'd talk them down, pretending to pull rank and taking the piss at the same time in such a way that we all saved face and nobody got hurt; a great result all round. Despite his age, he was one of the best doormen on the team, and a very effective bloke to have around.

And then there was me, at 21 years old very much the young apprentice and 'newbie' of the group.

The Varsity's new general manager, whom I'll call 'Aiken', told us that the reason he had reorganised the door team was because he wanted to make some big changes to the way the place was run. He also said he expected we would have trouble in the early stages, which was why he'd put a lot of time and effort into assembling a good crew who could talk as well as fight.

In the '80s, clubland consisted of mainly privately owned outfits run by local people, but by the '90s all this was beginning to change. Major corporations had taken over many of the small clubs and were starting to run them like cash cows, squeezing the punters of every available penny. Not surprisingly many customers became pissed off at this culture change and frequently those of us on the frontline copped for their anger. The Varsity had just received an expensive makeover and Aiken had been instructed by the brewery to make the club more upmarket in order to try and improve the clientele.

There were two major changes that I knew would cause us untold grief: the introduction of a £2 entry charge and the barring of customers wearing jeans. For the best part of ten years, it had been free to enter the Varsity bar and people could wear what they liked, so the sudden change in the rules, coupled with the new faces on the door enforcing them, would go down like a lead balloon. We were going to have to earn our pay the hard way.

Things soon got off to the worst possible start. One of the oddities of the Varsity was that we had a curious mix of clientele for a seemingly trendy town centre bar. The majority dressed smartly and visited us for perhaps a few hours before going on to another club. Although this group complained bitterly about the new conditions, they eventually (albeit begrudgingly) accepted and complied without trouble. The smaller second group to give us untold grief were the local seafront workers who would drop in for a drink after work wearing their scruffs. These were quite a rough-and-ready bunch, many of whom ran burger bars on the prom or sold dodgy pirate videos from backstreet market stalls. Trying to convince them to accept the new deal seemed impossible – they weren't the type to follow rules at all and were guaranteed to rear up against them.

Night after night they would turn up in jeans and trainers demanding to be let in, adamantly, indignantly and aggressively refusing to accept that things had changed. They also objected vehemently to paying an entry fee. Rather than launch into an all-out battle of wills with them Aiken sensibly suggested a compromise. As those complaining were old customers who had drunk in the bar for years, he agreed that for the first month or so they could enter free of charge in their jeans, provided they fully understood that it was only temporary. The idea was that as the rest of the clientele smartened up, the old holdouts would gradually get the message and follow suit – or find somewhere else to drink. Of course what happened in the end was that they just demanded these conditions continue, becoming ever bolder and more obstinate in their objections, throwing Aiken's diplomatic kindness back in his face. Aiken had done all he reasonably could to avoid trouble in his new club, but he now reluctantly told us to simply bar the lot of them. End of story.

The one man who was really struggling to enforce all these new rules was Chaz, mainly because he was simply too associated with the old routine, pre-makeover. Many of the punters to whom he now had to refuse entry had in the past bought him drinks and been pals with him. He was getting horrendous stick off the regulars and spent most of the night either fighting them off or apologising. This in itself was causing tension between him and Callum, who felt we had given too much leeway to the complainers; he also felt Chaz wasn't supporting him in facing them down. Although Callum was in favour of talking problems through with customers and avoiding violence – indeed, he was the undisputed master of door diplomacy – he made it clear that he felt Chaz was being too considerate and allowing certain customers to take liberties with the door crew – liberties that could backfire on us and get us badly hurt.

The rest of us agreed. Enough was enough. Previous friendships had to be set aside and a line drawn in the sand. The softly-softly approach simply wasn't working: it was drawing trouble to us, not deflecting it away. We'd reached the point where we had conceded so much ground by backing off so many times that we'd soon lose any remaining respect the locals had for us. If we had been dealing with reasonable people, then it might have been a different story, but we weren't; they were nasty types and violence was the only language they understood.

Things came to a head shortly after. Chaz and Callum had been sniping at each other, disagreeing over door policy in full view of everyone. As the new kid on the block, I tried to keep out of it, but I could sense a battle for control of the door was brewing. If it came down to it, I would be loyal to Callum, as he had got me my start in town, but more importantly I felt he was right. I trusted his judgement implicitly.

It was a busy Saturday night and by 10 p.m. the place was heaving. Punters were squashed in shoulder to shoulder, the toilets were overflowing and the bar was under siege. We were already overfull, way beyond capacity, and we simply couldn't admit anyone else, no matter how they were dressed. As we stood in the club porch, Callum let out a heavy sigh. Looking up the street, he muttered 'Shit' wearily to himself. Purposefully marching towards us were about a dozen scruffily dressed, banned punters.

As I scanned their outfits, I could tell they had come for a fight: yellow puffa-jackets, pale Joe Bloggs jeans. Dirty parkas with the hoods pulled up completed the look of defiance. They intended to wreck the place, whether we liked it or not.

There were four of us on the door, so clearly we were heavily outnumbered. At the Kennel I had faced down and fought off a few yobs, but never this many and I didn't fancy the odds.

'Well, fuck it! There's a first time for everything,' I nervously told myself.

Instinctively, I looked to Callum for leadership and asked him what to do next. I didn't do this to disrespect Chaz, rather just because I had more faith in Callum's methods. Chaz didn't object to Callum taking charge either, but he growled uneasy consent. I think it was at this point he subconsciously ceded control of the door, handing it to Callum. The ongoing squabbles with Callum and the never-ending rumbles with disgruntled punters had taken their toll and eroded his position to the point that I think he simply wanted an end to all the tension, rivalry and upset.

Callum said to leave the talking to him and told me to stand beside him in the narrow two-man-wide porch. The other guys stood behind us, backing us up. We were the first line of defence and if Callum couldn't reason with them (which was the likely outcome) then he and I were to strike first on the two ringleaders. If possible, we would then drag them into the pub, at which point Chaz would slam the shutters down and we would radio for back-up from Charlie's. We would have no chance against a dozen men, but with the entrance so narrow only two of them could attack us at any time. Our one consolation would be seizing the gang leaders and beating the shit out of them inside the club doorway as an example to the rest of the idiots.

The gang now stood outside the entrance, demanding to be let in. The two self-appointed spokesmen framed the doorway and began issuing threats. Callum attempted to reason with them, but it was clear they intended to storm the door and force entry. I looked at the opponent facing me and ignored Callum's tormentor. He looked like a druggie type and was short and skinny, his sallow skin framing pinched cheeks, blackened teeth and sunken, dead eyes. I didn't take my eyes off him as he stepped closer, snarling out threats through cruel and contorted features. In his own pathetic way, he was as venomous as a spitting cobra. But unlike that brave reptile this bastard could only fight in a pack.

My main worry was that he had a concealed knife: experience had taught me that these types didn't like clean fights and were very quick to resort to weapons, being inevitably 'tooled-up' wherever they roamed. I wouldn't let him get any closer now, as I didn't want him invading my personal space. He made a clumsy lunge towards me and I stepped forward and to the side to counter it. By keeping the distance between us, I was now able to launch my signature technique of a front snap-kick, my surging adrenaline and anxious focus ensuring that it had plenty of 'whoomth' behind it. I felt confident in the kick and let it go at full force, without hesitation.

Out of the corner of my eye I also saw Callum move on to his opponent.

Smash! The sound of breaking glass and an anguished yelp surprised me, and I wondered what it was. During the split second in which I threw my kick, I was also surprised to see the gang all step backwards, when it would have been more logical for them to charge forward. Anyway, fuck it, I would worry about them later, I thought. For now, it just felt good to have got my kick off.

I readied myself for the cunt's inevitable counter-attack, but strangely it never came. Then I saw what had happened, as my assailant sunk to his knees, holding out a bloodied hand with shards of brown glass sticking messily out of it. His friends stepped back further and stared at him in shock. On the floor lay a jagged broken bottle stained with blood.

Now I understood.

As the yobbo lunged at me, he had drawn the already smashed bottle, which he had concealed behind his back. His intention had been to stab me with it. By a stroke of sheer good fortune, my kick had connected with his hand as he swung it towards me – shattering the bottle in his grip. I had been aiming for his balls, so this was a piece of fantastic luck on my part. For a few seconds longer, I just stood on the spot, grinning in disbelief and savouring the sound of the rotten bastard's richly deserved screams.

I was brought back to reality as Callum shouted, 'Shutters down!' Chaz barged me aside as he slammed them shut, with a dreadful screech of protesting corrugated steel.

Outside an avalanche of punches, kicks, bottles and bricks rained on the steel shutters and I heard Chaz radio for back-up. I turned to Callum and saw that he was marching briskly towards the fire exit at the back of the club. In his grasp he had the writhing and twisting form of one of the chief yobbo tormentors. A few minutes later and Charlie's staff began hammering on our shutters that they had chased off the gang of pricks and we could open up now.

To his credit, Chaz really performed well and it was great to catch a glimpse of the formidable doorman he still was, deep inside, once he let his old self burst free. I think the sudden urgency of the moment energised him and instead of brooding about his position he was simply able to express himself instinctively and show his best self, 'taking care of business' the old-fashioned way.

When I was certain it was safe, I followed Callum into the fire escape to see what he was up to. He had the yob pinned against the wall and sank a heavy punch into his stomach; the lad doubled over and began to babble out fake self-serving apologies in between wheezes and drool. The lad had a screwdriver balled in his fist, which Callum thoughtfully removed by twisting his wrist in an arm lock, holding it away from him and crashing the offending arm into the wall. With a further yelp, the screwdriver slipped from his scrawny grasp.

I had expected to see the lad half dead by now, but that wasn't really Callum's style; he may have been many things, but he was never a bully and always knew when to stop. He instead lectured the lad in very threatening and graphic terms about what he would do to him and his associates if they ever plagued our doorstep again or brought 'tools' into our club. The gibbering lad promised to behave himself and also to sort out his errant pals. Lest he think Callum soft, he was given a sharp poke in the eye and a few more gratuitous but necessary digs, which I won't go into here, as a reminder of the frailties of the human body. By the time he stumbled from the darkened fire escape, the poor little lamb was wide-eyed with fear and paranoia – just as Callum had wisely intended.

This may sound particularly nasty and vindictive, but it wasn't – it was cautious, appropriate and justified treatment, fairly and patiently applied with no pleasure taken. A mindless thug would have simply beaten the lad senseless and put him in hospital. Instead he walked out of the pub with no real injuries to speak of – apart from a few aches and sprains that would be gone in a day or two – but a deep-rooted fear and respect of Callum. Lesson learnt. He had come at Callum armed with a screwdriver and a vicious intent to hurt him, and had got off lightly in return.

I later asked Callum if he enjoyed terrorising him, because from where I stood it looked like he had. Callum replied no, he didn't enjoy it in the least, nor did he mean a word of what he had said, but he was delivering a necessary and prudent warning. He wanted the yobbo to think he had enjoyed it and meant every word – so that we could do our jobs in safety and without fear. That was absolutely fine with me, and if having punters think that Callum was a warped psychotic was the price of peace then so be it.

When I think of the damage that the broken bottle could have done to my body, I still shudder. People have died from such wounds. If that scumbag's aim had been more accurate by just a few inches, then I might not be alive to tell this tale today.

I never wanted to have to face a broken bottle again, although, ironically, a few years later I did and I got the same 'lucky' result: this time my assailant broke the bottle in his own hand before he even had the chance to use it on me, so the fight was over before it started. The only small blessing that you can take from these situations is that most of the time when a thug attacks you with a bottle he doesn't know how to use it properly or how to break it cleanly in his hand, so he'll often end up hurting himself badly and will abandon his attack straight away, dropping his weapon in a bloody heap and becoming instantly consumed with his own welfare. Twice now I have seen this happen. Also, the fact that he feels unable to fight without first resorting to a bottle in his hand tells you that he's a pretty cowardly specimen. He is too afraid to take you on cleanly, bare-handed, because he feels he will lose.

But none of this is any consolation to you when you face it: you know he only has to land one lucky strike and it's you who'll be leaving in an ambulance or worse. I was very unlucky that I wasn't able to run from my would-be bottlers' clumsy attacks; if I could have done, I would have. In my own experience, when faced with a jagged bottle, it's always best to walk away if you can. You should only take it on if there's no other choice whatsoever. It was pure luck that saved me in my close-quarter confrontations with inept, armed drunks: it had nothing to do with skill or bravery whatsoever.

The one area in which we couldn't afford to play safe as doormen was in how we dealt with weapons; they were the things that worried us and gave us sleepless nights. If a punter was foolish enough to menace us with a weapon, then we simply had to crush that threat and vanquish him instantly – either in front of his friends (the preferable option) or down the fire escape with a few well-aimed slaps. No mercy, no apologies and problem fucking dealt with – quickly, cleanly and professionally, end of. To do anything else is to invite the local lunatics up to your doorstep with their knives, baseball bats, used syringes and knuckledusters every night of the week. You had to make them believe that it wasn't worth them attacking your door because the repercussions for them would be instant and draconian.

The vibe that Callum wanted to put about was that we weren't a tooled-up 'gangster door' (unlike some of the heavier private doors that we knew of) with a weapons stash of our own under the counter, but neither were we soft-touches either – down that road lies chaos and anarchy.

The rest of the night passed without incident, although there was a palpable tension between Chaz and Callum. Both men had performed exceptionally well but sadly there can only be one captain on a ship and the brawl had brought the unanswered question out into the open.

The kiosk girl had witnessed the entire fight and wasted no time in telling Aiken how professionally Callum had dealt with it, swiftly taking command and directing the action from start to finish. At the end of the night, we had a sit-down meeting and Aiken said he would be asking Pete – who was still our boss, really – to promote Callum to full-time head doorman, as he'd proven his worth time and time again and had surpassed himself that night. We were all to make no mistake; it was now very much Callum's command and the rest of us junior doormen would answer to him.

Inevitably, Chaz decided to put in a transfer request to another door. Sadly, I think he felt he had to. His closeness to many of our former customers – who were now our chief troublemakers – was making it nigh on impossible for him to do his job in peace. I felt sorry for him, and didn't particularly like the abrupt manner in which Callum had displaced him, but he was just too associated with the old regime to be able to enforce discipline on a meaningful level. Since he was such a nice guy, punters had begun to take advantage of his conciliatory style in a cynical and abusive fashion that was fair neither on him nor on his colleagues.

Chaz had rediscovered his old formidability and he'd just proven that he could still rise to the occasion when his back was against the wall. So I felt slightly uneasy that such an obviously capable man found himself in a position where he felt compelled to leave in order to preserve his dignity. Wanting to learn from it, understand it and avoid the same mistakes, I pondered on it deeply. On the surface he had simply found himself in checkmate with Callum – outmanoeuvred and outplayed by a skilful and cunning opponent. But there was more to it than that: I sensed he'd broken a fundamental but unspoken rule. Chaz was not a big bloke in the sense that many doormen – including me – aren't. That in itself isn't a problem if you handle and respect it properly, as the doorman concerned.

If you're not a really 'big guy' on the doors, then you have to make up for it in other ways: you need to be visibly strong, fit and on top of your game, with a sheen of health and conditioning – that's your 'aura of capability' and as a smaller doorman you need this more than anything else, otherwise who's going to listen to you? But not only that, you have to visibly try harder too, to project all of the right qualities and character traits that a doorman needs to maintain authority.

Chaz had simply stopped doing this, so the punters had started seeing him in a very different light. They became brave around him. Instead of seeing a lean, alert and confident man not to be trifled with, they saw something else and sadly that was the beginning of the end.

Now, if you're fortunate enough to naturally resemble King Kong – like my old bruiser pal from the Palace, Brick – without ever having touched a weight, then you can relax and let yourself go a bit because most guys won't fuck with you based on your natural size and presumed strength; but if you're a more modestly built chap then you can allow yourself no such luxury and must remain on top form at all times. Life isn't fair, but that's just the way it is. Some of us have to try harder if we want to do certain things.

I can't say I blamed Chaz for leaving. Aside from the actual yobs who physically assaulted you, you had to deal with some truly odious and thoroughly nasty types who delighted in goading, insulting and repeatedly challenging you; it took an immense amount of emotionally draining self-discipline to swallow it down and walk away. Every now and again a self-styled 'tough guy' would saunter over and quietly, mockingly ask you outside for a fight, for no other reason than to boost his own ego, embarrass you a little and secure bragging rights amongst his mates. You had to learn not to take it personally, to simply ignore the threats and to recognise the challenges for what they were: traps and banana skins. It wasn't easy to turn the other cheek, but unless it got physical – which rarely happened once they knew you weren't falling for it – then that's exactly what you had to do. I found that the best tactic to use when somebody strolled over and casually threatened you was to simply say nothing and silently look back at them. Most times they'd leave you alone and move on to bother somebody else, as bullies are wont to do.

Callum said that from now on we would run the door much more tightly. We would be firm but fair, the idea being to stop trouble dead in its tracks before it started.

A positive by-product of the incident at the door was that I was now briefly viewed as some kind of lethal karate expert. I most definitely wasn't – my kicking the bottle from his hand was a pure fluke and nothing more; I hadn't even seen the bottle coming. So I decided to tell the truth about my lucky strike. When I confessed to Callum, he laughed and said he suspected as much, it was simply too good to be true. The last time he'd seen shit like that was in a Jackie Chan film, he said. But he then cautioned me to keep the fiction going: he told me not to brag about it, but not to correct it either. When I asked him why, he once again revealed his streetwise wisdom to me: 'Think about it, Steve. It does this club the world of good if people think there is a karate expert and lunatic gangster in charge of security, even if it is a load of bullshit. The idiots will keep away.' As usual, he was right.

As the night wound down and the adrenaline dissipated, I found myself sitting alone with Callum in the bottle-strewn VIP area, his eyes glittering mischievously as we grinned and toasted our victory. It had been a hard night's work, but the dynamics and balance of power had suddenly shifted in our direction – from both the punters and the staff. He looked at me in silence and our eyes met across the sodden table, with its torn beer mats and wet, shrivelled fag ends. He shrugged his shoulders, raised his eyebrows aloft, leant heavily towards me and rapped his knuckles hard on the table, as if he'd reached some kind of decisive conclusion and arrived in a happy place.

'So what do you think, Steve?'

'I think it's good.'

'We've got control now, mate. This fucking door is ours.'

And so it was.

Not all of the fights we got into were such dangerous, bottle-breaking affairs; indeed some of them were downright comical, such as the occasion we tangled with 'Mr Shit'. During one noxious night, a barman marched over to the front door and asked us to evict a drunk from the toilets who'd collapsed and was quite literally causing a stink. As there were only three of us on duty, we left Big Sam to control the front door alone, due to his awesome 'deterrent effect', while Callum and I grudgingly skulked to the toilets. What we found there shall never leave my memory.

The cubicle door was locked and a pair of spindly white calves, trousers half-around ankles, were spilling out under the door. We didn't even bother banging on the door to stir the comatose idiot because we knew from bitter experience that he'd be stubbornly uncooperative. Getting a call-out to shift an unwilling drunk from a pub's toilets is a doorman's equivalent of a bad day at the office. We entered the cubicles on either side and stood on top of the toilet bowls to get a better peek at the delights which lay in store for us. The guy was clumsily spread-eagled, with his head lolling back against the bowl, a fountain of multi-coloured sick decorating his shirt and his pathetic white legs splayed before him. Worst of all was the ever-widening pool of diarrhoea leaking from his arse and smearing the hands that he held aloft to us with drunken groans, like some demented worshipper, as if he expected us to haul him up.

'Fuck me! Mate, I'd chop my fucking hands off before I helped you up!' roared Callum in his booming Brummie accent in tones of shock and disgust. Neither one of us had any intention of doing what we were supposed to do: that is, climb into the cubicle housing this drooling shit machine and unlock it from the inside. Fuck that!

In any case, the drunk had already half-kicked the door off its hinges with his repeated mad thrusts and the lock was the only thing keeping it up; the door was beyond repair and the only place it would be going was to the tip.

Callum couldn't resist teasing the guy. Every time he asked the drunk what was up, he would let out an angry groan and boot out hard at the bottom of the door, no doubt wishing that it was Callum's leering head. We both climbed down and I directed Callum to watch the door just in case the barman peered in. A split second later I booted it clean off its remaining buckled hinge. It clattered back and bounced noisily off the toilet wall, just above the drunk's head. We were resolute that we wouldn't touch him, no matter what, such was the shit-dipped state of him. He helped us along by angrily flinging the door back at us with curses and threats before unsteadily clambering to his feet, with his trousers still round his ankles, repeatedly slipping in his own shit until his hands were as brown as his backside.

At the sheer spectacle of him, we couldn't help but laugh and Callum remorselessly goaded him with insults and jibes.

Well, it's safe to say the stinky bastard took his revenge on us and had the last laugh.

'Now, mate, you're going to go fucking quietly, aren't you?' taunted Callum in between fits of hysterical laughter. 'Because, mate, I wouldn't go near you with a ten-foot fuckin' bargepole, you dirty cunt!'

'Yeah, yeah, you fuckin' twats,' came the grunted reply. 'Think you're so fuckin' hard, don't ya'? I'll knock you bastards out, I swear.'

Mustering as much dignity as he possibly could, and failing miserably, the dazed club-goer shuffled and stumbled out of the toilets and onto the impossibly packed dance floor. I walked warily in front of him, carefully parting the crowd and warning revelers of the approaching shitty mess. Callum was following up at the rear, deigning to go as far as to gently place a solitary guiding hand on the drunk's shoulder to veer him away from our immaculately attired crowd and towards the door. At the sight of the drunk, the crowd parted as if a CS gas canister had been lobbed into the middle of the floor – the man was covered in enough human body fluids to put a zombie off his dinner.

By now, his top half was like a rainbow of vomit, while his bottom half was brown, all brown, baby.

Periodically, I'd glance over my shoulder to check that Callum was OK and he'd greet my gaze with a turned-up nose, wrinkled eyes and an expression of abject disgust. Blessed release loomed in the shape of the exit door and we both breathed a sigh of impending relief – we'd be able to wash our hands soon.

Suddenly, a commotion erupted behind me. The drunk had spun on his feet and flung himself at Callum, deliberately running his shit-smeared hands over Callum's grimacing cheeks. He was now trying to intertwine himself with Callum's writhing form. He had taken his revenge and was madly laughing – as was I – refusing to go quietly. Normally, I'd be the first in if anybody laid a hand on Callum, but as this guy was no threat and I didn't fancy getting smeared too, I just stood back and watched. It was utterly hilarious, as Callum at first tried to dodge his slippery grasp but then realised he was failing miserably and accepted that he had no choice but to half-lift, half-wrestle him out of the door – shit-stained body and all. Callum managed to manoeuvre behind him and picked the wretch clean up off the floor in a tight bear hug, with his thrashing arms pinned firmly to his sides.

As I watched the two of them grimly waddle to the front door, looking like a couple of demented penguins locked in a bizarre mating ritual, I have never laughed so hard, nor seen anyone look so disgusted, in my entire life. When Callum flung the drunk to the pavement, he actually jumped back as if he'd been shocked by an electric cable. Callum shouted, 'Ahh!', then turned on his feet and ran back to the toilets to decontaminate himself. When he eventually emerged, it was minus his blue jacket, which had mysteriously become brown, and a scowl on his crap-flecked face that resembled an erupting volcano.

It wasn't every night you got to see one of Blackpool's most respected head doormen get 'happy slapped' by an enraged punter, especially not one who'd lost control of his bowels and was waving his shitty arms around like some rickety windmill in a Force-10 gale.

That night, for once, it was definitely one-nil to the drunk.

8

THE FIGHT

WE HAD SEEN OFF THE INITIAL WAVE OF CHALLENGERS AND imposed our new style of security on the club. Once word got around town how swiftly we quashed trouble, a lot of the idiots melted away like shit on a hot summer kerb. For now, we enjoyed the peace and tranquillity, but we knew it wouldn't last. Trouble is never far away in clubland, no matter how hard you try to keep it out or how hard you stamp on it once it's squeezed its way in.

If I had thought glass collecting was good for pulling girls, then I was sorely mistaken; it wasn't in the same league as working on the doors. Never before or since have I enjoyed such female attention. I could have had a different girl every night, and sometimes I did. If I saw a pretty girl, I would usually let her in for free, telling the girl on the kiosk that this was a special friend of mine – even though I'd never seen her before in my life. Another great 'bird puller' was to point out a girl in the queue and usher her inside like a VIP, making her the club queen for a night. Pretty soon I was her new best friend.

From my time on the door, it is my feeling that, in general, girls are far more obsessed with image and social status than men are. It never ceased to amaze me that some girls viewed being treated as a VIP in a local nightspot as the most important thing in the world. I have seen gorgeous professional women making drooling fools out of themselves and behaving like obsessed stalkers, just to be able to say they are 'with the doorman', 'with the DJ' or 'on the guest list' at a trendy club. I took full advantage of my privileged position and enjoyed every heaven sent second of it, eagerly ushering giggling girls into the VIP area and ultimately having my wicked way with a string of ever-willing ladies in a variety of fire escapes, beer cellars, toilet cubicles, cloakrooms and random hotels. Needless to say, when I eventually tired of clubland my romantic life returned to its sadly more sedate pace, the powerful kudos I had working on the doors vanishing like piss in the wind.

Still, I'd had my fill and I can't complain about the joys I've loved and lost.

While I got busy with the girls, Callum wasted no time in instigating small-scale, 'harmless' but undoubtedly mischievous scams. I suspect this was the real reason he wanted control of the door so badly. Some of them I joined in with, enthusiastically divvying up my share of the spoils, but others I chose to ignore, either because I didn't feel comfortable with them or I just felt they were plain wrong.

One I did partake of was the 'entrance-fee fiddle': the club didn't start charging punters until 10 p.m., but Callum simply moved that back to 8 p.m. and charged them from then on, generously dividing the cash between the door crew and justifying it as money well earned and much deserved due to the increasing risks that we faced. Another nice top-up that Callum devised was to charge an extra pound for each punter. A simple but effective ploy was to claim the pub was overfull – but for a few quid extra we might just let you in . . . as a favour.

By doing these extra little earners, we could usefully boost our wages on a busy night. I knew it was wrong, but I rationalised it to myself by saying that it harmed no one and the truth of it was that if I hadn't gone along with it I would have been viewed with suspicion and ostracised by my colleagues. We worked hard to hide any mischief that we got up to from Aiken and mostly succeeded. Out of respect for him and his position we'd never jeopardise our working relationship, so if he was in one of his periodic 'watchful' phases and monitoring the door team, Callum would order us to play it straight and cease whatever we were doing.

When we were overcharging people to come in or tapping up punters for an entrance fee, we very craftily walled off the narrow doorway with a couple of broad backs and stationed one of our lads immediately inside the club to give us advance warning. This way if any management approached us we could instantly play it straight and cease trading. We got away with it because a large, always packed dance floor separated us from the forever busy bar, so there was very little chance of us getting spotted or of a manager suddenly surprising us at the front door. We were also extremely careful and watchful about whom we charged and never pressed the issue, tending to restrict it to groups of genial holidaymakers who were simply grateful to be let in, rather than the savvy locals; we weren't daft and realised that if we tried to charge the wrong punter then they could complain about it and kick up a fuss.

On the rare occasions that we slipped up and a customer started complaining loudly, Callum would simply step in, turn on the charm and gracefully let them in 'for free'. Once they'd been subjected to Callum's disarming patter, they usually ended up buying him a drink and couldn't thank him enough for his 'generosity'.

Aiken's absolute top priority and focus was the physical safety, security and general success of the club – no easy task indeed and a job that kept him incredibly busy. Just as long as we performed well, kept troublemakers out and did our jobs professionally without causing any problems, then he'd leave the door side of life to us, trusting that we wouldn't let him down or go too far in enforcing security. I respected him as a man and as my boss, so I tried not to disappoint.

But it was a constant game of cat and mouse, and had Aiken ever known what we got up to then he'd have sacked us on the spot because he was a totally straight guy and had warned us fairly and squarely from the start that if he ever caught us taking the piss then we'd be finished on his door.

In the early days at least, I felt like I was nigh on indestructible whilst working the Varsity door, but occasionally life drops you a big fat hint that you aren't. Thanks to the long double shifts I worked, I was earning a nice wedge of cash. With my hard-earned funds, I treated myself to a bright red 125cc motorcycle that I liked the look of. I loved that bike and roared around town on it as if I were Barry Sheene reborn – despite not having a full bike licence, as I hadn't taken the full and proper test.

I learned the hard way that your actual skills on the road – just as on the door – had better match your imagined ones otherwise you'll come a cropper, which became apparent when I took a corner a tad too enthusiastically, foolishly trying to impress a bunch of kids nearby. Unbeknown to me there was a large invisible ice patch on the road and as I leaned into the corner I could feel the bike instantly beginning to give way beneath me. I snapped out my heel and frantically dug it into the tarmac, trying to get some traction and prevent the bike from slipping over and burning a hole in my leg. But to no avail. My foot only hastened my collapse and as I skated uselessly on the ice, alarmingly, the bike tilted almost horizontally over me. At the last possible moment, when a fall seemed certain, glorious, blessed luck kicked in and my boot heel at last found tarmac. I left the treacherous ice patch behind and instantly, like a whiplash, the bike was bolt upright and I skidded round the corner in an unintended but massively impressive balletic 'power slide', with the apparent ease and grace of a professional Speedway racer.

I was so shaken up by it that I had to pull over and catch my breath. The gaggle of kids ran over, exclaiming, 'Wow, mate, that was fucking brilliant! Amazing! Where did you learn to ride like that?' What to me was an absolute fluke had appeared to them to be amazing skill and preternatural bike control. I didn't have the heart to disabuse them of my true status, so merely replied 'Practice!', before slamming down my visor with trembling hands, desperately trying to look cool, and roaring off into the distance with brown-stained pants.

But I wasn't a fool. I took the near-miss as an omen of sorts that I'd better slow down my life in all areas – both at work and at play. Especially with Callum and his never-ending stream of 'ideas'.

The one scam I turned my back on because I felt uncomfortable with it was the 'charity' bucket shake. This involved a bucket being made up to look like an official charity collection – usually to coincide with a genuine public appeal – and somebody standing by the door shaking it and asking for donations. To be caught doing this by management would have meant on-the-spot dismissal – and rightly so – so this was one trick that Callum reserved strictly for those nights when the boss was either off duty or on holiday and safely out of the way. To my eternal shame, the first few times Callum ran it I turned a blind eye and took a cut of the spoils, but I quickly grew sickened by it and opted out. It was one thing to ask pissed-up punters for an extra pound or two to get in, but something else entirely to dupe them into giving money to a bogus charity appeal, no matter how I tried to justify it to myself that the collection hurt no one.

After I told Callum to count me out, I initially gave half of my 'look away' money – but not all, shamefully – to Oxfam in a failed and pathetic attempt to ease my conscience. I had hoped that this half-hearted act of contrition would ease my conscience and make me feel better to the point that I could actually enjoy spending the remaining cash without feeling like crap, but it didn't. I couldn't motivate myself to spend it and the pile of untouched coins lay in my drawer, contaminated and mocking, reminding me of what a shitbag I was. Eventually I ended up just walking into Oxfam and guiltily shoving the lot into the collection jar because it seemed the only way that I could go on looking myself in the mirror. I was making a tidy sum legitimately anyway because I was doing two jobs and reasoned that it wasn't worth getting involved in if it made me feel like shit.

Callum seemed to see it all as a big, harmless joke. He actually guffawed aloud when I opted out and told him I'd given my 'bung' away to a real charity, calling me a 'soft, soppy bastard' amongst other things. To Callum, these kinds of scams didn't even register on the scale of criminality – he knew there were blokes hovering around town who'd developed far more sophisticated schemes so that they were now bleakly humorous art forms. One burly trickster would regularly don outlandish fancy dress whenever a big event came round and would flit from pub to pub with his 'charity bucket' in hand, hustling and berating drinkers into giving him 'donations', whilst craftily and expertly disguising himself amongst the vast majority of genuine collectors. Innocent drinkers and real charity collectors would glance at him and simply assume that he was completely genuine. I think the fact that he was a large and forceful character also helped his cause somewhat. Towards the end of the night his bucket would get so full of change he'd have to empty it out several times. Of course, he met his match in Callum: as the saying goes, you can't kid a kidder. Whenever he visited our place, Callum always prised a crisp note off him as a tidy commission for 'entrance rights' . . .

You see, that's one of the problems in working on the doors and spending too much time around the wrong types in clubland: you just can't help losing a little bit of your soul with each compromise you are forced to make. You start turning a blind eye when you shouldn't; you start becoming friendly with people you'd normally cross the road to avoid; you start saying yes to things you should say no to. In effect, you start considering things that are abnormal as normal. Everything gradually becomes mis-wired: your values get slowly fucked up and confused, and the line between good and bad gets increasingly blurred. And in the end, you start condoning things that make you feel even less happy than when you started the job. I recognised this human weakness in myself and I could see it in others, too – especially Callum.

I learnt a lot about people's characters on the door and also that the simple stereotypes don't always apply. It frustrated and puzzled me that Callum thought his charity scam was acceptable, was just another victimless game. I knew Callum owned many fine qualities that so-called 'straight' society and business would value: he was kind, loyal, honest about things that mattered and brave. Yet, despite these worthy virtues, he had what I can only call 'moral blindspots' about certain pretty big things. I've got no doubt whatsoever that had Callum been more educated in the traditional academic sense (and been given a sparkling sheen of social polish), then he could have achieved a great deal in life and become a big-hitter in the business world. After all, he was a cunning, clever, impressively streetwise operator. Still, I suspect that even if he had had these advantages he'd have been sorely tempted to skirt on the edges of white-collar crime, using a cut-glass accent and whatever worldly wisdom he'd managed to accrue to get himself into and out of all kinds of sticky messes.

Unfortunately, the Callum I knew was a middle-aged man with a serious criminal record and a first-class degree in street survival from the university of life, so he found himself policing a door and struggling manfully to remain 'reasonably' straight amidst a whirl of glittering temptations. Society does not make it is easy for a man of Callum's age, experience and record to truly put his past behind him and go straight. The reality is few traditional employers and institutions are willing to give those with criminal records a place in their organisations, and thus a chance to reform, so often they'll end up working for themselves or gravitating to the black and twilight economies where sadly the cycle repeats itself and offenders fall back into old ways. And while it's true to say that some of the more extreme, unpleasant and unrepentant examples maybe don't deserve or want a second chance, I don't believe that applies to the redeemable majority who surely do.

Sometimes, believe it or not, there is honour even amongst thieves – but, as in the case of Callum, it has to be prodded and coaxed out of them.

It is a common practice to label all criminals and drug dealers 'evil scum' or 'predatory villains', but my experiences on the door contradicted this. I met and got to know all kinds of wheeler-dealers and con artists as a doorman – it is simply unavoidable, as they are drawn to the nocturnal economy – and while, in truth, I did encounter some very nasty types who deserved all the contempt and jail time a society could pin on them, it's a strange paradox that I also met some genuinely nice people who happened to be involved in some very shady practices . . . and that's putting it mildly. It puzzled me then, and it still puzzles me now.

In the end, I just tried not to get involved and I learnt not to judge too harshly those who did. Just so long as nobody innocent was getting physically hurt in my orbit, I tried to stay out of the way. Like the parable of the three wise monkeys, I kept my own counsel.

It was hard work removing myself from all that went on

and the struggle to remain detached from the clubland excesses could be exhausting. The temptation to dive in and commit myself fully and emotionally was a siren call I fought hard to resist.

One of the nice things about Callum being in charge was that as head doorman he could pull a few strings with the door agency if ever we were short of men and request that Zenon do some shifts with us if he was free. We did manage to bag him a few times but faced the insurmountable problem that we couldn't get him on a permanent basis, even though we wanted to, because he was proving to be in very high demand on all the top doors. Inevitably, once a manager got to know him, the club wouldn't want to let him go.

Zenon and Callum got on like a house on fire and grew close in their own way, just as I knew they would. Sometimes they'd do building jobs together and they had a great mickey-taking rapport going, with each man ripping the piss out of the other's accent, loudly and in public, but always with great warmth. Whenever we found ourselves working together at the Varsity, it'd be a bit like a high school reunion. We'd spend as much time laughing at each other as we did the punters; we were a triumvirate of piss-taking comics (a blond Pole on one side, a raven-haired gypsy on the other and a short arse in the middle) whom the customers couldn't quite fathom, such was the ludicrous stupidity of our jokes.

Callum was a difficult character to categorise, being not quite straight, and a bit of a risk taker, keen to have a laugh and make a few quid as he went along, but happy to keep things at a very low level. Any scams he ran were insignificant compared to the shady goings-on of some of the gangster types that occasionally visited the town from nearby cities. I tried to avoid them, but sometimes you just couldn't help rubbing shoulders. And even though you knew better than to keep company with such men, it was difficult to snub the allure of their lifestyle – the parties, the mystique, the authority – and some simply couldn't resist getting close. They soon found themselves drawn into all manner of trouble, however, and I heard stories of unfortunate downfalls and self-destruction from afar.

One particularly sad story involved a young and incredibly vulnerable man who had drifted into the Blackpool area from the Welsh valleys. His mother had died while giving birth to him and later in life he had also lost his father in a horrendous car smash, rendering him an orphan. Having recently come of age, he also found himself a millionaire, inheriting a large fortune from the estate of his extremely successful businessman father. Feeling lonely and rootless, he had come to Blackpool in search of friendship and a new start. He made the fateful error of displaying his wealth and generosity by openly going on a spending spree. Word travels fast in clubland when a new player arrives on the scene and in the space of weeks this innocent young man had caught the attention of some extremely serious out-of-town characters who visited Blackpool from time to time.

Living in a luxury new home, the young man was seemingly riding high, overextending himself in a never-ending round of champagne parties and ruinous casino gambles. Soon a rumour began circulating that he was looking to invest heavily in new ventures and wanted to become a major player on the scene – not in Blackpool itself but way beyond it, in the big clubs of London and Manchester.

Unfortunately, he hadn't inherited his father's extraordinary business acumen. Nor did his more modest abilities match his over-arching ambitions or his enormous all-too-temporary wealth. A few older heads in town tried to advise him to rein in his excesses, calm down a touch and avoid the company of the 'flash mobs' from down south and the Manchester crews, but he didn't want to listen. Defiant and undeterred, with his confidence bolstered by the fake sense of security that a bundle of hard cash brings, he eagerly sought introductions to the big spenders from the bright lights.

He became very friendly with a Manchester-based crew that occasionally visited the town. They always treated him like a long-lost friend whenever they bumped into each other – at least in the beginning.

He decided to dip his toe into business with the Mancunians after allowing himself to naively believe that they could achieve great things together. To cut a long story short, he was used as a virtual piggy bank to fund various failed enterprises, wild parties and lost causes – and to provide hefty personal loans to his new 'friends', both in London and in Manchester's own burgeoning Madchester club scene.

A few years later, a large chunk of his fortune had gone and his former associates had abandoned him. Feeling ever more depressed, he joined his departed father, the victim of a catastrophically misjudged, self-inflicted descent into chronic alcoholism. He had been searching for friendship and a fresh start – instead he had only found the dark side of clubland. Like a careless moth, he sailed too close to the flames and found himself cruelly extinguished.

I could well understand how this naive and innocent lad, mistakenly thinking himself streetwise, was taken in by the false glamour. I had been approached by a 'connected' doorman at a seductively decadent, out-of-control party and had found myself sorely tempted, my young ego flattered.

One of the perks of working on the door is the numerous party invites you receive. As it was a Saturday night, we had all been working late and a massive after-hours party was in full swing at a millionaire's mansion. The house was extremely impressive and as we congregated around the swimming pool it seemed that half of the doormen in Blackpool had turned up. We didn't get started till 3 a.m., but we managed to keep the party going for a full 24 hours. Bowls of cocaine and saucers overflowing with pills were doing the rounds.

The party was an unusual one because of its sheer largesse and the trashy opulence on display. While it was true that we got invited to a lot of after-hours parties in punters' homes, they were rarely like this. Most of the time we'd either be necking tins of lager and treading on toes in a crowded semi's kitchen or be squashed cheek to cheek on a scruffy sofa in a smoke-filled terrace, Technotronic's 'Pump Up the Jam' reverberating off the walls until the neighbours sent the police round.

At parties like this you could end up feeling a little awkward if you didn't have any real wealth (be it of legitimate means or otherwise) or connections because there was a lot of preening and showing off going on, as big egos battled to outdo one another with flashes of cash, champagne and vulgarity.

A particularly 'heavy' crew were there and occupied their own little corner. It was wise not to invite yourself into their circle unless you were explicitly asked. I saw one of the associates of this select crew get up and stride towards me. I felt a tinge of apprehension in my gut, worrying if I had committed some indiscretion: had I tried to chat up one of his girls? 'Chalkstone' (not his real name) was a senior doorman around town, which meant he was a clear division above me and normally we'd have nothing to talk about apart from the weather. He was quiet and polite, but he didn't waste time on small talk.

I felt relieved as he shook my hand and greeted me warmly – at least I wasn't in trouble – but I remained wary of him. Why was he bothering to speak to me, as we really didn't know each other? Even though he came across as calm and mature, I knew he had a veneer of steel beneath the silky charm. He steered me off to the side for a quiet chat and came straight to the point. He had an offer to make me.

Chalk explained to me that he always took great care to know what was going on in the clubs, especially with the doormen. He went on to say that he had heard good things about me and liked what he saw. He flattered me further by saying I was quiet, professional and discreet but also willing to get stuck in when the occasion called for it. In short, I was just what his employers were looking for on the strictly private club door where he worked. How did I fancy doing a few shifts alongside him and seeing how things went?

He finished off by saying I should consider his offer carefully because there were perks to be had and I would be looked after. My heart skipped a beat, as I knew I was being tapped up and asked to become potentially involved in something far more serious than just door work.

I think Chalk sensed my hesitation and he began to sweeten the pill: how would I feel about driving with him up to Scotland the following weekend? Think about it, he said, because we could have a blast as well as earn a few quid. I considered his offer, as he spoke to me in confidential tones. His voice had a soothing, reassuring quality to it. I was getting a good vibe off him and had to admit that the extra money and enhanced status would be nice. What was pulling me closer was the fact that on the surface Chalk was just about one of the coolest guys I'd ever met. He projected an aura of calmness, confidence and certainty – a grim sunshine, if you like – that I definitely fancied basking in. I'd seen him cruising through town in a flash car borrowed from 'friends', invariably with a hot girl with big tits beside him. How I could see myself behind the wheel of such a motor with an identikit pouting mega-babe beside me . . . Chalk was really fucking living the life, writ large and in glorious, garish Technicolor.

I was tempted . . .

Then I woke up and realised what I would be getting myself into. I let Chalk finish his pitch and pretended I was interested.

I couldn't just fuck him off there and then, as the wrong sort of 'no' could be interpreted as an insulting rejection; he could easily have taken offence and turned nasty. I told him I needed a few days to think it over. Chalk replied I was wise to do so, before adding one last piece of bait: 'That's why we want to try you out, you don't just jump in but think things through. We've noticed you. That's good, Steve.' We shook hands and I told Chalk I would give him my answer soon.

Callum had been watching our little chat with hawk-like eyes. He subtly beckoned me over and failed to hide his concern. I didn't need to explain things to him, as he told me Chalk had enquired about me several times. I asked Callum what he thought and he advised me to stay well away. Callum knew that bouncing was just a passing phase to me, not a lifetime occupation – and that I didn't have a criminal record and didn't want to end up with one. Chalk had correctly judged me as a reliable and decent doorman, but he had wrongly assumed I was a potential something else. As I was young and eager to get on, Chalk thought I could be groomed in a different set of ideals. A seductive sales pitch had momentarily swayed me, but as usual Callum helped me to see through the haze. This was how young lads got reeled in to the lifestyle. Pretty soon you have a serious criminal record and expensive tastes – and then you can't get out. When I asked Callum how he could be so sure, he replied that it had happened to him when he was a youngster. That's why he'd ended up living the life he had, constantly in and out of trouble, and eventually going to prison.

A few nights later I made the trip to see Chalk on the door he worked. I could tell by his reaction that he was disappointed and surprised that I was turning him down – a lot of doormen would have given their right arms to connect with the crew he associated with. Out of respect for him I listened once again to all the reasons why I should reconsider. I even began to feel guilty about wasting his time and fretted that I was making the wrong decision. It struck me that a lot of what he said made sense and I had to concede that I was ambitious after all. But Callum had warned me to expect this: it was all part of the sales pitch, all part of the flattery and seduction. I obeyed my instincts and gave Chalk a polite but firm no. It's true that I was ambitious for certain things – just not these kinds of things.

Ultimately, my ambition was for a different kind of achievement and that's where my interests radically veered away from the path that was being hinted at. We parted on good terms and remained friendly from a distance, with mutual respect and 'face' intact on both sides. Chalk knew never to repeat his offer to me and I have no doubt he soon found another willing volunteer. Strangely enough, I think my refusal increased his respect for me, as it took a stronger person to reject than accept.

Chalk's offer of employment wasn't the only piece of 'work' I'd had to turn down. During my earlier stint at the Kennel, I'd been approached by a market-stall trader who wanted me to beat up her stingy slum-landlord because he was constantly escalating the rent for no good reason other than his own rapacious greed. After listening to her hare-brained scheme, which would have involved me ambushing him and bundling him down a dirty back alley to be threatened and menaced by none other than herself (from the sight of her a terrifying prospect, if ever there was one), it took me about 20 sputtering seconds to turn her down. Her generous offer of payment: a night of passion and £50! I'd have refused no matter what she'd offered, mind you, because I simply wasn't that kind of bloke. The fact that she was about 30 years older than me and completely barking mad certainly helped speed up my decision.

On a regular basis you'd get ridiculous offers from a variety of customers regarding petty disputes, debt collection and squabbles – most of which were quite comical and utterly absurd playground fallouts. I never accepted any of them because I was a totally straight doorman – only a complete idiot would have. It simply wasn't my cup of tea. Judging by the IQ levels of most involved, it would've been a virtual guarantee of prosecution anyway.

Just as in any major holiday town, there was a thriving black economy swirling around the backstreets of the wider club scene and the huge tourist industry involving debt collection, drug dealing and the routine settling of 'scores' by fists, boots and 'other means'. Not surprisingly, a few of the less bright and more hardcore types did get involved and sure enough, without exception, virtually every single one of them got swiftly caught and lived to regret it.

Occupying a berth on the door of a hot club automatically meant you were fair game; it plugged you into every gaudy temptation and pitfall that the night-time, tourist and black economies could offer – if you wanted it, that is. The only problem for me was that I didn't and that's where the tension began to creep in. The first seeds of doubt had been sown in my conflicted mind about how far I'd be willing to go.

My idea of fun on a door was all to do with casual sex, a bit of banter with the locals and the odd jolt – I will admit it – of exhilarating fisticuffs violence. But that was it. The criminal side just didn't carry the same appeal. If you wanted in, then it was a great place to be. But if you wanted out, as I soon would, then it could be a hostile and unwelcoming place.

As the song goes: 'It's a mad world'.

The New Year of 1992 brought new problems on the Varsity door. We had managed to get rid of the first batch of troublemakers, but that was now last year's news. All sorts of new idiots were coming out of the woodwork.

After about a year of working on the doors, I made a stupid mistake that led to me receiving my first pasting from a drunken lout. My pride was hurt more than anything else and I was furious with myself for letting it happen because I had only myself to blame.

It was bitterly cold on the door in January and we had been issued with thick winter coats. The coats were a welcome relief but so incredibly tight and restrictive you could hardly swing your arms in them. Foolishly, I ignored this possible hindrance by preferring to keep warm, my dim wits not registering the likely implications in a fight when one is trussed up like an Eskimo and can barely breathe, let alone brawl.

I learnt the hard way when I suddenly found myself wrestling with a slippery young lad who'd objected to paying the entry fee. To add insult to injury, it was the genuine fee this time as well. Whilst I was struggling to hold him off, he was lashing me with hard, mule-like kicks and stinging punches from all angles at an increasingly fast and furious pace, his confidence and accuracy growing with the dizzying realisation that he might just score the spectacular public goal of 'battering the doorman' in front of his admiring pals. The super-heavy overcoat felt like a rubber tyre weighing me down; I couldn't even catch my breath, never mind get loose enough to plant a grip on him. Thank God the lad wasn't a big bloke otherwise I am sure he would have knocked me out. As it was, I was definitely coming off worse. To rub the humiliation in further, I had to suffer the indignity of the kiosk girl and a sympathetic punter having to help me eventually overpower him, as Callum had gone to the toilet. What an incredible embarrassment the beating was. That very same night I ditched the overcoat and vowed never to wear it again. I invested in some thermal long johns instead and stood on the door freezing cold in my shirtsleeves and blazer – but at least I was mobile and it was better than taking a thrashing.

In time I would see the above incident as comical, but other run-ins couldn't be laughed off quite so easily. The second fight of the year was one that I also almost lost, but the price of victory was so high I began to question if it was worth continuing in the profession. Once again this near-beating was my own clumsy fault – this time because I went in too heavy-handed and woefully underestimated my opponent.

The panic bell in the kiosk rang and Aiken's voice cut across the radio: 'Steven, I have a problem at the bar. Come and sort it.' I darted inside, over-eager for action, and spotted a guy of medium build, about 30, who didn't look anything special in clothes, arguing furiously with a barmaid. Without so much as a cursory glance or guess at his true physical condition, I leapt forward and locked a tight choke-hold on his neck, unceremoniously dragging him out; in fact, if I am honest, I was far more rough than was necessary. As ever, Callum watched my back. Once I reached the doorway I flung the offender hard onto the pavement – again, going a little overboard – to reinforce the message that he was no longer welcome. I sauntered back inside, congratulating myself on my strength, and feeling all aglow and rather manly.

That was my big mistake.

As the saying goes, pride comes before a fall.

A few minutes later the lean fight-scarred face of 'Isaac' appeared at the door in an agitated state, his trim physique taut with tension. Isaac was a twentysomething former boxer who worked on the door of several of Blackpool's roughest nightspots and had a reputation as a battle merchant who loved to fight. He contemptuously ignored my greeting and asked Callum why I had chucked out his good friend and fellow fighter, whom I'll call 'Juan'. I noted the stress in his voice and decided it best I kept my mouth shut while Callum tried to sort things. But they couldn't be sorted.

Isaac stated that Juan was a respected ex-boxer and training partner of his and that it was bang out of order and grossly disrespectful the way I had treated him. Juan deserved a 'square go' at me, here and now, down the back alley.

By this time, Juan had dusted himself off and stood silently outside, looking like he meant business. I noted the litheness of his step and worried that I might have bitten off more than I could chew – the first seeds of doubt beginning to sprout in my arrogant mind. Callum told me to go and sit inside the club while he tried to calm the situation down.

Ten minutes later Callum walked over to me shaking his head and I knew what this meant.

'I'm sorry, Steve, but you'll have to go outside.'

Fucking hell, I needed this like a hole in the head. As I walked out of the door, I said to Isaac sarcastically, 'Cheers, mate.' Then I turned down the darkened side alley of the club.

As I got my first real look at Juan, I instantly realised my mistake. He seemed to have sobered up quickly and appeared ferociously fit and determinedly focused. The purposeful, clear expression in his eyes and the icy calmness of his bearing told me he was a genuine threat. We both adopted fighting stances and warily circled each other. I tried a front-kick but missed miserably, Juan gracefully skipping back out of range. From Juan's nimble footwork I could immediately see that, as fast, fit and agile as I was, I was still no match for him in that department. Whenever I tried to land a fist or foot on him, he simply sidestepped it as if I wasn't there.

Suddenly, he was hitting me in the face with hard, crisp jabs that stung like angry bees. I had to rapidly blink to regain my composure before heavier shots rained down, snapping my head back despite my tucked-in chin. Clumsily, I attempted to swing back but missed pathetically, whilst every single one of his landed with hard intent. A professional boxer was beating me up easily. It was becoming humiliating and desperate. As more punches slashed and staggered me, I was running out of ideas about what to do next. He was just too damned fast. I could feel a faint panic stirring in my blood. I was the angry bull to his matador. He was cutting me to ribbons at will.

THE FIGHT

To say I was embarrassed and worried would be an understatement. I felt like I was on the verge of having the shit kicked out of me by a vastly superior fighter. Brutal turnarounds like this weren't supposed to happen to me. I was supposed to be the guy that did this to others. That was my job and I thought I was good at it. This is what I was paid for. What a fucking time to find out you are wrong.

Callum's voice cut into the fray angrily: 'Fuck boxing, Steve, use your strength! Take him to the floor!' This urgent message penetrated my muddled brain and I dropped my hands and stood back. I stopped throwing useless punches into thin air and instead dipped my shoulder like a rugby player in a scrum. I made sure my chin was dug well into my chest and charged like an enraged rhino. Crashing into Juan, I felt the wind leave his body as the momentum of my charging bulk pinned him to the floor. I heard a sharp grunt and felt a spasm of pain ripple through him as his head struck the concrete, giving a welcome bounce as hard bone hit cold stone. Hopefully, this would weaken him further.

My sudden change in tactics caught him by surprise and I could feel the tide turning my way now, giving me a massive morale boost and an extra spurt of adrenaline just when I needed it most. But I had to finish him off quickly because I was perilously tired and spitting blood – and I certainly couldn't keep the intensity of pace up for much longer.

Juan was eons faster and far more skilled on his feet than I was, but I had a lot more power and far greater wrestling skills. On the ground, he was in my world, with every one of his previous advantages gone because you can't punch your way out of a paper bag when you're winded and flat on your back, no matter how good a boxer you are. Once I had neutralised his boxing by taking him to the floor, there was only ever going to be one winner, just so long as I could keep him there. With a ferocity borne of desperation, I began pummelling his face, grounding and pounding him mercilessly with the last remnants of my fading strength. I didn't stop until Isaac and Callum hauled me off him.

Technically, I suppose, in the eyes of our audience, I had won – but barely – since I had finished up the man on top, 'leading on points', as it were. But from where I stood, swaying drunkenly in my quivering and rendered flesh, it felt more like an honourable draw from hell. Certainly neither one of us could have gone another round. We were both completely fucked. It definitely didn't feel like a victory to me; it was pure survival.

The fight had lasted about ten minutes, an utter eternity to be rolling around on the cobbles and operating at 100 per cent capacity. I was totally spent and had to be helped back into the club with my arms draped over Callum's shoulders, chin dribbling with red-stained saliva. Callum sat me down and told me I was finished for the night, shift over, end of story, not open to negotiation. Juan had taken me to the edge of my endurance and the absolute limits of my strength and ability. I had nothing left to give, no spare capacity or fuel to draw on. If he could have withstood my assault for just a few more minutes, then I'd have collapsed on his chest and he could have turned it around, rolling out from under me, flipping me over, switching positions and returning the favour. But this time I got lucky, Juan being even more fucked than I was. While I was worn out from throwing punches, he was utterly exhausted from receiving them.

If you have ever been there, you will know how sickening it feels after such a fight. The comedown is one of the most awful feelings in the world. There is no victory in it – only the sense of being a drunk and half-crippled, drooling baboon barely able to form words, let alone speak. As the adrenaline wore off, I began to shiver uncontrollably, my wounds becoming unbearably painful. I was so fucked I actually considered weeping – but I didn't have any energy, salt or fluid left for tears. Everything I had inside of me – and I do mean everything – had been left outside on that pavement or imprinted on Juan's bruise-strewn face. For the first time in my life, I could feel that every nerve and fibre in my body had been pushed to its individual maximum: my knees were cut and bleeding from friction burns, my fingernails split from clawing, my gums loosened and pummelled to mush, my fists two angry balls of bruised and cracked pain. I sat there feeling sorry for myself, quivering, looking as if I had been in a train crash. At that point in time, I couldn't have fought off an attack from Mary Poppins such was the aftermath of the fight. Without needing to look or feel, I could already sense golf ball-sized lumps of bruised tissue sprouting across my forehead. My eyes were already becoming dark purple, as the blood pooled under torn and shredded skin.

I suppose it is a sad measure of the sometimes warped values of fighting men that Isaac gleefully bounded over to congratulate me, seizing my hand in an apparently sincere handshake that caused my ruined mitt to limply creak and groan in protest. He had just seen his best friend and me beat each other to a pulp and he had played a major part in causing it to happen. Only 15 minutes earlier he'd been fixing to beat the shit out of me himself, a cauldron of angry agitation, menace and morally outraged offence. Yet now he seemed curiously sated, refreshed and relaxed, beaming with astonished joy at a night's good work. He enquired of punters enthusiastically, 'Did you see Steve fight, didn't he do well?' as if he was the proud coach of a schoolboy football team and had just seen his charges play the match of their lives. As he bounded off into the night with a cheerful skip in his step and a half-unconscious pal under his arm, I got the curious sensation that all was right in Isaac's world, everything was now as it should be in his battle-clouded, 'sentimental' eyes. Pride, honour and friendship had been restored with a bloody good punch-up to end a great night.

All I could think was this world of mine was getting fucking madder.

When I woke up the next day, my condition had worsened and I decided to go to hospital. Imagine my surprise when I hobbled in on wobbly legs and saw none other than Juan sat waiting obediently in casualty, waiting to be treated for various cuts and grazes and a broken hand (remember what I said about boxers and their fragile hands?). Great!

I slid over and plonked myself down uneasily next to him. He was as shocked as I was. But Juan was a game and proud fellow. The first thing he did was offer to continue the argument outside, there and then. 'Fuck that!' I told him. I said we'd make far better friends than enemies. I was relieved when he agreed. We had a frank discussion about the night's events and how we had both reacted stupidly – rising to Isaac's constant goading and allowing his relentless baiting to get the better of us. Apologies and compliments were exchanged all round. The same doctor treated us both and he chuckled as we told him our story. From then on, Juan and I became friendly acquaintances and would often joke about our unusual and bloody introduction.

Another positive by-product of our battle was that my status got a welcome boost and I was suddenly given a lot more respect from the hard-man types and senior doormen in town, many of whom hadn't seen me really fight before and considered me relatively untested. It's one thing to throw a guy out of a club, quite another to roll round on the pavement with him and until you'd been through that sort of desperate situation, older hands viewed you as unproven.

The next time I saw Pete, on wages day, he made a point of coming over and shaking my hand in full view of several senior doormen, congratulating me for 'having the balls to take on Juan', before planting a crisp note in my hand by way of a bonus. His compliment meant more to me than he could have ever known – I had a lump in my throat but hid it well – as I always wanted to be seen to be doing a good job in his eyes, as I regarded him as an inspiring example of success.

No matter how much I liked to kid myself otherwise, I still suffered from self-esteem issues, harking back to the rejections of my childhood, so to receive praise from an older and successful symbolic 'father figure' type gave me an immense morale boost.

In reality, Pete wasn't quite old enough to be my father and I was nowhere near that close to him – he was always very much 'the boss' in a stern, formal but friendly way – but because of the way my mind was wired as a result of what I'd been through praise always made me work harder to prove myself worthy of it.

I felt exactly the same way in the army whenever a colonel congratulated me on a job well done: it's hard to impress men of that calibre and they rarely give compliments, so when they do it really means something. It was the same thing with Pete: praise wasn't lightly given, so it put me on a high.

The cuts and bruises were worth it for the honour.

Around Easter time the Varsity door began experiencing problems from the remnants of the gang that had stormed the door the previous year, during which I had almost been bottled. There were some new faces amongst them and I guess this time round they were feeling stronger. It seemed like every other weekend we had to engage them in a scuffle or endure their insults. I wasn't particularly bothered if they kept it at this low level, but I was concerned they were planning something big for us. We found out one night as we were enjoying an after-hours drink following yet another wearisome mini-battle.

Sitting relaxing, we were startled by the sound of splintering glass. I was forced to duck as a barrage of bricks came hurtling against the windows. Mercifully the safety glass held out and none of the missiles got through. But this was getting ridiculous – what would it be next, petrol bombs, paving slabs? I was worried about one of their missiles one day finding its way to my head and mentioned this to Callum. His nonchalant reply – 'Don't worry, Steve, we'll do them if they do you' – hardly soothed my fears.

Another major concern was the appearance of their new ringleader, whom I'll call 'Irvine', who had served a prison term for repeated and extreme violence as a young man. Irvine was well into his 20s now, but alas, like many of his kind, he was becoming more volatile, not less, with the advent of his 30s. He was also well connected and his uncle in particular was a man to be wary of.

Irvine had a chip on his shoulder and seemed determined to wreak havoc whenever he turned up on our doorstep. On the rare occasions he was sober he would be humorous and approachable, but recently it was getting harder to catch him like that. He retained a smidgen of respect for Callum, but he had formed a deep dislike for the rest of the door team. When he had first appeared, he had tried to barge past us with his little gang of adoring pill-head acolytes – but we had stood our ground. He wasn't used to not getting his way and had interpreted it as some kind of ridiculously inflated 'insult' or 'disrespect'. We weren't looking to make an enemy of him, but we refused to allow him to intimidate us in front of paying customers. It was obvious he was the kind of man who couldn't resist creating chaos and pushing the boundaries, the sort who, if you did him one small favour, would demand and expect more, never being satisfied. On his part it was getting very personal and we could feel he was developing a destructive grudge against the entire door team. Callum quickly grew tired of his antics and decided to intervene before a really big fight blew up on the door and somebody got hurt.

THE FIGHT

Callum arranged an informal, private 'sit-down' with Irvine in a nearby pub and invited his respected older uncle to come along, too. Although his uncle had been a handful in his youth, he was now well into middle age and had mellowed wisely with the passage of time, nowadays preferring to resolve issues with reason and diplomacy than the more direct route. He had proven himself to be an exceptionally capable man many moons ago but had long since outgrown that phase of wanting to solve problems by force of arms alone. Whilst naturally backing up his errant relative, he confided in Callum that he was getting heartily sick of bailing young Irvine out of trouble and intimated that his patience only went so far; in other words, if Irvine one day received the shit-kicking that he thoroughly deserved and was so royally courting, then he wouldn't be getting too upset about it, provided the said shit-kickers didn't go too far. It seemed that Irvine would have to finally learn this lesson and face the consequences alone.

Callum wanted Irvine's uncle along so that he could hear our side of the story, as opposed to Irvine's self-justifying bullshit, and hopefully rein him in. The meeting was a success and Irvine accepted he would have to behave himself and treat the door staff with a bit more respect – otherwise it wouldn't just be Callum that he'd be upsetting, he'd be letting down his uncle, too.

Irvine confessed that it was personal with him, purely because he objected to 'new faces' on the door crew treating him like an 'ordinary mug punter' and making him pay in front of his pals. As ridiculous as it was, he said he regarded it as a gross insult and he was struggling to accept it. Callum wearily explained – yet again – that we were only doing our job and he backed us up 100 per cent on that, but as a gesture of goodwill and out of respect for his uncle he would let Irvine back in the club and he wouldn't have to pay.

A reluctant truce was called and normal service resumed.

I was enormously relieved that Callum had been able to sort out our problems with Irvine. It wasn't that we were physically afraid of him, but we were all fearful of the consequences of a fight. Unless you were prepared to really hurt him, you would struggle to beat somebody like Irvine because his inflated ego and volatile nature would simply not allow him to accept defeat. In a one-off fistfight, I think most of us on the door could have taken him without too many problems. What we couldn't have taken was the knife in the back he would stab us with the following week. Or perhaps the baseball bat wrapped around our heads as we visited the loo. If he couldn't beat you with his hands, then he'd resort to weapons in a heartbeat, constantly escalating the conflict and turning a fight into a battle and a battle into a war. So it just wasn't worth going there in the first place.

See what I mean?

In clubland, as in everyday life, it is not always the strongest man who prevails but the one who is willing to use the most violence, risk everything or go to the greatest of extremes. And depending on the morality of the situation or the character of the person involved, this can be a very good or a very bad thing. In Irvine's case, it was unquestionably the latter.

Despite knowing this, we let Irvine back in. He shook our hands with a resentful glare and we all made up, just as we had been ordered to – but I always watched my back whenever he was around and I didn't kid myself about the nobility of his intentions. No matter how fair, reasonable or 'respectful' you were with him, you could never, ever totally relax because inevitably that would be when he decided to do you. Mercifully, the problem fully resolved itself when he grew tired of us constantly watching him and abruptly announced he'd no longer be drinking in the Varsity. I can't say we were too displeased. At the time, they were the sweetest words we'd ever heard.

In later months, whenever the club went quiet we'd often

lean against the porch walls and natter away the hours. It never failed to raise a laugh when one of us would mutter aloud, 'Fucking hell, do you remember that shit with Irvine last year? Do you reckon he'll ever come back? I could do with some action tonight. Where is he when you need him?' Cue groans, guffaws and exasperated protests from the entire crew of 'Fucking hell, not that again, mate. No way!'

Most of those we ended up fighting were stupid beyond belief. I am sure some of them truly believed they were indestructible. One mad-eyed lowlife turned up on crutches steaming drunk and demanded to be let in. To compound his state, every single woman that attempted to squeeze past his lardy frame was subjected to a mauling that bordered on sexual assault. When we turned him away, he exploded into a predictable rage, screaming that we 'couldn't put a fucking match out' and offering to take the entire door team on.

He took a particular dislike to me and lunged at me repeatedly, half falling over, his huge belly spilling over his stained jeans like a pregnant whale's.

'What's wrong with you, man?' I retorted. 'For God's sake, how can you fight with a broken leg?'

While poking me sharply in the chest with his crutch, he spat back that he could batter me with every bone in his body broken, going on to inform me of the sexual delights he intended for the female members of my family and my girlfriend of the time. The guy went so far that I am ashamed to say I actually considered whacking him in his leering fat face. Callum read the mood and wisely sent me to cover another exit. I know in my heart that I would never have hit him, but I hated the fact that my job actually forced me to consider striking a disabled man. The glamour of the door work was rapidly wearing thin for me.

Occasionally, an unseen and as yet unknown enemy would slip by you undetected – a false friend or disgruntled dealer who was unhappy that his gear had been confiscated or one of his acolytes refused entry. They'd let their displeasure be known in a variety of ways, either subtle or malicious, but all equally disturbing.

One night after closing I went to a hot club to meet a girl that I had arranged a date with in the Varsity. Patrolling through the club looking for her and failing to find her, it would seem that I found somebody not quite so enamoured of me instead. As I walked out of the club alone, it was with the tail of my jacket cut into several distinct ribbons, the work of an expertly wielded craft or Stanley knife. I wasn't aware of my torn jacket until a pal pointed it out. I had never felt so much as a tug on it the whole time it had been on me. Even more disturbingly, this kind of thing became normal to me; you couldn't help but make enemies if you were doing your job properly, controlling the space tightly and ejecting the riff-raff and lowlifes. In time, each and every one of us on the doors had collected a grim harvest of similar tales, bizarre encounters and battle scars, ranging from malicious 'accidental' cigarette burns, 'warning slashes', collapsed drunks in puddles of vomit and shit, organised gang attacks on the door and full-on stabbings. My pal Zenon even had to contend with a tooled-up gang of football hooligans throwing a smoking canister of CS gas through the door of the rowdy seafront pub he was working on before weathering an ambush of bar stools, beer bottles and overturned tables as the mob invaded. At the height of the summer season, not a day went by when you didn't hear of something kicking off and wonder if you'd be next.

That was the hardest and most dangerous part of being a doorman: trying to soothe, calm, control and police the fragile egos of some absolute fruitcakes. Looking back, I don't know how I got through it all.

I'm sure the worst of these men were clinical psychopaths – and there was a worrying abundance of them swirling around the clubs like flies on shit. The most difficult and frankly disturbing task was trying to dissuade someone who was intent on violence – in a cold-blooded, determined and completely unwilling-to-see-reason sort of way – not to do it. Or at least not to do it in your club. No amount of diplomacy or reasoning would work with such types because they'd already made a firm decision in their mind that they were going to 'hurt someone' purely for a momentary ego boost. You could spend an hour of your time trying to talk them down and they'd just stare back at you with blank and depressingly resolute eyes. They would find a victim and a self-justifying excuse for themselves no matter what you said and only then would their eyes clear. I got the sense that it was almost like an orgasmic reflex action for them – some kind of mis-wired default emotional setting they reverted back to after a few tiresome, draining months of 'being good' or behaving normally.

Many such instances and scenes remain in my mind.

One night outside the club a pushing and shoving match broke out between two chubby, fresh-faced pals over the usual non-issue – whether it was girls, taxi fare or whose turn it was to pay for the kebab, I can't even remember. What I do remember, though, is Callum and I going over to them and asking them if they'd mind moving their dispute away from the club's walls because it was disturbing our customers and interfering with the queue. Typically, at first the lads told us to fuck off and mind our own business, but even more typically again Callum shot back with a wisecrack about their sweaty beer guts and the logistical difficulties of getting blowjobs. Within moments the lads had completely forgotten about fighting each other and were wetting themselves with laughter. Callum patted them on their shoulders, told them to behave themselves and wished them a safe journey home. He then sprinted back to the club entrance to get the queue moving again. I hung back briefly to hail a taxi for the two miscreants, then walked back to rejoin Callum.

One of the lads shook his mate's hand and jumped into a taxi. The remaining lad leant back against the wall, just about recovered from Callum's relentless piss-taking but still bravely battling the giggles, gulping in huge breaths of cold air to try and stop himself from dissolving into hysterics. In between bouts of laughter and quivering spasms, he'd look up at the night sky and shake his head in mock self-disgust. And then the laughing would start again. Truth be told, I was enjoying the show too because it was a joy to see someone in such a happy state and a privilege to witness Callum's magic at work. Yet again he'd achieved a brilliant result with his cheeky-chappy charm: a bruising fight and damaging row between two great friends had been averted.

But apparently somebody else didn't feel that way.

An all-round nasty piece of work casually walked up to the young lad and smacked him hard in the mouth with a straight right sucker punch. He cracked him square on the jaw, mid-laugh, and the poor kid slid down the wall like a techno-shirted blancmange. I felt utterly sick at what I'd just seen and angrily started towards the man when Callum's rough hand seized my arm and half-dragged, half-hauled me back into the club doorway, loudly commanding me to 'fucking leave it well alone because it just ain't worth it'. Before I could even protest, he sternly waggled his free finger at me in the way that a father admonishes his son when he is about to commit a careless blunder or trip up on a great big fucking banana skin. As I peered round the corner, the man was standing over his victim stock-still, admiring his handiwork as an artist admires a finished masterpiece. After a few minutes, he fastidiously straightened his tie, thoughtfully rubbed his bruised knuckles, then swivelled on his heels and briskly strode off into the night without so much as a backward glance at the bleeding heap he'd created.

I'm not a shrinking violet, but what most disturbed and

offended me about the unprovoked attack was the sheer arrogance of the assumption behind it; the guy felt that because he had a bit of a reputation he could just barge into this argument, one that Callum had spent time and effort resolving, and smack the guy in the face and walk away. And neither me nor Callum nor anybody else would reprimand him for it.

Depressingly, he was right.

A few minutes later a policeman appeared and helped the lad back to his feet. He ushered him into a taxi with some sage advice to get his fat arse home. Once he was satisfied that the lad was safely on his way, he came over to the door and asked us if we'd seen anything. As ever, because nobody was seriously hurt, the answer had to be no. Callum helpfully volunteered that it looked like the lad had been clumped by some holidaymaker, although he couldn't be sure because he hadn't seen anything. Feeling ever more cowardly, I solemnly nodded along. The golden rule was that you didn't 'shit on your own doorstep' and as this 'fight' had taken place well outside of the club and the lad was all right, there was no way we were going to get involved.

I briefly became acquainted with the bloke who'd thrown the sucker punch, as from time to time circumstances meant that I was forced to endure his company. He was a shrew-faced, lean and wiry type who reminded me of a coiled-up cobra, always ready to strike and forever looking for fresh, unsuspecting victims. I never learned exactly what he did for a living, but from his frequent long absences and the way his fortunes seemed to surge and dip erratically, being loaded one month and seemingly skint the next, I had a pretty good idea. He wasn't what you'd describe as a regular face in Blackpool, as it wasn't his hometown and he neither lived nor worked there; he was more like a piece of toxic flotsam that drifted into shore periodically, hurt somebody and caused a bit of trouble, then floated back out to sea again, to Manchester, London, Glasgow or God knows wherever else he plied his trade. His one saving grace was that even though he'd never been a doorman himself he did seem to like us and never gave door crews any trouble – probably because we all let him in for free, as we were desperate to avoid trouble with him. Ironically, I don't think he even realised this; he simply assumed it was because we all thought he was a great guy and not a complete lunatic. I soon learnt why Callum wanted us to keep away from him.

Thankfully, he never drank in the Varsity, but there would be awkward moments when he'd be visiting the town and you'd bump into him in another bar, when he was in one of his good spells and flush with cash. He'd absolutely insist on buying you a drink and you'd have to sit there laughing at his jokes through gritted teeth, lest you cause offence. Worse still would be when he'd begin bragging about his skill with 'tools' that he was so immensely proud of and you'd feel obliged to nod along approvingly at his stories of Stanley knives and screwdrivers being used to 'stripe' and 'plunge' enemies. I used to dread bumping into him and would gulp down whatever he'd bought me as quickly as I could without making it obvious, all the while thinking to myself, 'Yes, you're laughing and joking with me now, but if I said so much as one wrong word to you, you'd whack that pint-pot straight over my head.'

It was disturbing to have to endure 'civilised' chit-chat with blokes such as this; you had the unnerving sense that every word you uttered, however carefully phrased, was being scanned for signs of offence or disrespect. A convenient, flimsy excuse could always be found to turn their wrath on you. When they turned their back on you for the night and you walked away unscathed, it was always with immense relief. The only good that came out of briefly encountering this type of person was that your powers of patience, diplomacy and reasoning were increased tenfold – because your survival and bodily health depended on it – and your understanding of the crueller and darker aspects of predatory pond-life was usefully enhanced.

Still, I was learning a valuable lesson the hard way. As the great philosopher Nietzsche once said, 'What doesn't kill you makes you stronger.'

9

STEROID BOYS

CALLUM AND I HAD GROWN AS CLOSE AS FATHER AND SON DURING our time together on the Varsity door. Some nights I would go to his house for a beer and he would regale me with tales of his misspent youth or his latest moneymaking scam. He was a prodigiously talented craftsman and his house was a testament to his remarkable skill and extraordinary sensitivity with hammer and chisel. Looking around his handcrafted home, I saw it as absurd that he was so addicted to small-scale scams and trifling, unnecessary schemes when he could have carved out a career as an in-demand master builder, if only he could have forced himself to go completely straight. The problem for Callum was the buzz he got from being 'a bit naughty'. It seemed to add spice to his life – and it was an ingredient he was unwilling to go without.

I was amused but not surprised when he told me he got most of his building materials from midnight scavenging raids on carefully selected building sites. Beautiful tiles and top-of-the-range kitchen units abounded – all free of charge and courtesy of various property developers.

But beneath the laughter and jokes I could sense he was worried about his position at the Varsity. It meant a lot to him being the top man there, but the atmosphere was becoming strained as a result of his incessant and needless mischief. As wise and capable as Callum was when it came to running a door and leading men into action, he just didn't know when to stop when it came to his less admirable traits.

We were on to a good thing at the Varsity, but the management had made it abundantly clear from the very beginning that we weren't indispensable and would be sacked if we went too far. I suggested to Callum that perhaps it would be wise to ease back on overcharging punters behind management's back, to stop pushing our luck and just appreciate what we had, but I dropped the subject when Callum, as usual, fobbed me off and told me to stop griping like an old fishwife.

Callum's behaviour was becoming increasingly erratic in all areas of his life and I felt that he was putting our friendship at risk. The closest we ever came to falling out was during one nightmarish night when I made the near catastrophic error of accepting a lift home from him.

Callum had begun to develop a worrying drink-driving habit that annoyed me greatly and that evening, due to my own naive and misguided sense of responsibility towards his safety, I accepted his offer of a lift, seeing it as a chance to point out how crap a driver he was when drunk and to hopefully prevent him from having an accident or mowing down a group of innocents. Like an idiot, I genuinely believed that having me sober and alert beside him would make him safer. Well, that was a big mistake.

Callum quickly grew fed up of me constantly hectoring him like a driving instructor and occasionally grabbing the wheel to avoid him hitting anything from a drunken stag party to a ton of approaching white-van metal. 'For fuck's sake, Steve, I'm all right,' he'd grumble, then to prove it would weave across the road quite deliberately, singing a ridiculous chant of 'I'm forever blowing bubbles, pretty bubbles in the air' just to wind me up.

If you're going to do this sort of thing, then Blackpool promenade at 2 o'clock on a Sunday morning at the height of the summer season, when it's teeming with revellers, police and ambulances, probably isn't the best place to indulge yourself.

Growing ever more tired of the charade, I hissed at Callum to stop showing off, get off the main road quickly and take me home the back way because I was fed up of his carry-on and not in the least impressed.

But Callum had something else in mind entirely. With a devilish grin and an impish twinkle in his eye, he sang out 'No problem, Stevie boy!' and lazily swerved his van into a side street, almost flattening some peroxide blondes in 'Kiss Me Quick' hats in the process.

I began to feel a little less stressed and relaxed into my seat as the sea of beachfront traffic, dazzling illuminations and weaving punters thinned away into nothing. We had made it thus far mercifully incident-free. Maybe we'd get home safely after all – my second stupid thought of the night.

Callum had gone unusually quiet and seemed suddenly more alert. It was almost as if he was looking for something but couldn't quite find it, his baby-blue eyes scanning side to side suspiciously in gleeful, wicked anticipation. I should have guessed what he was up to when he began to make an unexpected detour, cheerily announcing that he wanted 'to check out a site'. Next thing I knew we were noisily crunching gears, bouncing wildly and spinning up dirt on a muddy lane before coming to a stop in the dark shadows of some trees and thick bushes.

I might have known.

'Oh, for fuck's sake!' It was all I had the energy to mutter as Callum bounded out of the van like an overgrown Springer Spaniel, sniffing the air, suddenly alive and on the scent again.

Momentarily paralysed with a now all-too-familiar weariness, I let out a long sigh before following him, once again feeling some absurd sense of responsibility to make sure that this middle-aged man, old enough to be my father, was OK and didn't get hurt. The trouble was I could never say no to Callum; he'd done so much to help me get my start in town and looked after me so well on the doors that I felt I had to back him up.

Now that I'm a middle-aged man myself, I can look back and see that there was actually no obligation on my part at all: it was a free and equal exchange. Callum got a lot out of my strong support and total loyalty, and in reality I owed him nothing more than the decent friendship that we shared. I can see now that he took crafty – but never malicious – advantage of my feelings of indebtedness and often dragged me into situations he shouldn't have, supposedly being the older and wiser man. I was subconsciously looking for a father figure and he knew it, and I guess he used this to get away with things at my expense when it suited his purposes. But since there wasn't anyone else around to fill that void, I clung to him tighter and longer than I should've done.

'Callum, where the fuck are you going?' I sighed resignedly.

'Shh! Just keep fucking quiet and follow me,' he replied mischievously.

Five minutes later, after wading through a muddy assault course of cement mixers, dust, sand and piles of brand-new red bricks, Callum found his target: a closed garage door next to a half-built semi.

'I reckon that's where the stuff'll be,' he whispered theatrically to himself.

As Callum lifted the unlocked door, we were confronted with a virtual Aladdin's cave of bathroom tiles, granite worktops and cement bags.

'Aha!' was Callum's gleeful response.

'Shit,' I sighed, shaking my head and sulkily stalking back to the van, much to Callum's amusement. I was already covered in building-site crap and had no intention of ruining my work clothes by relieving this carelessly unsecured site of its much-coveted 'supplies'. Undeterred, Callum resolutely marched into the garage and began wading back across the rubble with boxes of tiles precariously balanced in his arms, such was his eagerness to grab all he could. I slunk further into my seat, cursing my own stupidity and generally feeling sorry for myself. I was so angry at Callum for involving me unwittingly in one of his escapades.

Of course, he was quite deliberately being oblivious to my scalding disapproval and whistled cheerfully as he began filling up the back of the van with repeat loads, asking me if I wanted 'a box or two' for my own bathroom. But the merriment soon evaporated when he got a nasty surprise of his own. The cockiness seeped out of him in an instant.

If I hadn't been on hyper-alert, I don't think I'd have seen the police car that was slowly cruising directly towards Callum and his building-site paradise. The loud crunch of gravel stung me awake and I sat up sharply in my seat, straining my eyes towards the creeping threat and Callum's prized bounty. The van was parked at an awkward angle and well hidden under trees: from where I was sitting, I could see the policeman, but he couldn't see me. What really alarmed me were the soft blue lights that were flashing silently and ominously, casting an eerie, threatening glow into the night air that seemed alien and out of place. I think now that it must have been some kind of random security check, or perhaps neighbours had complained of strange noises – Callum's loud mutterings and curses as he stumbled over the site debris in the pitch black – hence the silent lights but no signs of obvious hurry or alarm.

Whatever, the car slowly drew to a halt and a reed-thin PC jumped out, casting a brief glance around the site and casually ambling up and down the road, squinting into the darkness for a couple of unbearably tense minutes, which felt like an eternity to me. As he beamed his powerful torch into the blackened shadows, I had visions of him catching Callum, a rabbit frozen in the headlights, snared in the act.

No sound, no movement, nothing cut the air; satisfied, he jumped back into his car, noisily banged the door shut and made a speedy three-point turn before revving off into the distance. Immediately, a cooling wave of relief washed over me. I almost slid from my seat and under the dashboard, like a slippery egg white.

Eventually, I summoned the energy to go and retrieve the hapless Callum, who'd been stuck to the spot, a burst bag of cement at his feet, plastered against the darkened semi's walls like a petrified daddy-long-legs while the curious PC had made his blessedly brief sweep of the site, none the wiser about our presence.

Inwardly, I was seething, boiling with contempt for Callum that he'd tricked me into such a ridiculous, almost farcical, but potentially serious 'midnight excursion'. I think the shock sobered him up a bit, but sadly not enough, as he giggled uncontrollably like an overgrown schoolboy. I told him that working with him was like starring in a Carry On film, such was the sheer stupidity of the situations he got us into, and I didn't know how much more I could take. But, as ever, Callum disarmed and calmed me with his roguish charm and irrepressible humour. He began laughing hysterically as he explained how he'd dropped 'this fucking great bag of cement on my feet' as the torchlight swept menacingly in his direction and he'd flung himself against the wall so hard, he said, 'I banged my head and didn't know if the stars I was seeing were real or in my fucking mind!'

Pretty soon I was laughing uncontrollably too, as the madness and insanity of the moment released its icy grip on me. But that was Callum: he had that rare quality of finding an infectious joy and humour in any situation, which made it impossible to stay mad at him for long and so much harder to leave him alone to his madcap schemes and scams.

Beneath the laughter and bravado I could tell Callum was shaken up by his near capture, so I decided to take advantage of the situation and suggest that he might not want to take all of the gear he'd so painstakingly loaded the van with, after all, lest the police were on the lookout for a white van and pull him over for a stop-and-search. He hummed and hawed about it and I could tell the decision pained him, but in the end he begrudgingly conceded that I might be right and it wasn't worth the risk. Between curses and tuts of bitter disappointment, he unloaded his illicit 'supplies' into the cover of some nearby bushes – no doubt to be picked up at a later date, but I'd most definitely not be around for any return visit. If Callum was foolish enough to risk coming back, he'd be on his own because one close shave was enough for me. I made the decision there and then to never accept a lift from him again, whether he was drunk or sober, because he simply couldn't be trusted. I'd managed to dissuade him from raiding the building site on this occasion, but, Callum being Callum, I doubted I could do it again.

As Callum emptied the van, I still felt shaken up, so I purposefully told him I'd walk the rest of the way home and he could unload and tidy up his mess alone; I wanted nothing whatsoever to do with it and it was none of my affair. I told him to drive carefully and for Christ's sake to take it slowly – one brush with the law was more than enough for one night. He was so engrossed in heaving out the boxes onto the wet grass that he didn't seem to register my concern and was absent to my fears. I stood watching him for a few moments longer as a fine, misty rain began to fall, washing the dust from his jacket into a milky white pool. The clear moon lit up his broad man-child face and at that moment a gulf opened up between us. I sensed that something fundamental had shifted in our relationship – however oblivious Callum remained to it. We bade each other farewell and I began the long, lonely walk home, all kinds of conflicting emotions, divided loyalties and pressing anxieties swirling around my head. I had a growing sense of foreboding that we'd have to part ways soon and bid farewell to our precious friendship: we were alike but not alike, and I had decided to choose a different path in life.

Back at the Varsity, things seemed to have gone from bad to worse. The air was thick with tension. Our dealings with management were under increasing stress as things rapidly turned sour, thanks to Callum getting completely carried away with his scams to the point of embarrassment. Our business relationship was still salvageable if only Callum could have reined himself in and stopped galloping through his nine lives like a cat on speed. Aiken had given us a firm and unequivocal warning to 'sort ourselves out and stop taking the piss' and I reckoned we owed it to him to take it on board in the generous spirit that it was offered. No matter how good we were at keeping trouble out, we weren't indispensable. There were plenty of other door teams who'd delight in our downfall and couldn't wait to take our place.

Just as Callum should have been cutting back on the scams and trying to build bridges, he was actually increasing them. Once, he held a fictitious 'charity raffle' behind management's back with unintentionally hilarious results. The grand prize was a bottle of vodka; however the bottle itself only contained tap water, Callum and an accomplice having carefully drained it the night before to be guzzled at a later date.

Callum had carefully organised the raffle to ensure that a certain number would be drawn, which he had given to a pal. All went according to plan until the winning ticket was announced and a delighted genuine punter stepped forward. Somehow the wrong ticket had been pulled out. Callum's face turned a deep shade of purple as the punter, egged on by his cheering friends, unscrewed the vodka and took a long gulp. A second later his lips sputtered and he yelled, 'It's only fucking water! What's going on here?'

The bar supervisor, who was totally innocent in all this, and was in fact acting up in Aiken's absence, hadn't got the faintest idea what was going on and was understandably livid, as she had to calm the irate 'winner' down. She swiftly put a lid on it by ordering Callum to run to the nearest off-licence and buy a new bottle of vodka out of his own pocket – an extra-large one, as a goodwill gesture – to be given to the punter straight away or else there'd be further consequences.

Callum darted off to buy the vodka and begrudgingly did as he was told but with a scowl on his face; he'd screwed up and he knew it. Ironically, having to pay the full retail price for the big bottle meant he lost money on his raffle.

He used his banter and charm to win over the disgruntled punter and managed to convince him that it was all part of the joke, presenting him with his king-size prize, but then he slunk off and lay low for the remainder of the night.

The incident might well have been hilarious, but it was also one more of those silly things that helped seal Callum's downfall at the Varsity. It was becoming crystal clear to me that his days there were now numbered. He had broken his own golden rule: he had begun to take the piss, completely ignoring the warning to behave that he'd been given.

Over the next few months the working atmosphere deteriorated further. Worryingly, we also began to experience an escalation in violence as the summer season took hold. Dealing with drunken holidaymakers was far more difficult than controlling the locals. Tourists have nothing to lose if they upset you, as it is not their own hometown, plus they are usually so intoxicated they resort to fighting very quickly. We couldn't arrange a sit-down or counter the tourists with the same coercion that we used on the local troublemakers if they refused to see reason and challenged us. You couldn't win either way with them: if you refused them entry, they would kick off, and if you let them in they kicked off anyway!

Whenever we saw a gang of rowdy tourists approaching, we would use the same old well-rehearsed lines: 'Couples only', 'Members only', 'No groups of lads'. The trouble was they knew this was bullshit and frequently took offence at it.

But the Varsity wasn't a holidaymakers' beer-hall type of place and our clear brief from the management team was to morph it into an upmarket bar, so they insisted we kept them out and concentrated purely on keeping our local customers happy.

Soon enough we were involved in a predictable brawl with a bunch of holidaymakers. We sensed trouble the very second they appeared, wobbling drunkenly down the high street, swaying from side to side, arms aloft and chanting football slogans in that universally recognised yob-like style. There is always a gobby ringleader in these situations and, sure enough, our man promptly revealed himself to be a classic example: spotty, mid-20s, ginger hair, plug ugly and all topped off with a dainty, blood-stained tea towel wrapped around his fist. His back-up man and clear number two was a blobby character who smelled like he had pissed himself and wore a sick-stained shirt.

No sooner had the words 'couples only' left our lips than a sneaky slap landed on Callum's head and I found myself being dragged outside by the ginger-haired one, who'd angrily seized my lapels. These bastards hadn't even bothered with a cursory dialogue before launching their attack and we had been caught out cold by it.

The kiosk girl screamed and hit the panic alarm, sending an urgent red light pulsing through the doorway. Meanwhile Callum and I were on the pavement, praying for back-up to arrive, as we jostled with the gang and frantically tried to stay on our feet, lest our heads be used for football practice. Taken by surprise, heavily outnumbered and clearly on the back foot, we were taking a beating. Lashing out blindly, caught up in the fierce struggle and with an adrenaline-fuelled strength sparked by grievous moral offence, I inwardly cursed, chastising myself that sooner or later I was going to take a hammering on this fucking door, but I'd be damned if it was that night. I had witnessed the weekly ritual of council cleaners chemically washing the weekend blood off the pavements and vowed that it wouldn't be my tissue getting flushed down the drain next Monday, the fight already forgotten but my wounds still raw and agape.

Back-up arrived in the nick of time and we began to even the score, beating back the attackers with a righteous rage and an anger borne of desperation. Thankfully, most of the yobbos crumpled like papier-mâché when they saw the numbers were now equal, but a few die-hards hung on, eager to take a doorman's scalp or two as a weekend souvenir. What was particularly galling was that out of the corner of my eye, as I continued battling with his blobby pal, I could see the ginger bastard that had started it all just standing there watching the fight unfold, as if it had nothing to do with him.

Mr Blobby deflated like a sack of shit as he ran out of puff and I could feel him rapidly weakening. I was bone-tired myself by this stage but managed to struggle free from his sweaty grasp and pushed him backwards against the wall with a hard palm-thrust to his jiggly chest. We stood wordlessly staring at each other without moving, both gulping in lungfuls of much-needed air, lost in the moment of combat. But, as fucked as I was, I could see that he was totally spent and in a far worse state, barely able to move, quivering feebly. Sensing a golden opportunity to finish him off, I shuffled back to give myself a couple of yards' space and then, with my remaining energy, I launched forward with a left roundhouse kick to his fat face. It was an extravagant gamble that I normally wouldn't have tried, but my instincts screamed at me that it would work. My leg landed heavily on his jaw and neck. He was too fucked to move out of the way, just as I suspected, simply dropping his arms and sliding down the wall like a burst bubble of pus.

It seemed like the brawl was over as I began sucking down air to catch my breath. But it wasn't. Unbelievably, the ginger gang leader had finally decided to do the 'macho' thing by deigning to get stuck in himself – on the five-foot-nothing, petite-as-a-pixie kiosk girl. As I was dragging him off her, the slippery swine started to bite my forearm. I managed to wrestle him out of the doorway, but he insisted on kicking out wildly at the girl, causing me to lose my balance. His writhing snake-like form fell on top of me as we tumbled out onto the pavement again and I landed flat on my back, still holding him in a choke-hold. We were surrounded by his scrum of scum-like pals, ever ready with their boots and fists, but luckily for me they hung back: if they'd obeyed their natural instincts and stomped me, there was every chance they'd have ended up stamping on their pal, too.

No matter: my sole focus was the woman-beating scum in my grasp. His assault on the girl had enraged me. I got out from under him by twisting my hips and flipped him onto his back before pummelling him, as he writhed and wriggled, clawing me with his blood-stained hands.

Callum roughly pulled me away as the familiar sound of police sirens pierced the air. Heavy black boots came running towards us from all angles as blue Sherpa vans screeched to a halt.

Whilst all the doormen dusted themselves down, licked their wounds and returned to their respective club entrances, true to form the gang of yobs who had actually started the fight sprinted off into the night, melting away into the seething mass of fellow drunks and stag parties.

The ringleader had caught me with some bruising blows and my nose was bleeding messily down my white shirt. A uniformed police constable motioned me towards him with a sympathetic nod: 'You look like you've been in a hell of a scrap, lad, do you want to tell me what happened?' I composed myself and started to tell him what had gone on, still wheezing and struggling with the frantic exertion of it all. The constable said not to worry, as he had no interest in arresting anyone now it was all over; he just wanted to know what had gone on and if we knew who the instigators were because he could see that they'd all run off. He seemed like a decent man and as I relayed the night's events he nodded knowingly.

Then suddenly I felt the atmosphere change. A sharp dig in my back caused me to turn around. A tall man, wearing the standard early 1990s 'drug dealer' uniform – baseball cap, black and silver LA Raiders jacket, pretentious goatee beard – was standing over me, glaring down at me with an expression of cold arrogance and mocking disdain. At first I thought he was an Ecstasy peddler or a hardcore raver, taking advantage of the heavy police presence to ridicule and insult. But then, in a challenging tone, abruptly stabbing his long, bony finger into my chest and invading my personal space, he said: 'You need to calm down a bit, dickhead.'

Still thinking he was an opportunist troublemaker or deranged attention-seeker, I ignored him and turned back to the constable, swallowing down a rising urge to tell him where to go. Unbelievably, I felt his sharp knuckles in my back again. I took a deep breath, turned around and said to him, in my most patronising tone, one I reserved strictly for idiots, 'Look, mate, don't be stupid. I don't want any more trouble tonight. OK? Can't you see I am talking to a policeman?'

And that's when he drew out his ID card and handcuffs. I stood there open-mouthed. To say I was shocked is an understatement.

'I am the fucking police, prick,' he spat at me. 'And you're under arrest.'

I turned to the uniformed constable to appeal for support and reason, but as my tormentor had very forcibly taken charge of the situation he merely shrugged his shoulders. The plain-clothes officer glared at the constable as he walked away, as though he was a gormless pleb, only fit to dish out parking tickets and help old ladies across busy streets. It was crystal clear to me that there was no love lost between the pair. But whatever their feelings towards each other, it didn't alter the fact that I was now under arrest.

Handcuffs on, I was frogmarched over to a police van and unceremoniously flung into the back of it by the big undercover type and a burly pal. Callum shouted through the locked doors to me not to worry, it would all get sorted out – everybody knew I'd done nothing wrong – and I'd be out by morning. But worry I did. It all felt a bit surreal, as I was whisked off to Blackpool central police station with sirens blaring; you'd have thought Hannibal Lecter was in the back from the fuss they made. Minutes later I was processed by the custody sergeant, fingerprinted and led into a room for questioning. I made it very clear that I would not say a word until a solicitor arrived and I had spoken to him in private, as I felt that I was being held on false pretences. Privately, I was worried I'd be unable to keep calm while being questioned because already a gnawing sense of injustice was growing inside me and I was seething at how I'd been treated.

The tall guy who had arrested me was now joined by another equally cocksure cop of the same 'undercover raver' variety and as we waited for the duty solicitor to arrive they questioned me. I worked out within minutes that their preferred style of interrogation was based on mockery, provocation, insults and intimidation.

Sadly, the uniformed services occasionally attract these types;

I encountered a few similar sorts in my army days – 'little Hitlers' who'd allowed a tiny smidgen of authority and power to go to their heads as they ruled over their personal fiefdoms.

As soon as I met the solicitor, we had our private chat. I told him the absolute truth of the incident from start to finish and also that I felt I had been wrongfully arrested. When I returned to the interview room, I repeated the story for the benefit of the tape. The policemen then gave me their version of events. I was totally stunned by what I heard and said so. As far as I was concerned, they had completely concocted a story out of thin air. That they could sit there as warranted policemen and invent this fiction shocked me; from where I was sitting, it bore no relation to the reality of the situation. What really got to me was that they seemed comfortable bullshitting me. I asked them why they were doing this and they just grinned at me. The interview was getting nowhere and I was returned to my cell. They released me without charge in the early hours, just as Callum had predicted.

Before I left I asked the solicitor for his honest professional opinion and he said to just forget about the whole thing: 'They don't have witnesses or victims, or even a complaint against you. They are just trying their luck. Even if only half of what you told me is true, there'd still be no case to answer. It's obvious that you were only defending yourself and doing your job. Set your mind at rest and put it behind you.'

Despite the solicitor's soothing words, I returned to the Varsity feeling down in the dumps about the arrest episode and the escalating violence. Aiken was pissed off about the arrest, too, but he had some good news for me. By incredible good fortune, a group of tourists were being shown around town at the exact same moment that the door was stormed. The group had stopped opposite the Varsity and begun to take photos of the nearby iconic Blackpool Tower, but as the fight on the door of the Varsity erupted they couldn't believe their eyes and had turned their cameras on us, capturing the whole incident on film from start to finish. During the week, they had visited Aiken at the Varsity to hand him the photos and their addresses for witness purposes, should they be needed. The tourists said they were disgusted by my arrest and felt I should have been given a medal – not handcuffs.

Natural justice, you might say.

I took the pictures off Aiken and filed them away for safekeeping, as they were irrefutable proof that I was telling the truth.

Before this incident I had always been resolutely pro-police: I felt they were doing a difficult job for little reward and I held them in high esteem. Whenever a defendant cried foul, I tended to believe the police version of events, seeing it as the gospel truth. Why on earth would police officers lie? They were honest – weren't they? If I hadn't been able to join the army, I had always thought I would join the police instead. Well, that's what I had thought before this incident anyway. My experience that night made me think differently. It profoundly disturbed me.

The man who arrested me against the uniformed constable's better judgement was, in my opinion, a fundamentally flawed officer with little interest in genuine justice. Instead, he perhaps had an unhealthy fixation with boosting his arrest figures by what to me seemed like dubious and questionable means. I wouldn't have minded if I'd actually been guilty – and let's be honest, I wasn't exactly an angel – but to be arrested for something that you're completely innocent of shakes your sense of security and self.

Weeks passed and the whole sorry arrest saga began to fade from my mind. My attitude towards the police had hardened, but I resolved to put it behind me. On more than one occasion on the Varsity door we'd gone to assist police officers taking a beating; Aiken even had a commendation we had received for help given framed behind the bar.

On that occasion, we had overpowered a gang of Saturday night hooligans who were in the process of giving two plain-clothes policemen the hiding of their lives. They had attempted to make a legitimate arrest of two known louts without realising a dozen of their thuggish accomplices were about to stream out of a nearby bar and steamroll into them. They swarmed across the streets like locusts and began kicking shit out of the policemen. I'll never forget the noise of the shop shutters, rattling and rippling like crashing drums, as they were pounded against them. Callum had led the charge into the fray and within a few minutes we'd turned the tide – even managing to hang onto the original two yobs until uniformed back-up arrived. It was one of those moments when violence erupted in seconds and you realised that if you didn't do something there'd be blood on the pavement and worse.

I questioned whether I'd be so enthusiastic about coming to the aid of the police again, risking my own neck in the process.

During my time working in the clubs, I formed a dim view of certain select elements within the police (especially the non-uniform ones), as I saw what some of the very worst ones got up to and how they behaved 'after hours' and off duty. In my opinion, letting some of these guys go anywhere near Blackpool's nightclubs was like letting a fox guard the chicken coop. It unsettled me that a select few of them would brazenly cosy up to gangster sorts and gush around them at parties, laughing at their jokes, sitting shoulder to shoulder as if they were schoolboy prefects invited to dine at the headmaster's table. It seemed that whenever the free champagne went round these types were the first to get their noses in the trough, waving their warrant cards around, demanding free this and free that. It was embarrassing at times; you just didn't know where to look.

The very worst of them seemed to view their official status as some kind of magical free pass: free entry, free drink and, as it appeared to me a few times, apparent freedom from arrest if their mates saw them drink-driving or getting a bit carried away during an off-duty 'disagreement'.

Of course, if you ever queried it, you'd be given an innocent-sounding ready-made explanation: as part of their work, they needed to be seen to be 'out and about in the clubs as a visible deterrent, watching what was going on, etc.' or how they 'needed to know who the local players were' and 'unfortunately the only way we can do that is by speaking to them, in their language and environment, mixing and mingling with them, and leaning on them'. Which all sounds fair enough and was undoubtedly true most of the time, but people aren't idiots and sometimes you just look at a situation and know instinctively that no matter what explanation is given it somehow isn't right.

I'm not suggesting that all the police I encountered back then were like this because they weren't – that would be a grossly unfair and deeply wrong belief to assert. I also feel honour-bound to point out that the vast majority were, and always have been, totally straight and thoroughly decent, honest professional sorts. (Indeed, I learnt this first hand from the first-rate policemen that I've been privileged to know or work alongside through my writing, military contacts and charity work; men of true character and nobility in every sense.) But nonetheless, in my opinion, from close observation, it appeared that a very small hardcore minority from 'my time' were not quite so well inclined, and at the very least displayed poor judgement and decision-making skills in the choices they made. Whenever police become intimately involved in the nightclub world, there are dangerous temptations and glaring conflicts of interest. And, sadly, the worst of these cases will always involve the young non-uniform guys who operate on the fringes of clubland due to the nature of their work – and then get fully sucked into it and hopelessly, unwittingly compromised a tiny piece at a time. (In much the same way that a doorman might . . .)

I got my first glimpse of what I shall discreetly term 'unwise' policing when I spent several months in the early 1990s training at a notoriously hardcore gym that shall remain nameless, and which very rarely got raided even though it was widely rumoured and later proven that its owner was a major supplier of anabolic steroids. Other similar gyms had been busted in the past, but this one rarely got touched – and whenever it did it was almost totally clean, containing only vitamin pills and protein powders, despite what was known to go on there.

There were some seriously big fanatical bodybuilders working on the doors at the time, most of whom were already well down the road of becoming full-on 'steroid doormen' and developing ruinously expensive 'gear' habits. I knew a few of them, thanks to my own lifting, and rather stupidly accepted an invitation to train at their gym, thinking I could resist the allure of easy gains and muscles that hadn't been earned by sweat and blood. I rationalised (i.e. bullshitted) the decision by telling myself it was because I lived close by and it was more convenient to reach than the far superior, completely clean Olympic Gym.

The place was literally awash with steroids and during its darkest heyday it could only be described as a chemical hub. A few clean individuals aside, virtually every single lifter that trained there was 'juiced up' to the eyeballs and virtually rattling with steroids; at times it seemed that there were more chemicals in that claustrophobic and hormonal space than an entire pharmaceutical factory. Huge men would waddle around chatting openly – bragging even – about how much gear they were ingesting, discussing how they were struggling to stop shaving nicks turning into raging red torrents, such was the sky-high blood pressure that the drugs induced. For no apparent reason, their noses would erupt and bleed like a tap mid-conversation. Their faces seemed permanently flushed beet-red.

When I arrived there, I was already 13 stone of solid, natural muscle. I had 15-inch biceps that were visibly lean and 'ripped'. I was totally drug-free and could bench press 250 lb, squat 300 lb, run 13 hard miles and do 120 strict press-ups with ease – a fact of which I am justifiably proud because it took a hell of a lot of hard work, blood, sweat and tears to achieve it. I was in fantastic shape and had never felt or looked better – yet by a vast margin I was still the lightest and least muscular man in that gym. Which I think tells you all you need to know about that place.

Whichever way you turned, your view was inevitably blocked by some 19-stone dinosaur puffing and panting under a surpisingly light weight, his arms bloated with stretch marks, finger-like veins and the burden of too much water retention. Angry acres of furious pimples and scarred acne glistened under unnaturally oily skin and freakishly broad backs. In that place, if you weighed less than 16 stone you were considered an anorexic – and if you weren't 'on the gear', you were viewed with suspicion and outright hostility from some of the more extreme steroid heads in there.

Whenever you were in the showers, you couldn't help but notice the scabbed-over and occasionally infected injection scars that spotted their bull-like buttocks and thighs, the result of endless shots of assorted bodybuilding chemistry.

Looking back, it was undoubtedly the most surreal and culturally warped 'health club' that I've ever had the misjudgement to train in. It was the complete polar opposite of the Olympic Gym, where Ivor had spent so many hours patiently tutoring me in how to lift weights as nature intended. At the Olympic Gym, there was a strictly enforced 'no steroids' rule; here, the opposite seemed to apply. I felt instantly out of place, but against my better judgement I resolved to give it a try, as it was so damn close to home and the Olympic was several frustrating miles away. I was constantly pushed for time, doing long night-time shifts on the doors – not just on the Varsity, which was my main door, but occasionally at other clubs too – and struggling to hold down a day job at the same time. That, more than anything else, made the decision for me.

But surprisingly, given what was known about the place and what would later transpire, a few perhaps misguided policemen apparently felt right at home there and appeared to embrace the culture. And it was definitely not the sort of place that you'd expect off-duty police to socialise and train in, for glaringly obvious reasons, no matter how innocent intentions.

The owner of the gym was a boisterous, larger-than-life character who lived an increasingly opulent lifestyle, despite the fact that he only had a solitary gym with a smattering of members to fund it. He had a luxurious pad and drove a succession of exotic European sports cars that he seemed to change almost daily. On many a night you'd pull up outside to be met by a new Porsche or Mercedes, with the owner showing it off to his admiring friends. If it was summer time, they'd probably all be bare-chested – their huge barrel-like chests and bloated bellies virtually blocking out the sun. They'd stand around nattering about sports cars, girls and 'gear', acquiring curiously deep burnt-orange tans.

One of the most popular members of the gym was the owner's frighteningly large but surprisingly docile American pit-bull terrier, which he fed on a daily diet of anabolic steroid pills, injections of growth hormone, bowls of protein powder and pounds of the best meat. It seemed to be his mission in life to turn this already large dog into some kind of super-beast that could scare a lion from its kill. It spent its days wandering round the gym, in between shiny chrome torture machines and bulging weight racks, accepting tidbits of protein bars and vitamin pills from the amused and awed lifters, many of whom were green-eyed with envy of its formidable muscularity. I ruffled his ears a few times when he ambled by and was rewarded with a lingering but menacing sniff of my calves, so concluded that he was best ignored if he happened to bump into your straining, tempting sinews.

Even though many of the gym's clientele were surly and careered about like cannonballs, thanks to the constant stream of testosterone they routinely ingested, the owner himself was charming and affable; he hadn't become a successful businessman by being a braggart or a bully. Whatever your view of his activities, the fact remained that he was friendly and welcoming – hence his cultivation of new clients. Occasionally, however, you'd get unwelcome glimpses of the price he was paying for his lifestyle and the dangerous risks he was taking. One day he'd be sporting a black eye and bruises, another he'd angrily fling a phone to the ground with 'roid rage'. Quite surreally, you might find him sitting behind his counter with a needle full of 'Deca' or 'Syp' stuck in his massive thigh, barely concealed with a tiny towel, looking as though he were defiantly proud of it. Sometimes he'd wear a skin-tight T-shirt emblazoned with the legend 'Die big, die young: Dianabol', a menacing skeleton illustrated underneath with a dripping syringe in hand.

I think he truly believed in this warped philosophy to the point that he felt like an immortal superman. Sadder still is the fact that instead of the eternal strength and vitality he craved, he instead got his jocular wish of an early death.

It was around this time that I made what I now consider to be one of the most stupid mistakes of my life and began training with some 'steroid doormen', allowing myself to be talked into taking a starter course of gear. Even as I was doing it I felt guilty about it and knew it was wrong, but like the naive idiot I was I gave in to the temptation. In truth, I should really never have trained there in the first place – that was the bigger mistake – but now that I was, I inevitably succumbed to the social pressures and negative allure of the environment. At that point in my life, as a kid in my early 20s, I didn't yet have the maturity or good judgement to say no.

The owner gave me a three-month supply of Dianabol tablets and simply told me to carry on training as I was but to supplement my workouts with five pills a day in between meals. He assured me that it was a safe low dose and that after a few months I'd be shaping up tremendously with no side effects whatsoever. His advice was to basically go away and enjoy the experience: 'You've got nothing to worry about,' he said. 'It's normal here.'

And that was the trouble: it was 'normal' there (indeed you felt abnormal as a clean lifter!) and in a twisted way he was telling the truth. So like the idiot I was, I went away and took the drugs.

Up until that point I had always prided myself on my natural physique and the extreme fitness that I'd been able to achieve from hard work alone: I'd go for long endurance runs for the sheer fun of it and at times it felt as though I had an extra couple of gears in my heart and lungs, such was my conditioning.

But almost from the first day I started taking the pills I began to feel queasy, sluggish and completely out of breath. Looking back, I don't know what was in them, but I'm completely certain that it wasn't what it said on the tin. At best, I think they were poor counterfeits because I seemed to be getting all of the bad side effects, i.e. feeling bloated and breathless, and none of the good, such as energy and definition. I had a sneaking suspicion that he saved his purest medicines for his close associates, personal training partners and bear-like dog – and that curious amateurs like me got the weaker stuff. In fact I don't even know if they were genuine 'medical grade' steroids, so bizarrely I might never even have taken proper gear, even though I thought I was at the time. Now, I can see that it was a tremendous blessing: in reality, it did me a favour and got me off them quicker.

I did seem to pack on a few pounds and found myself lifting a little more than usual, but nothing spectacular and certainly not enough to justify continuing with them, feeling as permanently ill as I did. Most of the weight seemed to be nothing more than a bloated, temporary wateriness and I think the extra strength was purely down to the placebo effect and the fact that, as ever, I was training freakishly hard and refused to allow a temporary pill-induced illness to derail my routine. So ironically, straight away I felt that these pills – whatever they truly were – were giving me absolutely nothing. I decided to stop using them almost as soon as I'd begun. In any case, I didn't really need them because I was already in great shape and getting steadily stronger without them, so the decision to ditch the Dianabol and get rapidly clean again was a no-brainer.

After a month or so on the drugs I got my first hint that I wasn't right physically when I found myself struggling on my morning runs. My cardio-vascular endurance, which had always been so strong and vital, was utterly deserting me. After a couple of miles I had to turn around and jog gently home with my heart pounding furiously like a novice runner's. The second hint came with a series of sharp spasms and agonising cramps that felt as though my kidneys were being squeezed dry by some malevolent giant hand.

I considered going to the hospital to explain my predicament but didn't because I was too embarrassed and ashamed. Besides, there wasn't any need: I instinctively knew what was wrong with me and how I could put it right.

In an impulsive flash of clarity and shame, I opened my bedroom drawer and dug out the remaining Dianabol pills from where I'd guiltily hidden them. I then stomped outside, found the nearest bin and dumped the entire stash into it. It crossed my mind that it was a foolish thing to do because I could have easily sold them on to one of my now ex-training partners and clawed some cash back, but I decided to seize the moment of inspiration and act boldly; I didn't fully trust myself and worried that if I hung onto them for any longer I might slip back and start using them again.

No, it was better to be rid of the things quickly because I knew in my heart that the whole time I was using them I was lying to myself: my gains weren't genuine, they were damaging my health and I felt like a fraud – both physically and psychologically. I wanted them out of my home and out of my body, the sooner the better.

Within a couple of days the pains in my gut passed and I returned to my normal state: fresh, alert and fighting fit. I found a new gym to train at and punished myself with a series of long cleansing runs, partly to get the crap out of my system and to blast away any remnants of Dianabol, but also to clear my head and undergo a little long-overdue penance and cardio-vascular suffering.

I had learned the hard way that when you're living a lie and making easy gains that by rights shouldn't be yours then the only person you're kidding is yourself. The truth was I never felt right at that gym, it wasn't my kind of place and I didn't belong there. I would find peace and happiness within my own skin away from that pin-pricked meat market and the misguided souls who doped there. My brief flirtation with the world of steroids and the dark side of gym culture was over as soon as it began.

The owner and his band of chemical brothers continued training long after I'd left and for several more years it was business as usual and seemingly happy days all round. But eventually all crazy parties have to come to an end, no matter how much they're being enjoyed, and inevitably empires that are built on foundations of sand have a habit of crumbling away.

The owner's notoriety had grown to the point that he could no longer avoid police attention and after a deal too many he was sent to prison for a number of years and lost virtually everything he had: his false friends, his wealth, his fast cars and the chemically induced 20-inch arms and 55-inch chest that he was so immensely proud of. But saddest of all, he lost his life, succumbing to a shock illness at a tragically early age. I'm not a doctor, so I can't speculate on what killed him, but what I can guess at is that decades of heavy steroid use probably didn't help things.

I was sorry when I heard of his death because I always felt that he had a decent core of warmth and humanity in him, despite the toxic nature of the stuff that he was involved in. He was always very friendly and helpful to me during the months that I trained at his gym and, to be fair, he did know a hell of a lot about weightlifting and nutrition, but alas he knew even more about 'the other stuff' too and that was what brought him down. Fundamentally, I believe that he was a good man. I think that like many he just took a wrong turn in life and found himself very far down a certain path and couldn't turn around. It takes a special kind of strength to recognise when you've really screwed up and to put things right; very few of us have it in us and we shouldn't judge too harshly those who don't. I certainly make no assumptions that I've got that kind of strength in me.

Whatever became of the others who trained there during my time in the early 1990s – policemen, doormen or otherwise – I haven't a clue; it was a very long time ago, it wasn't my kind of place and we were different kinds of people.

10

'GET OUT WHILE YOU CAN'

I COULDN'T BELIEVE MY EYES, AS THE POSTMAN DELIVERED THE brown envelope to my door. My hands shook as I read the court summons: I was being charged with threatening behaviour. Stung with resentment against a seemingly all-powerful persecuting state, with numbed hands I phoned a solicitor and arranged an urgent appointment. He patiently heard my story, examined my photos and dissected my account with ruthless efficiency before coolly denouncing the case against me as a pile of manufactured bollocks and carefully constructed poo. It had been too long, he cheerfully announced, since he'd had the opportunity to demolish a concocted prosecution case in court, so he was going to relish this one indeed. I was a little taken aback by his zeal and failed to share his overarching confidence, still feeling that faceless and unscrupulous powers were aligned against me, but he read my worry and immediately set about banishing my doubts.

Calmly, he explained to me that it was purely a police charge, meaning that there were no prosecution witnesses or so-called victims – it was simply their word against mine and, having seen my rock-solid evidence, he was certain the whole case would collapse at the first hearing. There was no chance of me being convicted – no matter what mud was slung – because it would be a gross miscarriage of justice. The police were chancing their arms and flexing their muscles, trying to get an easy conviction to justify the unnecessary arrest. It was a serious charge, he said, but we would prove it a false one.

When the court day finally came round, I was a wall of angst despite my display of false confidence. By this stage, the shock and anxiety of the official charge had worn off and I was simply morally offended and disgusted by it – and resolutely determined to have my say in court. I felt wounded that I was being put through this ordeal and mused that if there was any justice in this world then those who cast stones and accused me should have to stand in my shoes and be judged too.

I had to struggle to keep my mouth shut as the prosecutor repeated the bullshit account word for word, in a solemn tone, as if she were uttering the very essence of Godly truth itself. The officer concerned hadn't even deigned to turn up, furnishing the court with some feeble excuse about other 'urgent matters' and his intention to attend at 'later hearings' (when it was glaringly obvious there wouldn't be any). I think his non-attendance said a lot about how seriously it was being taken and how flimsy the case against me was. The magistrate didn't seem too impressed.

Finally, my solicitor stood up and gave our version of events, coldly rebutting and ripping apart every single sanctimonious dollop of slop that had been laid against me. He finished by loudly asking the prosecutor: 'Where are the victims? Who are these invisible traumatised victims of my client's titanic wrath? And why aren't they in this court?' He ended with a flourish, producing our bulletproof, unimpeachable, photographic evidence showing how the fight had unfolded, backed up by a list of independent witnesses – all out-of-towners and completely unknown to me. The magistrate motioned me to stand and asked if I had anything to add myself. I told him what had happened again and, as he examined the pictures with a troubled brow and perplexed mutters, I pointed out the ginger nut and Mr Blobby launching their completely unprovoked surprise attack and storming the door.

The prosecutor asked to see the pictures; as her face became flushed red, I could see she was mortally embarrassed by the trap that had been sprung. It meant the complete collapse of the case against me and the cruel exposure of her pious wind. She stood up and told the court she would be dropping the charges against me in light of the new evidence. The magistrate said he'd seen and heard enough by now. He asked me to stand again and withdrew the case against me. As soon as I thanked him, he sternly asked the prosecutor – who was unable to meet my eye and didn't even have the grace to nod at me – to see him for a private chat. It seemed surreal that in a matter of moments the trumped-up case that had been giving me sleepless nights for months was completely vanquished. I was free to go.

The trauma of the overblown court case obliterated any remaining enthusiasm I had for working on the doors. All right, even a guilty verdict wouldn't have been the end of the world – but what about the next time or the time after that? And the way things were going, I felt the overwhelming odds were that there would be a next time sooner rather than later. Time and again I had seen brutish yobs and seafront flotsam cause fights and then run away once the blue lights started flashing, vanishing into the night air like spectres. But where could the doormen run to, rooted to the spot, employed to do a job and having to defend themselves and their lawful customers? The answer was nowhere.

We represented easy meat for vans of police officers arriving en masse after a fight had finished but still with a pressing 'professional need' to 'make some arrests' for the incident of violence just gone. It seemed to me that often the police had a 'play it safe' policy of just rounding everybody up after a nightclub brawl and making arrests of both the guilty and the innocent. I understood the pressure they were under to 'make arrests' and had even been sympathetic to it in the past – but now that I had fallen victim to it, my opinions abruptly changed. I'm aware that this might sound hypocritical, but unfortunately human nature works in such a way that we often don't care about injustices until we become a victim of one ourselves. I guess it comes back to the old cliché, 'It will never happen to me.' When it does, it certainly strips away all naivety and makes you see things in a different light. Having faced what I considered to be a grossly unjust court case, my overwhelming feelings were that I never wanted it to happen again.

The ginger-haired idiot who'd almost got me a criminal record was probably safe at home now, in London or wherever, having a laugh at my expense in some smoke-filled backstreet pub full of soccer hooligans: 'Fuck me, we got the doorman nicked. Nice one, bruv!'

And I wasn't a fool either. I wanted a life outside of clubland. That's why I had turned down Chalkstone and steered clear of the heavier elements in town. A serious criminal record could screw that up, hinder my plans and make life harder. It weighed heavily on my mind, too, that if I hadn't had the photographic proof to demolish the case against me, then the magistrate may have believed every word the prosecutor said and I might have been found guilty. The photos had landed in my hands like a gift from the gods; they were a literal million-to-one coincidence. Somebody was looking after me that day, but what would have happened if the snappers hadn't been there?

The company I was forced to keep while policing the doors was causing me concern too. When I sat down and analysed the very worst of my associates, I realised that I had unwittingly become a friend or foe to druggies, thieves, conmen and thugs. I had entered into conflict with 'GBH men' with multiple convictions and had bumped chests with men who had killed. I had become an enemy of the sort of people any sensible soul would avoid like the plague. And all for just doing my job properly, running a tight door. It didn't take the brains of Einstein to work out that the longer I remained a target for such types, blocking their path on the door, then the more chance I had of becoming one of their victims.

Sod it, it was time to pack it in and move on. I had done enough fighting and fucking in the clubs and was tired of it. I was quitting while I was ahead – sanity, balls and conscience intact. My cup was overflowing. There were more important things in life to do. Better choices and different paths.

I had grown to understand that the problem with working the doors was that you risked losing your soul a tiny sliver at a time; it was down to the drip-drip effect, the constant strain and tension that it placed on your core principles. If I'd carried on much longer, I'd have ended up losing count of the values and beliefs that I would have been forced to betray on a daily basis – and I wouldn't be me today. I'd already compromised myself way more than I should have done. I recognised this creeping danger early on and that's why I bailed out.

Things that I swore I would never do, I had ended up doing, albeit briefly: I'd dabbled with drugs; I'd allowed dealers to ply their predatory trade in front of my own eyes and pretended not to see; I'd got involved in Callum's stupidity and had been dragged into his escapades, even though they made me feel hollow and guilt-ridden; I'd got into bloody battles with hard men and scuffles with drunken yobs, and these so-called victories had only led me to a magistrate's bench and the open arms of the law, which brought me nothing but anguish.

Once the court case was over, I immediately gave my notice

in at the agency and told Aiken that sadly I'd be leaving the Varsity and quitting the doors altogether. He understood my reasons. Aiken had been a fantastic manager to work for. He'd always backed up the door team: whether it was the police, yobbish punters or troublesome hard men facing us, we always knew we could count on his loyalty and support, no matter what. As a crew, it gave us a feeling of security and certainty to know club management would be in our corner, fighting for our rights, justice and proper treatment if ever anything went wrong and we found ourselves being unfairly screwed. I felt guilty about some of the shenanigans we'd got up to in his absence or whenever his back was turned and he was swamped with the duties of running an incredibly busy bar on a steaming hot Saturday night. We'd been a crafty bunch, and with a ringmaster such as Callum we did things and kept secrets from Aiken that had he known we'd have been sacked on the spot. You can make mischief on a door when a thick crowd separates you from a bar under siege and you ring yourself off with a strategically placed circle of ever watchful doorman steel. We did and I'm sorry for that because Aiken deserved better; it was a breach of trust on our part. I owed him a lot, too, because it was Aiken who had agreed that I could work on the Varsity door when in many ways I was still an unknown commodity. This, of course, made it all the harder to leave and say goodbye.

Telling Callum was harder still because we were so much closer. We had literally bled side by side and I knew how heavily he relied upon me to watch his back. We had enjoyed some tremendous times together and got ourselves into some comical scrapes and near-misses. But now it was time to call it a day; the fairground ride had stopped and the lights had ceased to glitter. To his credit, he didn't try and dissuade me. He accepted my reasons with his customary grace and humility.

In the absence of a father figure in my life, Callum had

been like a surrogate dad to me. He knew I looked up to him, but he rarely took advantage of it or tried to manipulate me – at least not in a malicious sense anyway. Yet I think we parted ways at just the right time: had we stayed together much longer, I fear I would have picked up some of his more unsavoury ways.

As it was, I tried to take on board the best of his lessons and to discard the rest. I didn't always succeed, but I did my best. He taught me to be streetwise and how to better read people's true intentions beneath the silky words and surface charm – not to trust too easily nor to condemn too quickly, but to wait until you've got the full picture. And most importantly he gave me a fascinating and useful insight into the criminal mind and all of the cunning tricks it employs.

Developing an understanding of those not so well intentioned is a valuable skill for any man. That is not to say I can't become a victim or be conned like anyone else – because I can and have been – it's just that I can maybe read the signs a bit more quickly or judge a character a little better. And that's in large thanks to Callum. He sharpened up my instincts and made me more aware.

We parted warmly, on good terms, and amid much sadness. I could never bullshit Callum, so I told him that I doubted we would see each other socially again, other than the occasional catch-up. When he asked why, I said that I wanted to make a clean break from clubland and all of its temptations, and that if we stayed in close touch we both knew I would end up back on the doors again, watching each other's backs but lapsing into old ways – and I wanted to leave that behind. Like the true friend he was, he said he understood and agreed with me. The last thing he wanted was for me to get sucked back into it all again because he knew I had different dreams.

The private words of thanks and farewell that he uttered to me whilst we shared our last night on duty together would prove to be grimly prophetic and have never left me. We hugged and gripped hands in that fiercely close, unembarrassed and sentimental fashion that only men who have stood shoulder to shoulder in battle can understand. Callum had bled for me and I had bled for him; it meant something. There was unashamed warmth, respect, regret and affection in that embrace – for me, it was special – tinged with brotherly love.

'Get out while you still can, Steve. Look after yourself, mate. Get out while you still can.'

And so it ended.

I faded from clubland as quickly as I had arrived in it: a burning bulb extinguished with a pop. I deliberately didn't venture into the clubs again for well over a year. After years of incessant thumping, I retreated to my natural habitat of books and a bedside lamp, devouring words and living vicariously through the printed imagery of others. Jaded and burnt out, nothing could coax me back into that smoky excess – not even Callum's sparkle and mischievous promise.

In the beginning, I had wanted to make my mark downtown, but once I'd accomplished that goal it proved a hollow victory and not a good enough reason to hang around any more. And once it was over, surprisingly I didn't miss it. Giving it all up came as a relief and welcome release. I felt like I could relax more and be myself – no longer having to worry about projecting a certain image in that insular and claustrophobic world. I had filled my cup and enjoyed my taste of the wild times – fought, fucked, faced down challengers, been arrested and got my fingers burnt. Now it was someone else's turn – time to pass the baton on.

When I'd begun working on the doors, all I ever wanted – apart from having some fun – was for the landlord to feel he was getting good value for money when he paid for my services and that when trouble flared he'd be glad he'd got me on the door to deal with it. Once the din of violence subsided, I wanted him to say of me, 'Stevie Mac? Yeah, works for me on my door, a decent lad who gets stuck in but not a troublemaker.' It was very important to my sense of pride and self-worth that I was perceived in this way. I always felt like I had to do a good job in my own eyes; it is how I measured myself. By and large I think I succeeded, and when I left the doors, although I was never regarded as a so-called 'hard man' – a label I never sought – I was considered to be a good doorman – I suppose what you'd call a 'handy lad'. And that was more than enough for me.

One of the first things I did after quitting was to blast off to Corfu to wash the crap off and tan away the post-clubland comedown blues. As the plane roared off, I remember looking round me and thinking that none of it really mattered, the troubles that had plagued me in the clubs were mere pinpricks in time and utterly meaningless. On this plane and in this foreign land nobody knew me, gave a fuck about who I was or where I was coming from. For the first time in years, I felt free. Past conflicts and mutual dislikes that had at times erupted into hatred burnt up in the jet's fuel and evaporated in the blazing sun. Individuals I'd once fantasised about kicking fuck out of and beating into a bloody pulp vanished in the sun-streaked mist and powdered into nothing in the sands. It was all a million miles away. The 'stocky little fucker' called Steve who had once stood on a few square feet of Blackpool's noisiest clubs had already ceased to exist. I lost myself in early morning ocean swims and mountain treks, parasailing against a hot blue sky and bungee jumping from towering cranes till my head shook stars.

In later years, whenever I made fleeting visits to clubland I'd feel like a stranger – I wasn't surprised to find that many of my contemporaries had moved on, too. Inevitably, Callum had tried one trick too many at the Varsity and decided to jump before he was pushed, while once-prominent nightclubs had been closed down and banished to the history books forever, taking their good times, bad times, memories and guilty secrets with them. Ever bigger and brighter 'superclubs' had sprung up in their place. Darwinian evolution in concrete and neon.

The galloping pace of change was electric. A few of the 'fresh faces' who had come onto the scene with me still remained but were now looking decidedly more battle-scarred, shopworn and tired out – as ever, a pack of new young bucks were snapping and snarling at their heels.

I was glad to be out of it.

There'd been some other major changes, too: a doorman's compulsory training and police registration scheme had been launched that had caused a mini-exodus of some of the more brutish types almost overnight. Not surprisingly, police record checks had thrown up quite a few surprises and several dubious faces vanished or were barred from policing a door.

I had been among the first batch of doormen to go through the initial voluntary trial scheme when it was launched in a blaze of publicity by Blackpool Council in 1992. Basically, you got a day of first-aid training, did a crash course in security and pub law, and were shown how to use supposedly effective control and restraint moves on unruly customers. Unfortunately, the self-defence element of the course failed by assuming a best-case scenario and semi-compliant drunks. Those of us with experience on a door knew that in the real world it's impossible to always fence off and 'control' attacks with a minimum of legally acceptable force. Two things will happen if you go down that route: first, you'll get seen as a soft touch, and second, a weapon-wielding lunatic and his mates will smash fuck out of you and put you in hospital – or worse.

It's all very nice and civilised to be training in a pleasant hotel function room in your comfy tracksuit on how to use minimum reasonable force; it's a different matter altogether when a 20-stone pub monster is trying to tear your face off, and use your head as a drum kit and your ribcage as a trampoline. He's using maximum unreasonable force and unless you're prepared to defend yourself in the same fashion, you lose very badly indeed.

The course is an entirely different affair today. It has been toughened up considerably in recent years, thanks to the council eventually making the wise decision to employ one of Blackpool's most senior and highly respected security bosses to lead it. He knew instinctively what was required to make it truly effective and worthwhile from his own vast experience on the doors; I regret that I missed out on this quality of training in my day. I'm glad the current generation of lads benefit from it, however, because the passing-on of hard-won knowledge and frontline experience can literally save lives. It beats the more theoretical and ideal-scenario type training hands down every time.

When I returned to clubland, I noticed the culture on the doors had visibly changed, too: there wasn't a dickey bow or black suit in sight. It was all black polo necks, bomber jackets and walkie-talkie earpieces. The doormen looked like wannabe CIA agents.

There had been an explosion of CCTV cameras, which plastered virtually every street corner and peered into every pub porch like an Orwellian nightmare. CCTV would play a massive part in toning down the violence and fights that spilt out onto the streets, however it could never eradicate them completely – the criminal types just developed greater cunning and worked out where the blind spots were. But certainly the days when a 'score' could be settled down a dark alley or in a deserted fire escape were long gone. Any doorman today found smacking shit out of a persistent troublemaker to lance the boil will certainly have some explaining to do.

But the same applied for the police, too. There were some pretty hefty bruisers amongst the police in early 1990s Blackpool and to say that you didn't want these guys arresting you during a Saturday night scuffle, with no cameras around, was an understatement indeed. Let me put it this way: the old standby of 'he was resisting arrest' was used with a frequency that wouldn't be possible today. Sometimes it was true, sometimes it wasn't. It was a very different era back then.

Another big change – and definitely not one for the better – was the state of some of the doormen themselves. While we've certainly kissed goodbye to most of the bruiser types, in my opinion we've replaced them with a far greater menace: the 'geared-up steroid doorman'. You can spot them instantly because they'll be the baby-faced ones with necks that bulge from behind their ears, biceps that swell like watermelons from their shirtsleeves, chubby cheeks and a generally puffed-up, watery look.

In my day, there were certainly a few of these types around, but they weren't exactly a menace. They were just a definite, albeit growing minority – in both numbers and bulk. The very worst of them tended not to stick around long because they soon got battered and exposed for what they were, if they didn't have any skills or qualities to back up the obvious beef on display.

A lesson learned very quickly, and often painfully, is that muscles bloated and waterlogged by steroid abuse in no way signify conditioning, capability or fighting skill, only that their owner has got his physical priorities wrong and has some 'issues' that he needs to deal with. You can have all the muscles and body weight in the world behind you, but it's utterly useless – counterproductive, in fact – if after one minute's hard fighting you're blowing like a hippo, running out of gas, totally spent, and have no more tricks up your sleeve. Most of the big 'steroid boys' are so unfit that after a couple of minutes' exertion they're done for, their strength has evaporated and their powers have deserted them. What that then does to their minds is to cause an inner collapse of confidence and a moment of self-doubt, which then leads to their getting the shit kicked out of them by a man half their size.

An average steroid bloater would not even get a third of the way round an army assault course without collapsing in a quivering heap, if he really had to go flat-out and test himself.

The nightmare scenario for these geared-up idiots is to face a strong, fit and determined normal-sized man (say 12 or 13 stone) who gets stronger and more efficient as the fight wears on, whilst they get rapidly weaker and more demoralised.

The sheer volume of modern-day doormen – and sadly some policemen, too – who appear juiced up to the gills shocks and disturbs me. In my opinion, across Britain we've got scores of potential ticking time bombs working the doors, and possibly even walking the beat, just waiting to explode.

While writing this book, I researched this subject intensively and what I found out only cemented my beliefs and developed my thesis further.

On 27 November 2009, the BBC News website broke with a major story in which the Chief Constable of the anti-corruption squad, Mike Cunningham, and several other high-ranking anti-corruption officers spoke of their growing concern and alarm at the rise in steroid use amongst serving police officers and their subsequent links to supply and criminality. This was followed up on 14 February 2010, when the *Guardian* newspaper's crime correspondent Sandra Laville revealed that the Serious and Organised Crime Agency (SOCA) was launching an investigation into police corruption that would be centred heavily on steroid abuse, drug dealing and collusion, emanating from within nightclubs and dirty gyms.

So it would seem that I wasn't the only one concerned about policemen placing themselves in vulnerable positions where they could become potentially compromised. If you wish to delve into this topic a little further and do some research of your own, I suggest you start by typing the phrase 'steroid use amongst police' or something very similar into an internet search engine. Most likely you will be troubled by what you learn about the growing scale of the problem. Bear in mind, too, that for every individual who is caught either dealing or ingesting in the clubs and gyms, there will be others who escape detection.

In my opinion, this is one of the major police and security issues of the twenty-first century. It has been hushed up by the powers-that-be, who have turned a blind eye to it because they don't know what to do about it or how to stop it since it comes from within their own four walls. And it's my belief that a significant minority are 'on the gear' – which straightaway means they are potentially compromised. One possible solution to this could be random compulsory drug testing – or the dreaded CDT, as it is known in the army – where if you fail, your licence or warrant is revoked. It's doubtful that it would ever be instigated because of the cost to the council and the police authorities administering it, which is a shame.

My research also revealed that Blackpool itself had expanded ever deeper into the burgeoning drugs culture – that the town was becoming mired in it and undeniably socially decayed. On 9 October 2007 a major newspaper report in the widely read *Blackpool Evening Gazette* sent ripples through the town when it revealed that Blackpool was now officially the 'drug death capital' of Britain. In the same vein, the *Gazette* reported on 5 July 2010 that mainly due to drug use men in the resort had the shortest expected lifespan in the country. Police statistics published in the same newspaper in April 2011 proclaimed Blackpool 'tops the drugs league', with by far the highest number of drug arrests in the entire Lancashire region.

These worrying statistics weren't mere estimates but the

officially accepted government figures at the time of their publication; utterly startling figures when you consider that Blackpool is a relatively small – albeit culturally significant – seaside town. Some local council bigwigs proclaimed surprise; I didn't. I had seen it coming more than 15 years earlier from my own position on the frontline, where many of those selfsame 'drunks and druggies' literally wound up on my doorstep in the clubs, occasionally armed and spitting venom.

The Varsity, Illusions and the Palace are now, of course, long gone. They belong to a different century, relics torn down, rebuilt, rebranded or renamed. Clubland is an organic subculture that is constantly changing and evolving; the nightclubs I inhabited are now mere ghosts of the past – as indeed am I.

Then it was my time; now it is someone else's.

And so it goes on, endlessly.

For my part, I have never regretted working the doors and consider it to be a major factor in moulding me into who I am today, as a student, writer and observer of the human condition. I learned an unhealthy amount about human nature, survival, fear, intimidation, comradeship and the way the world really works – whether we like it that way or not. It encouraged me to stand my ground, face my fears and try to conquer them; to confront bullies and deal with them; to be patient and wait for my moment – and then to strike hard when it came, not just in the physical sense but in the daily battle of life itself. So many essential life lessons that no school could ever have taught me. I definitely treasure the experience and would do it all over again in a heartbeat if I had to relive my youth and was dealt the same set of cards.

If you're willing to accept the risks and have the physical wherewithal, I would recommend working on the doors in the same way that I'd recommend serving in the army – and I've been fortunate enough to have done both – just so long as you've got the presence of mind to stay away from the excesses.

It is a violent subculture where shit goes on, as they say, but if you can steer through the bad parts you'll come out better and stronger once it's over. For me, it was a life-enhancing joyful journey, tinged with occasional sadness and bittersweet loss.

I've often pondered on the irony that I'd have been a far better doorman in my 30s than I ever was in my 20s. Time had calmed me down and I was a more reflective individual (although I could still have my moments, if and when a perfect storm brewed). Physically, I was stronger and fitter than I had been in my first flush of adult youth because I'd never really stopped training, had evolved as a martial artist and had gained the mindset and experience of a professional soldier who had seen active service. So I could have brought new skills to the table and was a more confident and complete package. Writing this book and exploring my innermost feelings and memories triggered all kinds of shit in me and at times I was sorely tempted to abandon the keyboard and go back. But ultimately common sense and the artist in me won out, and I decided it was a lot more fun to look back, write and reminisce about clubland than it would have been to live through it again. Besides, I'm a great believer in moving forwards in life rather than going back; you have an experience – either for good or bad – and you learn from it and move on. And for me that's what writing this book has been all about.

But I will admit that when I sit back and think of all the crazy adventures we had, I often miss it. A piece of my heart will always remain in the early 1990s clubland of Blackpool – the notorious rave era – when we could breeze in and out of the hottest clubs for free and had the sexiest girls hanging off our arms. Taking ourselves into insanity or dream tripping to whatever else was the song of the day.

Throughout the late '90s I would still catch occasional glimpses of Callum down town. We would stop and chat and he would tell me of his latest scam or moneymaking scheme. It was always good to see him, but at the same time I was relieved whenever we parted and went our separate ways – before the allure of his clubland tales could take hold. He never once tried to tempt me back, and I appreciated his consideration. It was actually more a case of me not trusting myself when I was around him rather than the other way around. But once the new millennium dawned and the decade turned, I lost touch with him and never saw him again.

I've often wondered whether, if I'd stayed in Callum's life, I could have somehow 'saved him' or nudged him away from the path that he seemed to resolutely and helplessly follow. I don't believe I could have done – and it would have been arrogant of me to have tried any harder than I had already. The reality was that Callum was old enough to be my father and the choices that he made – often against the protests of those of us who cared about him – were wholly his own. If I'd stayed in Callum's orbit out of some misguided sense of rescuing him, I'd have probably only ended up destroying myself.

In the run-up to our parting, my instincts had begun to scream at me to get out and I received several sharp omens that it was time to go. Callum had an enormous Rottweiler dog that looked like something out of a horror movie but in reality was soft as shit; when he went on holiday abroad with his wife, I stayed at his house to look after it and to keep his property safe. It was a half-empty house and God only knows what was in it or around it, as there were boxes all over the place and most of the rooms were unlived in. I was dozing on the sofa one night and almost jumped out of my skin when a lone policeman loudly rapped on the door, asking if I knew where the owner was as neighbours had been complaining about his noisy late-night arrivals and careless, obstructive parking. A cold chill speared my entrails when I surveyed the policeman's sceptical face and explained that I was merely a housesitting friend. He told me not to worry, as the police often called late at night to catch people in who they were having trouble finding. Prickling with fear, I realised that I hadn't a bloody clue what was in the house or what Callum got up to outside of our friendship, on his trips away and in his life beyond clubland. I also realised that if anything was in the house that shouldn't be, then I was exposing myself to an enormous risk.

Counting down the days to his return, I was troubled and sad that our close friendship was coming to an end but I accepted it as necessary. I couldn't go on living like that. I knew Callum would never deliberately expose me to a really big, serious risk, such as the one that had sent him to prison, but I also sensed that if he ever did start 'doing that shit again', as he would say – and I don't believe he ever did – then all it would have taken was for me to be around him, or in the wrong place at the wrong time, and I could get caught up in it. There was no way I could let that happen and the only way to be sure was to cut myself off from his company completely, no matter how much it hurt.

When I began writing this book, I looked up a few old pals from the crazy days to see what they were doing now and to fill in some of the gaps. Zenon had carried on working the doors for a full decade after I left and had collected enough tales of his own to more than fill any book. He was now married to a wonderful girl from his Polish hometown near Krakow and was working in tunnelling all over the UK. It was a joy to rekindle our friendship. We've since travelled to Eastern Europe several times together and Poland has become my near-second home. After a long and successful career, Aiken finally retired from the pub game altogether. A few unfortunates were either dead or in jail. Many, like me, had simply chosen to get out while the going was good and consigned their doormen days to happy, youthful memories. One former hard case had even found religion and become a counsellor, which I have to say was quite a surprise but a wise, impressive one nonetheless – good for him and I salute his courage in choosing to follow a different path.

But the man I really wanted to catch up with was Callum. I felt it would be fascinating to see what had happened to him in the years since we'd parted. No matter who I spoke to, though, I could find no trace of him. I didn't bother speaking to the bouncers of today, as they belong to a totally different era – to them, Callum would just be some faceless and insignificant old man, as would I.

Finally, I managed to get some information, but it was not what I wanted to hear: he had become involved in a messy on-off relationship with a stripper that hadn't worked out and had ended up committing suicide after sliding into depression as various things in his life – both business and personal – went wrong. I researched this further but couldn't find out if it was true or just a misplaced rumour. The coroner's office and local press didn't seem to have any suicide reports in his name. (He had several aliases, though, so this doesn't rule it out. I can remember being gobsmacked one lazy Sunday afternoon in Callum's backyard as he showed me several different documents each displaying a different identity. I realised with a jolt that although I knew a lot about Callum there was a hell of a lot more that I didn't know. Despite our closeness, there would always be things he kept from me – and probably for my own good, too. Even the actual name that I knew Callum under, he told me once, wasn't his real name.)

But Aiken reassured me that it was true; our old friend from the crazy days was no longer with us. As I listened to him tell the tale of Callum's chaotic love life and mounting troubles, I found myself nodding along and agreeing in sad resignation; he was telling me what I feared in my heart to be true.

The stripper had a long history with Callum and in the beginning it was she who did all the running and wouldn't take no for an answer. In the end, the roles were reversed. He'd met her during a one-off shift at a gaudy strip bar that had seen better days (long before the current proliferation of trendy lap-dancing bars that litter Blackpool today). It was the very definition of a fateful meeting and they formed an instant, prickly and tempestuous bond. The only problem was that they were each to the other forbidden fruit.

One day when I visited Callum at his house the stripper turned up unannounced while his wife was at home. We were sitting in the front room drinking coffee and discussing the weekend's plans when Callum's cheery red face paled ghost-white, he jumped up from his seat and mumbled, 'Oh fuck me, she's here again!' We both tiptoed to the window and twitched the net curtains back as stealthily as we could, so his wife in the kitchen wouldn't hear us and the stripper outside wouldn't spot us. A glamorous, heavily made-up and busty blonde sat in the seat of a purring sports car, staring intently into Callum's window. She locked eyes with Callum, grinned lasciviously, gunned the engine, turned the car around and sped off. Callum sighed heavily and hung his head to the floor, as if in silent defeat.

Straight away I knew there'd be trouble because there was simply no way he could resist this girl – and there was no way she was taking no for an answer, she'd made that much abundantly clear.

A few moments later Callum's unsuspecting wife walked into the room with a beaming, blissfully ignorant smile; she was a sweet girl and didn't deserve all the heartache that I sensed was coming her way. I'd got to know Callum's wife very well over the years and she felt almost like a second mum to me, such was the kindness and consideration she showed me. I felt too that she was his true soulmate and that if he ever walked away from her he'd be making the biggest mistake of his life. But a man cannot look into another man's heart and ever truly know how far he'll go or what he's willing to give up.

Callum went along with the laughter and chatter as we drank our coffee, but I could see in his deep-set eyes and the handsome cragginess of his face an anxiety and doubt that hadn't been there before. The buxom stripper with her dangerous curves and penetrating stare had cast a spell on Callum and he was powerless to resist – sooner or later they would be together.

Ultimately, nobody but Callum is responsible for the choices he made and the places they led him to – and as long as I knew him, he always chose to live life in the fast lane – but if this is what became of him it breaks my heart to think of him facing such a crisis. Despite his silliness, he had immense character and warmth, and his story deserved a happy ending.

Now that I am older, and have lived almost as much life as Callum had when we first met, I can sympathise with him more than ever, for I too had an affair once that ended with my heart being dashed against the rocks and my world apparently collapsing. I made the exact same mistake that Callum did. And when I was younger, and depression struck me, I'd even sought my own suicide solution, too. The cruel irony is if things had happened at different times and we had still been in each other's lives, then I could have commiserated and counselled him, and he me. But of course he'd have to have been prepared to listen and I don't know if he could have done by that stage.

I sincerely hope and pray that this is not how my old pal ended up. Wherever he is now – be it dead or alive – I hope he wore a smile on his face whenever he thought of the special time we shared. It's strange, but I've often reflected that during the early stages of our friendship Callum was like a father figure to me, but during its latter stages, when he began to slip back into old ways, I became more like a father to him. I tried and mostly failed to keep him out of trouble.

I prefer to think of a happily retired Callum in a mythical parallel universe, living in the Costa del Sol and indulging himself in a never-ending cycle of sun, sea and laughter – with his ever-loving wife still beside him, gently scolding him and watching over her beloved man-child of a husband, cheerfully reining in his greater excesses. Callum will be bronzed deep copper brown, his thick black wire-wool hair now streaked with grey, and his big proud belly a testament to his love of food, wine and life itself. He'll have pulled off a big score that put him right back on top and enabled him to leave Blackpool and the doors behind, so he could live in the Spanish sun and enjoy a golden existence. And in the evening he'll sit on the sandy veranda and watch the warm sunset sink beneath the sea with a smile on his face, a cold beer in one hand and his wife's steady grip in the other. Perhaps he'll grin and mutter under his breath in that thick Brummie brogue: 'Well, it all turned out all right in the end, babe. It all turned out well in the end...' And as the reassuring squeeze comes back he'll smile and nod his head.

That is how I like to think of my old friend.

Whatever happened to Callum I shall always treasure our time together on the door and I will never forget the generosity of spirit he showed to me. He made time for me when a lot of his contemporaries would have just fucked me off. I was a lost and lonely kid searching for an identity and support – and for a while at least he was it for me. When we first met, I was still deeply damaged and felt like a hollow man – the world's biggest loser, despite the never-ending self-improvement programme that I was on. Callum brought joy into my life and a sense that anything was possible. He made me believe in myself and told me that one day I could be somebody

– because he saw that I felt like nobody and was carrying a ton of baggage. You can't put a price on a friend like that. He was full of contradictions but had a curious dignity and a manly honour that is rare. For all of his foibles, when you contrast him with some of our so-called leaders in society – from politicians to bankers – for me, he is the better man. I used to be a soldier once and I know who I would rather share a trench with. To others, he was a rascal, but to me he will always be a great man.

I only have to hear a tune on the radio from those crazy days and I am instantly transported back; it is always Callum's face I see first.

Miss you, bro.

DOORMAN'S TRAINING CERTIFICATE

Certificate of Attendance

This is to Certify that

Steven R McLaughlin

has attended and completed the

Blackpool Borough Council

"Doorstaff" Training Programme

and has achieved a standard

permitting him/her to obtain

registration under the scheme

.... Chief Executive

Dated 3rd June 1992

ACKNOWLEDGEMENTS

IT'S NEVER AN EASY TASK SETTING OUT TO WRITE A BOOK – AND this has been no exception. The following individuals, in various ways, were all a great help to me during the living and writing of this, my second book.

For their friendship and support when it mattered: Nazia Khan, Andy Roper, Mark Turner, Craig Holden, Les McSalley, Barry Evans, Jason McLemon, Joan Halton, Jayne Fletcher, Maja Patek and Marina Ciba. For his lessons in life as well as drama, Brian Hindle. For sharing his knowledge and friendship with me, voice teacher extraordinaire and Shakespearean scholar Stuart Morrison.

I'm indebted to my fellow military authors, in particular A.F.N. Clarke, ex 3 Para, author of the Northern Ireland classic *Contact*; Ken Wharton, fellow Royal Green Jacket and Britain's foremost Troubles historian; Alexander Khan, ex-British airborne forces and author of *Orphan of Islam*; and D.C. Alden, former Royal Signaller and author of the sci-fi masterpiece *Invasion*. Thanks also to Shaun Attwood, author of the prison memoir *Hard Time*.

For inspiring me to live as full a life as possible in the physical sense, I must humbly thank my training partner and lifelong friend Paul Clayton, former Mr London and natural

ACKNOWLEDGEMENTS

bodybuilding champion Ivor Markham, and phenomenally skilled master of ninjutsu Ralph Dunow. For his support of *Squaddie* and showing me his great chess play, Paul Evans.

A special thank you has to go to my Polish friends for opening doors to me that would otherwise have been closed and welcoming me into their homes and hearts. For his hospitality and counsel, Marian Hreska: from Blackpool barman to East European industrialist – wow! For their strength and support, Zenon Malkuch and Ewa Malkuch. For her kindness, class and wit, Kinga Ziolo – you're a great lady. I also owe a debt of thanks to rising Polish journalists Joanna Berendt and Magda Qandil – I respect your talent immensely.

Closer to home, I must thank Andy Mitchell of Blackpool's Radio Wave, Jacqui Morley and Chris Dixon of the *Blackpool Gazette*, and the following individuals, champion journalists all: Mike Peake from *FHM* magazine, Mathew Squires, Chris Thornley, John Barnes, Gordon McCully, Richard Hunt, Neil Docking, Gareth Vickers, Lindsay Jennings, Ian Sinclair, Yvonne Ridley, Ginko Kobayashi, Dr Roger Cottrell, Sally Naden, John Gilmore, Carole Turner, Mick Coyle, Johnny Wardy, Olivia Foster and Paul Mackenzie. Special thanks are also due to Vicki Woods of the *Daily Telegraph* and Terri Judd of *The Independent*.

For inviting me to complete their conflict resolution leadership programme and sharing their peacekeeping knowledge and skills with me, as generous mentors and skilled guides, I must thank Rosie Aubrey, Kelly Simcock and Jo Dover. For their inspirational example and guidance during three wonderful months as a Prince's Trust volunteer, I humbly thank Louise Rainford and Allan Brickman. I salute you for the amazing work you do.

I must say a huge thank you to all of the team at Mainstream Publishing, in particular Bill Campbell, Peter MacKenzie, Graeme Blaikie, Fiona Brownlee and Fiona Atherton. As ever, it has been a great pleasure to work with you and I'm honoured and humbled to be a Mainstream author for a second time. Special thanks are due to my editor Deborah Warner, for her perception and patience. It is no easy task honing down one of my bulky manuscripts and, you're right, I do use too many adjectives. Debs, your critical eye was razor sharp, you were a joy to work with and I can't thank you enough.

For his heartfelt support from afar, I thank my dearly departed brother, Damian McLaughlin. Bro, we did it again. I hope you like the book and find that I've written of you well. You were my Braveheart and I will make sure you are never forgotten – my promise to you. If ever the dreams we spoke of come to pass, then they will not be the same without you by my side, here to share them with me. I wish I could give you the world, but I can't. You were a light in the dark, and I miss you so.

For giving me the gift of life itself, I must thank my parents – a man can't ask for more than that.

And finally to the great John Rad. It's fitting that your name is the first and last in this book and that's exactly how it should be. Well, what can I say, old friend? Sometimes words aren't necessary, but sometimes they are: thanks for watching my back and making it special.

BY THE SAME AUTHOR

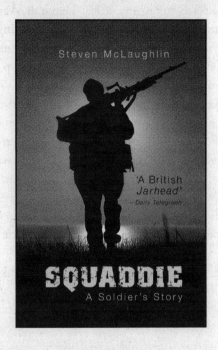

ISBN: 9781845962425
Price: £7.99
Extent: 320pp

'The British *Jarhead* . . . I'd like the entire MoD to read Steven McLaughlin's book'

— Vicki Woods, *Daily Telegraph*

'A candid look at life for the average enlisted soldier . . . offers a powerful insight into the motivation that drives youngsters to sign up, as well as the fear which follows when they realise they're off to Iraq'

— Teri Judd, *The Independent*